Small Dog Breeds

Dan Rice, D.V.M.

P9-DHN-140

BARRON'S

About the Author

Dan Rice retired from veterinary practice several years ago to embark on a well-loved writing avocation. His daily association with small animals in urban areas of Colorado accounts for his understanding of animals and their owners. Researching dog breeds and their problems and endless reading maintains his knowledge of veterinary medical developments. His continuing interest in companion pets is his reason for writing.

Little Dog Breeds is Dr. Rice's fourteenth book for Barron's Educational Series. Others include *Bengal Cats, The Complete Book of Dog Breeding, The Complete Book of Cat Breeding, Dogs from A to Z, Akitas, The Well-Mannered Cat, Brittanys, Chesapeake Bay Retrievers, Training Your German Shepherd Dog, The Dog Handbook, The Beagle Handbook, Big Dog Breeds,* and *West Highland White Terriers.*

Dedication and Acknowledgments

I've dedicated each book to the individual that inspired me to write it. This book must therefore be dedicated to all the little dogs that managed our family over the years.

Koko, the Amertoy; a Miniature Schnauzer called Delilah; Skip, a tiny little shaggy mutt; a Cardigan Welsh Corgi named Mike; a Yorkie that we called Rowdy; and Muggs, our beloved Pug.

Most of these little characters were adult castoffs and several came with extensive previous human experience but no references. A couple were excellent examples of their breeds, some were only average, and Mike looked like a throwback to some distant ancestor, but he was a solid individual. A common thread ran through all of our little companions; without exception these diminutive pooches enriched our lives by bringing us love, joy, and entertainment!

For trusting me with this project, I'm grateful to Mr. Barron, CEO of Barron's Educational Series, Ellen Sibley, President of Barron's Educational Series, Mark Miele, Managing Editor, and Wayne Barr, Acquisitions Editor. Many thanks to my editor at Barron's, Anna Damaskos, and my live in proofreader, Marilyn.

All inquiries should be addressed to:
Barron's Educational Series, Inc.
250 Wireless Boulevard
Hauppauge, NY 11788
http://www.barronseduc.com

International Standard Book No. 0-7641-2095-6

Library of Congress Catalog Card No. 2001056684

Library of Congress Cataloging-in-Publication Data
Rice, Dan, 1933–
    Small dog breeds / by Dan Rice.
        p. cm.
    ISBN 0-7641-2095-6
    1. Dogs. 2. Dog breeds. I. Title.
    SF426 .R543 2002
    636.7—dc21   2001056684

Printed in Hong Kong
9 8 7 6 5

Photo Credits
Kent and Donna Dannen: front cover, inside front cover, and pages 1, 3, 8, 10, 11, 12, 19, 20, 21, 24, 25, 30, 31, 32, 33, 42, 44, 49, 56, 62, 65, 71, 78, 92, 95, 99, 100, 107, 109, 118, 144 (left), 145, 146, 149, 152 (bottom), 154, 155, 159 (left), 160, 165, 169, 176, 178, 181, 188, 194, 200, 203, 209, 210, 211, 212, 215, 218, 220, 221, 224; Tara Darling: back cover (lower left), inside back cover, and pages 4, 5, 6, 27, 72, 84, 85, 86, 87, 88, 89, 90, 91, 93, 94, 96, 97, 98, 101, 102, 103, 104, 105, 106, 108, 110, 111, 112, 113, 114, 115, 116, 117, 119, 121, 122, 123, 124, 125, 126, 127, 128, 129, 130, 131, 132, 133, 134, 135, 138, 139, 140, 141, 142, 143, 144 (right), 148, 150, 151, 152 (top), 153, 156, 157, 158, 159 (right), 161, 162, 163, 164, 166, 167, 168, 170, 171, 172, 173, 174, 175, 177, 179, 180, 184, 185, 186, 187, 189, 190, 191, 192, 193, 195, 196, 197, 198, 199, 201, 202, 204, 205, 206, 207, 213, 214, 216, 217, 222, 223, 225, 226; Pets by Paulette: back cover (inset) and pages 76, 147; Close Encounters of the Furry Kind: page 136; Nance Photography: page 23; Norvia Behling: pages 15, 26, 182, 183, 219.

Contents

Introduction   1
The Many Faces of Small Dogs   1
Who Buys Small Dogs?   1
Dogs Are Dogs   1
Origin of Small Dogs   2
Goals   2

Section One: Small Dogs

Chapter 1 Shopping for Your Small Dog   7
Impulse Purchases   7
Small Dogs and Little Children   8
Look to the Future   9
Jobs That Small Dogs Can Do   9
Big Gifts in Small Packages   10
Two Small Dogs Are Better Than One   10
Gender Differences   11
Trustworthy Breeders   11
Internet Shopping   12
Pet Shops   13
Puppy Mills   13
Backyard Breeders   13
Crossbreds and Mixed Breeds   13
Age of Availability   14
Eight Signs of a Normal Puppy   14
Temperament Evaluation   15

Congenital Defects 16
Veterinary Examination of a Small Dog 16
Life Expectancy of Small Dogs 16

Chapter 2 Advance Preparation for Your Small Dog ... 17
A New Shadow in the House 17
A Refuge 18
Small Sharp Teeth 18
Backyard Traps 18
Sheds and Garages 20
Neighbors 20
Temporary Caregivers 20
Health Insurance 21

Chapter 3 First Experiences 22
Meet the Family 22
Picking Up and Carrying 23
Bonding and Socialization 23
Small Dog Housebreaking 24
Sandbox and Paper Training 25
Crate and Pen 25
Small Dog's Food 26
Exercise 26
Identification 27

Chapter 4 A Small Dog's Education 28
Manners 28
Teaching the Small Dog Its Name 28
Teaching *Come* 29
Collar and Leash 29
Teaching *Sit* 29
Canine Good Citizen (CGC) 30
Obedience 30
Terrier Trials 31
Agility Trials 31
Flyball 31

Therapy Dogs   31
Correcting a Small Dog's Bad Habits   32
   Jumping Up   32
   Begging   32
   Mouthing or Chewing   33
   Running Away   33
   Biting   34
   Separation Anxiety   34

Chapter 5 Your Small Dog's Health   **35**
An Early Bloomer   35
Your Veterinarian   36
History and Physical Exam   36
Ask and Understand   37
Diagnostic Aids   37
Prognosis   38
Therapy   38
Normal Isn't Necessarily Normal   39
Medical Kit   40
Shock   41
Artificial Respiration (AR)   41
Cardiopulmonary Resuscitation (CPR)   42

Chapter 6 Protective Care   **43**
Preventive Medicine   43
Active Immunity   44
Vaccines   45
   Passive Immunity   45
   How Much?   46
   When?   46
   Boosters   47
Vaccinatable Diseases   47
   Canine Distemper (CD)   47
   Canine Hepatitis (CAV-1)   47
   Leptospirosis   48
   Kennel Cough   48
   Parvovirus   48

Corona Virus   48
Lyme Disease   48
Rabies   48
Nosodes   49

Chapter 7 Small Dogs' Hereditary Problems   50
Atopy   50
Dental Disorders   50
Diabetes Mellitus   50
Circulatory Diseases   51
Cleft Palate   51
Elbow Dysplasia   51
Epilepsy   51
Hydrocephalus   52
Hypoglycemia   52
Hypothyroidism   53
Intervertebral Disc Disease   53
Facial Deformities   54
Kneecap Luxation or Slipped Stifle   54
Legg-Calvé-Perthes Disease   55
Ocular Diseases   55
    Keratitis Sicca   55
    Progressive Retinal Atrophy (PRA)   55
    Glaucoma   56
    Distichiasis   56
    Trichiasis   56
    Epiphora   57
    Microphthalmia   57
    Cataract   57
    Entropion   57
Tracheal Collapse   57
Reproductive Disorders   58
    Dystocia   58
    Testicular Retention   58
    Eclampsia   58
Sunburn   59
Umbilical Hernia   59

Chapter 8 Urgent Care   **60**

Poisoning   60
Vomiting and Diarrhea   60
Chocolate Poisoning   61
Heatstroke   62
Auto Injuries   62
Muzzle   63
Body Wounds   63
Pad Wounds   63
Tourniquet   64
Fractures   64
Ear Wounds   64
Nosebleeds   64
Deep Punctures   65

Chapter 9 Small Dog Nutrition   **66**

Water   66
Free-Choice Feeding   66
Meals for a Small Dog   67
Dog Food Terminology   67
Energy Requirements   68
Reading Labels   68
Calories   68
Fat   68
Protein   68
Starch   69
Minerals and Vitamins   69
Supplements   69
Feeding Trials   69
Dog Food Types   69
    Canned   69
    Semi-Moist   69
    Dry Food   69
    Premium Quality   70
    Other Commercial Foods   70
    Homemade Diets   70

Puppy Rations..70
Special Diets..70
Treats..70
Human Foods...70
Overfeeding and Obesity.....................................71
Sudden Weight Loss..72

Chapter 10 Small Dog Reproduction......................**73**
Questionable Motives for Breeding...........................73
Right Reasons...74
Plan, Plan, Plan..74
Small Dogs Have Big Problems................................74
A Full-Time Commitment......................................74
Life After Whelping...75
Spay Benefits...75
Castration Benefits...75
Age to Spay or Castrate.....................................75

Chapter 11 Small Dog Geriatrics........................**77**
Generic Drugs for Geriatric Dogs............................78
Making a Small Old Dog's Life Easier........................78
Grouchy Old Dogs..79
Arthritis...79
Dental Disease..79
Deafness..79
Lumps and Bumps...79
Nuclear Sclerosis and Blindness.............................80
Canine Cognitive Dysfunction (CCD)..........................80
Incontinence..80
Metabolic Weight Gain.......................................81
When to Give Up...81
Why Euthanasia?...81
When Euthanasia Is Really Necessary.........................82
An Act of Kindness..83
Finalize a Small Dog's Life.................................83
Grief Support...83
Starting Over...84

Section Two:
Purebred Small Dogs

Affenpinscher	87
Australian Terrier	90
Basset Fauve de Bretagne	93
Bichon Frisé	95
Border Terrier	98
Boston Terrier	101
Brussels Griffon	104
Cairn Terrier	107
Cardigan Welsh Corgi	110
Cavalier King Charles Spaniel	113
Cesky Terrier	115
Chihuahua	118
Chinese Crested	121
Coton de Tuléar	124
Dandie Dinmont Terrier	126
French Bulldog	129
Klein German Spitz	132
Mittel German Spitz	134
Havanese	136
Italian Greyhound	138
Jack Russell Terrier	140
Japanese Chin	143
King Charles Spaniel	145
Lhasa Apso	148
Löwchen	151
Lundehund	153
Maltese	155
Mexican Hairless, Toy	158
Miniature Dachshund	160

Miniature Pinscher	163
Miniature Schnauzer	166
Norfolk Terrier	169
Norwich Terrier	172
Papillon	173
Patterdale Terrier	176
Pekingese	178
Pembroke Welsh Corgi	181
Podengo Portugueso Pequeño	184
Pomeranian	186
Pug	188
Scottish Terrier	191
Sealyham Terrier	194
Shih Tzu	197
Silky Terrier	200
Skye Terrier	203
Swedish Vallhund	206
Tibetan Spaniel	209
Toy American Eskimo	212
Toy Manchester Terrier	215
Toy Poodle	218
West Highland White Terrier	221
Yorkshire Terrier	224
Index	**227**

Introduction

THE MANY FACES OF SMALL DOGS

The monkey-faced little Affenpinscher or the Pug's morose countenance will bring a smile to your face and maybe even a giggle or two. A trio of charming and angelic Shih Tzu faces peeking out of a box is sure to evoke everyone's maternal instincts. Athletes are drawn to the clean-cut Italian Greyhound's countenance that's as streamlined as its aerodynamic body. The stuffed-toy appearance of a Norwich Terrier puppy invites you to pick it up and give it a hug.

WHO BUYS SMALL DOGS?

Why are you considering the purchase of a pocket-sized pooch? Practicality may be the answer. Little dogs eat less food, require less space, are easily trained, and can be taken anywhere. Apartment dwellers who prefer not to take the elevator to exercise a dog in the middle of the night might consider one of the toys that's trained to use a litter box. Little dogs thrive in retirement communities and many common folks like them just because they're good lap-sitters.

Some people unconsciously obtain dogs that complement their own personalities. Have you ever tried to classify people by the types of small dogs they choose? For example, the burly weight lifter is as proud of his brace of French Bulldogs as he is of his

Small dogs come in every size, shape, color, and coat type, and they're all fun.

bulging physique. The laughing, fun-loving young lady is at the height of her glory following the wake of a prancing Jack Russell. The concert pianist prefers the quiet trainability of a Bichon, and the exquisitely groomed matron is quite happy with her equally elegant Yorkie.

Little dogs have very individual personalities and no two are alike, but one fact remains: a tiny dog is every ounce a canine.

DOGS ARE DOGS

Small dogs are different from big dogs in many ways that will be explained in the following chapters, but dogs of any size are still dogs. A common misconception

The large and small of dogs.

is that tiny dogs are really not dogs at all but are forever our little children. This book doesn't support that idea; a canine is a canine regardless of its size. Readers of this book will receive tremendous benefit if that premise is accepted up front. Temporary insanity allows every small-dog owner to demonstrate a tiny pinch of anthropomorphism when people can't overhear, but when important issues such as feeding, health care, training, and similar factors are considered, we'll be speaking dog language.

ORIGIN OF SMALL DOGS

DNA testing has proved that all domestic canines' progenitors were wolves. Because wolves are all about the same size, we can assume that miniaturized dog breeds were the result of selective breeding or human mutation management. Most small dogs were developed to fill specific needs.

Rural Europe was the origin of many terriers that were selectively bred from bigger dogs. These quick and clever little dogs were willing and able to catch and destroy farm pests. Terriers received their name for the terrain in which they tunneled to bolt (put to flight) or kill foxes, rats, otters, badgers, and other undesirable critters. Tiny dogs were selected to fit into their quarries' subterranean dens but they had to be scrappy little dogs with the power and perseverance to kill their quarry wherever they were found.

> **Mutations, selective breeding, inbreeding, and crossbreeding is the answer.**

> **Little dogs fill a void and quickly find their niche in family gatherings.**

Ancient Oriental ruling classes and monastery residents mastered the art of breeding miniature dogs to warm imperial feet or sit prettily on royal laps. These little Asian pooches were small, decorative, and had amenable personalities; little else was demanded of them.

North American Indian nations may have borrowed their original brood stock from the Orient, but the wee Chihuahua was developed within a Mexican Indian culture. Chihuahuas were prized because of their diminutive size and agreeable personalities, although for a time they occasionally were cooked and eaten (presumably as appetizers).

French royalty developed a small, highly intelligent, and amusing dog known as the Bichon Frisé to please the ladies of the court and to entertain one and all. During hard times these little canines were saved from extinction by serving as trick dogs in circuses because of their trainability, natural balance, and good humor.

Americans sneaked into the picture much later and quite successfully developed several small breeds, including the Boston Terrier and American Toy Fox Terrier. These tiny dogs resemble their larger European progenitors somewhat and their sole purpose in life is to socialize with their families.

GOALS

Virtually every type of small dog from many different countries is represented on these pages. The breeds have been selected because they fit a single arbitrary standard of 12 inches or smaller. Tiny dogs have many common attributes, some good, some not so good. Here we've discussed some of the infectious and genetic problems shared by small dogs as well as the joys and dangers that are often experienced in little-dog ownership.

If you're in the market for a little dog but first want to learn about their compatibility with children, pets, or strangers, this is the place to look. If you want a good little watchdog or one that will socialize with practically everyone without sounding an alarm, we've covered that as well. We've discussed small Spitz types, little terriers, most toys, some Lilliputian scent hounds, and even a diminutive sight hound.

Big or small, dogs are dogs.

> **Treat your little dog according to its species and you'll appreciate it more than ever.**

This book is written to help you plan for your small dog and to teach you to care for it after it's obtained. The similarities and differences between small dog breeds are explained. How to select a healthy little dog and how to train it are described at length. A little dog's hereditary problems are discussed and suggestions are offered to correct or live with these difficulties. Every type of health question is answered, from vaccinations to emergency therapy.

Because every little dog has a name we've elected to call our dogs Sprig and Sprout. In half the chapters Sprig is the male hero and, in others, Sprout is the female heroine. This should satisfy any questions of sexism and make our text more interesting.

Small 1 Dogs

Shopping for Your Small Dog

Buy in haste and repent at leisure is an axiom to remember when seeking a little dog.

A great deal of joy and comfort comes with your small dog, but it must be the right dog for you. It must fulfill your expectations and you are obligated to satisfy its needs. This little companion should provide thousands of hours of delight and diversion as you share the next dozen or fifteen years together. Do your homework well and take as much time as necessary to make a prudent choice.

IMPULSE PURCHASES

Never obtain a dog of any size, shape, or color without careful planning. This excellent advice applies whether you've owned dogs all your life or Sprig is your first puppy. A whimsical canine purchase will cause you more heartaches than any capricious act you can imagine. Take time to carefully consider your lifestyle and the opinions of everyone in your family even if you invest no money and the small dog carries no baggage.

Impulse buying is the curse of lazy Americans. Shopping malls are handy and useful in many instances; everything you could ever want is available in a single gigantic space. The downside of this convenience is that many people are sucked into that vacuum with such force that they buy everything that strikes their fancy without planning for tomorrow. Tiny pups in the windows of a mall shop may set in motion a chain reaction that will be regretted for many years to come.

First decide on a specific breed or type and progress from there. Do you want a tiny terrier that's active and ambitious or a slick-coated, streamlined Toy Manchester type? Are you attracted to the wrinkled face of a Pug or a fuzzy little Shih Tzu? Small dogs' personalities, physical traits, colors, and habits vary significantly from one breed to another. Gather all the information that's available about your breed of choice before you select an individual, because after taking him home he's going to be with you for a long time.

Have patience; don't rush to the nearest dog store and buy the first pup you see before you check out his temperament, genetic traits, and state of health. Every buyer is entitled to a healthy puppy that's sound of mind and limb. Don't accept a shy or aggressive pup or one that's a little lame just because you're fearful of his future and feel sorry for him. This advice

> **A very wise person once said that failing to plan is the same as planning to fail.**

Many small breeds appear in various coat types.

becomes urgent if you're inclined to choose a teacup variety. Ultrasmall dogs are often a great disappointment although most owners will deny it. This is especially true if Micro is the first teacup type they've owned.

SMALL DOGS AND LITTLE CHILDREN

Choose a larger and sturdier pup or an older dog if you have young and active children who are not knowledgeable about handling a tiny dog puppy. Infants and toddlers are given stuffed animals to play with and their parents approve tossing a fuzzy toy across the room, grasping it by a leg, and poking fingers in its eyes. How will baby know that Sprig isn't a toy to be treated in the same way? Small children can easily lift, carry, and sometimes accidentally drop or fall on tiny pups. Paying a veterinary bill for setting a fracture is an expensive lesson. For this reason little dogs are better suited to young adult families, school-age children, and seniors.

> **Small dogs often aren't compatible with babies and toddlers.**

Some little-dog breeds are reportedly snappy toward children, but why shouldn't they be? A small dog's sharp teeth are the only defenses it has. Snappy and untrustworthy dogs are made, not born. They're sensitive to the quick movements and high-pitched squeals of small children, and they resent being grabbed. Small dogs will resist having their ears pulled or their feet handled, and they often show fear of being stepped on or kicked in children's rowdy games. The cause of snippiness is another generality that may be proven incorrect, but why take the chance of having your baby or toddler's face disfigured or scarred?

However, every dog and each child is an individual and generalities are sometimes proven wrong. A few of the small breeds are tough little brutes that can withstand the forces of small children's activities.

Housebreaking the pup takes on new meaning when infants and toddlers are involved. Little dogs aren't difficult to housebreak but their training is often neglected because of the size of the mess left when a small dog has an accident on the floor. It's no trouble to blot up a teaspoonful of urine or pick up a thimble-sized pile of feces with a tissue, but if a crawling baby is sharing the floor, this mess seems much greater.

LOOK TO THE FUTURE

Don't shop for a real live dog if you actually want a novel decoration for your home. Instead, buy a beautifully crafted ceramic figurine or a stuffed toy that barks when you walk by. Before you begin shopping for a small dog, consider Sprig's destiny and his happiness. He will consume a significant amount of your time, attention, and love. He will securely bond with the person who spends the most time training and playing with him. How many hours each week will you devote to his grooming? Is it quicker or easier to brush out a shorthaired breed than to comb out a longhair? All dogs need grooming; the question is, how much time is available? Dogs of every description require exercise. A little dog's need for strenuous play is decidedly less than that of a retriever, but Sprig needs playtime, walks, and at the very least some simple obedience training.

JOBS THAT SMALL DOGS CAN DO

If you treat Sprig like a moppet with the mentality of a zucchini, that's probably just what he'll be. It's distressing to see a tiny dog relegated to riding around in someone's pocket. The clever nature and gigantic attitude of a little dog proves that it's an intelligent canine with an active mind and superb learning ability.

Sprig's training limitations are real and his size becomes a risk when he's put in con-

tact with larger dogs, but you shouldn't pass up training challenges just because he's tiny. Give him something to do, some schooling, a purpose in life. Your little pal will appreciate your consideration.

Tiny dogs are found in all-breed shows, and attending a conformation show is often the best place to begin looking at the many small breeds available. Take a notebook to the show, talk to owners of the many small breeds, discuss breed traits, and discover why you should or shouldn't choose each breed. While you're picking the brains of show dog owners, ask about their dogs' undesirable features. Don't rule out buying your puppy from show dog parents and training and grooming Sprig for competition. Dog show competition is certainly a fine method of providing challenging goals for both dog and owner.

When choosing a tiny breed think of obedience work that's well within the smallest dog's capacity. Attend several obedience trials and watch the competition. You'll see tiny dogs performing alongside the big ones. Then after you've obtained your pup, join your local all-breed club's obedience group and attend classes by yourself at first to watch how other small-dog owners deal with the problems of size.

In case you're contemplating purchase of a small terrier, consider terrier trials as a place to watch the various breeds perform. Learn the true purpose of the breed and choose accordingly. You'll be amazed by the cunning resourcefulness of these diminutive creatures.

> Postpone buying a dog of any description if you have very limited spare time.

> Is your little pal to be a watchdog or a watch fob?

You might select your little dog with an eye to other types of athletic avocations. Agility trials and flyball contests are timed events that require some specialized training. If considering an athletic little dog such as a Jack Russell, watch one perform in one of these events before you make your final selection.

Therapy dog is another avocation that's well suited to small breeds. The gentle, well-behaved, clean little dogs often delight in bringing pleasure to shut-ins and nursing home and hospital patients.

him when you're gone to the business meeting next week? The yard fence has gaps that a half-pint pup squeezes through. Your children graduate and move away. Your husband is promoted to a post in Great Britain. Your family increases by an infant and Sprig has never been around tiny tots. These possible changes should be seriously considered before you select your small dog. For these reasons no dog should be given to anyone without the recipient's express consent and agreement to provide all needed care.

BIG GIFTS IN SMALL PACKAGES

All members of your family should be included in the small-dog selection process. Not everyone loves a furry little companion that licks faces, chews shoestrings, and scampers about, begging to be loved.

Once it's purchased a small dog becomes a giant responsibility. Sprig will be no exception regardless of his good manners, loving personality, and minimal care. He won't housebreak himself. Without someone's tender and affectionate attention any little dog will become an immense nuisance. Who's going to care for

> Never give someone a surprise gift that requires daily care.

TWO SMALL DOGS ARE BETTER THAN ONE

Many facts and fallacies are implied because two dogs are small and easy to care for together. Appetites may be enhanced when two dogs are fed together, but sometimes it results in one fat and one skinny dog. Playtime competition may result in a tie that stimulates jealous growling and scrapping and neither dog is comfortable. Puppy games become overly rowdy and you return to find shredded furniture and torn drapes.

Two little dogs will keep each other company while you're away for the day. Competition is offset by the companionship they offer each other. They curl up in the same bed, groom each other, and contentedly spend the day without you.

When adulthood is reached, two intact males may begin bad habits such as fighting or marking their territories. One marks the furniture with urine and the second mimics the first. Scrapping is

This Pembroke Corgi is displaying its herding ability.

minimized if one is dominant and the other willingly accepts a secondary role, unless the more timid dog is on a lap and the dominant one enters the room. The meeker dog may become reticent, withdrawn, and notably unhappy when repeatedly chastised by the dominant one.

Your dog is getting up in years and you decide to introduce a new pup to increase vitality in the old-timer. When an older dog is joined by a younger one, the bad habits of the newcomer may be adopted by the older one and you find that you now have two barking dogs when previously you had none. Small dogs bond tightly with their owner and families, and this attachment increases with age. Introducing a new puppy into the realm of an extremely aged dog often is a bad idea. The golden oldie may resent the pup, refuse to rise to the youth's challenge, and retire to a dark corner and become incommunicative. About the only way you can be sure that a second dog will be good for old Sprig is to try it, but if the plan doesn't work out, what do you do with number two?

If you're sure you want two small dogs, it's okay to obtain a second dog of the opposite sex and about the same age as the other. Then neuter both. That doesn't always work and a better plan is to obtain two young pups of about the same age at the same time. They need not be of the same breed, and sex is not an issue if you have each one neutered.

Two small pups can often be kept together.

Schooling may be a problem because the dogs will need to be separated for training sessions and one dog will undoubtedly be easier to train than the other. Littermates can work just fine but the creative minds of two sibling puppies will result in doubled mischievous activities, and what one doesn't think of, the other one will.

GENDER DIFFERENCES

Sometimes the attitudes of little female dogs differ from those of males. In some breeds males are more dominant, more stubborn, or less affectionate than females. In other breeds the exact opposite is true. Differences related to sex generally are slight if the dogs are neutered when young. Sprig's breeder is the best source for specific information about personality differences related to sex.

TRUSTWORTHY BREEDERS

Visit as many breeders as possible, take notes, and compare your experiences in each kennel. Pup selection would be far easier if all breeders honestly portrayed every aspect of the breed and sold only high-quality puppies. Unfortunately no governmental agency inspects, certifies, or sets standards for dog breeders. Neither does the AKC have a regulatory function. Litigation is possible if you're cheated outright or if your purchase contract misrepresents the value of a pup, but most of the time you're on your own and must use common sense and experience.

Study Sprig's breed standard closely. Attend dog exhibits of all kinds and scrutinize the winners. This experience will certainly help you make an appropriate choice. Research Sprig's pedigree, meet his sire, handle his dam, and look at pups from past breedings. Note the blue and purple rosettes

hanging from the walls and ask about the breeder's plans for improving the breed.

Perhaps the best proof of breeder trustworthiness is the barrage of questions asked of you. A good breeder will always quiz potential buyers and some may even request references.

Invest only in a puppy that's guaranteed to be in sound and normal health at the time of purchase. Read your contract line by line before signing and always study your options if a veterinarian finds some obscure deformity. Then take Sprig to your veterinarian immediately and, if any problem is discovered, exercise those options. Never buy a sick or injured puppy and never assume he'll be normal after treatment or at a later date. Every buyer is entitled to a sound, healthy puppy!

INTERNET SHOPPING

Buying from a picture and pedigree is always dangerous. Internet listings may represent legitimate, trustworthy breeders but not always. How can you tell if the picture is an image of your pup or his parents? Can you be sure that the pedigree belongs to Sprig? A picture doesn't indicate conformation or gait and it certainly can't illustrate personality or genetic problems. Have you ever purchased a bathing suit from a mail order catalog? It looks good on the mannequin but how good will it look on you? You need to see, feel, handle, and try on the puppy to assure that it fits you.

Computer imaging is an excellent way to find breeders, and national breed clubs usually are represented by a Web page. Contact the club secretary and get the addresses of breeders who are close enough for you to visit in person.

Dam and sire's attitude is important when choosing a pup.

PET SHOPS

Pet shops are much the same as other mall stores. They buy from wholesale suppliers and sell to the retail trade. They're middlemen and their products are as good as their suppliers' guarantees. If the shop has the puppy you want and you feel comfortable buying from that source, ask for help from a knowledgeable friend with more dog-buying experience. Study the breed standard, handle the pup, scrutinize it for abnormalities, and evaluate its temperament. Read the guarantee's fine print and look for every escape clause. Examine the papers accompanying the pup and if they seem legitimate, go for it. Remember that you haven't seen the pup's parents. You've seen none of the siblings and you know nothing of the litter's background. All you know is what you can see and feel. That's more than you have when you order from Internet shopping, but you're still standing in the shadow of doubt about hereditary features.

> **Buying from a pet dealer may be a little less risky because of their guarantees, but beware and read the guarantee carefully.**

PUPPY MILLS

Unscrupulous dog breeders are found across the country specializing in raising pups purely for income and without regard for quality. A puppy mill usually raises several different breeds. Bitches are bred every time they come in season regardless of their health. They acquire average or below-average bitches from backyard breeders and their only criterion is that the bitch is AKC registered. Bitches are repeatedly bred until they're too old to produce live litters. Then they're disposed of. Ads in newspapers may lead you directly to a puppy factory. You can spot one by its questionable surroundings, unkempt breeding stock, and pups of various breeds running together in unclean pens. Small dogs usually are well represented by these mills because they eat less and require less space.

BACKYARD BREEDERS

A backyard breeder is one who breeds an average or below-average small dog to a similar dog without regard for personality, hereditary health, or conformation. Backyard litters' production costs are low and that usually lowers the price of individual puppies. Low prices are the motive for selecting such a pup, but backyard breeders' ignorance of hereditary problems often will offset the lower price with veterinary bills. Often neither the dam nor sire conform to the breed standard and no one checks genetic problems. You're relying on blind luck to give you a healthy representative of your chosen breed when you buy a backyard-bred pup.

> **Small-dog puppies are commonly produced by amateur breeders.**

CROSSBREDS AND MIXED BREEDS

The term that describes the increased hardiness of crossbreds and mixed breeds is *heterosis* or *hybrid vigor*. If small purebred dogs of different breeds but with similar conformation are bred together, the offspring's adult size and general appearance is somewhat predictable. Sometimes personality and temperament can also be predicted if the parents' dispositions are flawless. A crossbred puppy occasionally grows beyond expectations, and its coat may resemble neither of its parents. A few relatively new breeds have resulted from purposefully crossbreeding.

Mixed-breed small puppies are generally the result of unplanned breeding, and their heritage, size, and appearance is totally unpredictable. Skip, our tiny mixed-breed puppy, was found in the middle of a little-used country road when she was about four or five weeks old. She and four curly little siblings had been abandoned to fend for themselves, but a kind woman found them and brought them in to the clinic for vaccination. I adopted Skip immediately because my youngest son had asked for a little black shaggy dog nearly every day since his old Schnauzer had died in her sleep. Skip lived with and loved our family for many years and was one of the finest and smartest pets it has been my good fortune to know. I've known thousands of similar little mutts that were hardy pets with wonderful personalities.

> **Tiny breeds mature quickly but the first weeks of life are strewn with potential problems.**

By all means investigate that option if you aren't interested in exhibiting your tiny pal and you happen to find a crossbred or mixed-breed puppy. You should still handle the parents, siblings, and other relatives when possible. Remember that bad temperaments may be found in any canine, regardless of its breeding.

> **Thousands of tiny mixed-breed pups are accidentally produced each year. Some of these pups are adorable and many are more stable than their purebred counterparts.**

AGE OF AVAILABILITY

Breeders often keep little dog pups until they've outgrown their propensity for small-puppy ailments. Size and strength are important reasons to allow tiny puppies to mature for a longer period before going into a new home. Small dogs usually deliver relatively small litters, and keeping two or three tiny puppies for a week or two longer doesn't impose a physical or financial burden to a breeder. Small-dog puppies may not be ready for the stress of vaccination until they've matured a few weeks longer, and honest breeders won't release a pup until it has received its first vaccination. The best age to acquire Sprig depends on those and other factors.

Rarely is a small puppy ready for a new home at six weeks of age. A more likely time is eight to sixteen weeks of age. Take the advice that's been proven by years of experience if you're buying from a trustworthy breeder. Discuss housebreaking and other puppy training with Sprig's breeder if he isn't available until after three months of age. Be certain that he receives plenty of personal attention, and if possible visit him often to begin your bonding relationship.

EIGHT SIGNS OF A NORMAL PUPPY

Eyes should be clear without redness, tear stains, or pus.

Gums, tongue, and palate should be moist and bright pink.

Teeth should be white and never stained with brown patches.

Ribs shouldn't be visible but should be easily felt under a thin layer of fat.

Skin should be supple, not leathery or dry, and without hairless areas or redness of skin.

Leg joints shouldn't be enlarged or tender to mild pressure.

Movement should be a normal, straight, smooth gait, without any sign of lameness.

Never choose a pup that remains quiet and unsociable when siblings are playing.

TEMPERAMENT EVALUATION

Sit on the floor and let the pups climb on your lap and note any that run and hide. Toss a paper wad and watch the puppies chase it, making note of any that aren't interested. Roll a soda can with a few marbles inside and note any pups that run away in panic.

Stand behind a door and peek through the crack. Choose a pup that's bouncy and curious, playful and mischievous, but not aggressive or hyperactive.

Pick up a pup and walk into another room. Sit on the floor and place the pup beside you. If he immediately climbs on your lap, tries to reach your face, and covers you with wet puppy kisses, you've probably found a good match. Hold him on his back in your arms and rub his tummy. If he accepts that without excessive struggling, he's yours!

> **These are simple signs to look for but are not meant to take the place of a veterinary exam.**

CONGENITAL DEFECTS

A marble-sized enlargement in the center of his abdomen is probably an umbilical hernia that could require surgical repair in the future. This minor problem shouldn't discourage you, but the breeder might lower the price to compensate for the surgical fee. Sprig's testicles should be descended into the scrotum. If you don't find them in place make a note on the contract and discuss it with the breeder and your veterinarian. That point is critical if you're buying a show or breeding prospect. If you're in doubt, wait a week before taking him home or have him examined by your veterinarian. The hidden testicles can be surgically removed when he's mature if he's being purchased at a pet-quality price.

Your final choice of a small dog should be based on a robust constitution, a strong body, sound teeth, and a great personality.

VETERINARY EXAMINATION OF A SMALL DOG

Never guess about Sprig's health, especially when he's tiny and has a small energy reserve. The only way to be sure that he's in normal health is to take Sprig directly from the breeder to a veterinarian for examination and advice. Take the professional's advice, regardless of any preconceived ideas. If advised to return the pup to the breeder, do so, even if it breaks your heart. A far greater heartbreak will result from taking him home and suffering with him through a life of disability.

LIFE EXPECTANCY OF SMALL DOGS

Length of life is somewhat inversely proportional to the dog's size. Little dogs usually live longer than big ones but not always. Day-to-day health and nutrition can dynamically affect the longevity and happiness of your diminutive companion. Poor eating habits, congenital weaknesses associated with bone structural deformities, repeated illnesses, or hereditary deformities can create painful problems and shorten Sprig's life.

If you begin with a strong, healthy pup, feed it responsibly, satisfy its exercise needs, and give it all the love that's in you, the little dog should live for at least twelve years, and fifteen years or more isn't uncommon.

Advance Preparation for Your Small Dog

Puppies recognize familiar scents, sounds, touches, and faces much earlier than you might think, and their memories are phenomenal. Ask the breeder to allow you to come and visit Sprout before she's weaned. Take her into another room or if weather permits into the yard and play with her on the lawn. Having her alone will allow her to concentrate on your scent and your gentle handling before she's weaned. Take an old towel (momma towel) to the breeder's home a few days before you collect her. Ask the breeder to wipe her dam's belly with the towel and place it in the puppies' nest for the next two nights. When you arrive to take her home, pick her up in the towel and leave it with her as she rides home on your lap or in a carrying cage.

> **If possible, visit Sprout several times before bringing her home.**

The momma towel will bridge the scent gap between your home and the breeder's house, and Sprout will identify with these smells and be more comfortable. She'll also remember your visits and your kindness and she'll respond quicker than if you suddenly appear, pick her up, and move her to unfamiliar surroundings.

A NEW SHADOW IN THE HOUSE

Little dogs generally require less space than big ones, but Sprout's diminutive size also creates problems. Your plans don't include keeping her in a pen or carrier forever, but the little tyke dons a cloak of invisibility when she's on the floor. She's at her food dish one moment, then suddenly appears out of nowhere and is under your feet. You change direction to avoid stepping on her, lose your balance, and spill your iced tea on the carpet, but that's better than a squashed pup. You'll soon learn to move about with a shuffling gait when Sprout's out of her pen.

She's able to escape from practically any barrier designed to keep infants from crawling up stairs or falling down basement steps. She investigates every open cupboard door and may even learn to open them with her nose if they aren't securely latched. You realize that her small bones are fragile, but her ability to squirm from your grip is alarming, and numerous times you've done a juggling act to avoid dropping her.

> **Sprout can curl up in your palm but she may be a fistful of trouble on the floor.**

You're terribly concerned about the number of toxic substances that are kept in your household, and you're aware that a lethal dose is infinitesimal for your tiny pal.

Solutions to these problems must be found and Sprout's new home made safe before she arrives. Think small, very small. Magnetic latches on kitchen cabinets will render those places safe for your tiny pup, and solid-panel stair gates are a must, because most infant gates allow passage of Sprout's small body.

A REFUGE

It's been proven that all dogs were descended from wolves. Certain wolfish hereditary traits such as denning instincts are evident in little dogs and these instincts can be used to advantage. A fiberglass carrier is critically important for small dogs. This small crate should be furnished with your unwashed T-shirt or a pair of unlaundered socks that are heavy with your scent. The carrier becomes Sprout's haven, a place of refuge from the hustle and bustle of the day. At night it serves as a warm, quiet, and secure bed.

A carrier has many other uses. In the yard it's her den and doghouse that protects her from the wind or neighbor kids. It's the safest way to transport Sprout to the veterinary hospital for vaccinations, and while in the office, it's her protection from other pets.

Another fine investment before Sprout arrives is an exercise pen (X-pen). An X-pen is an expandable, portable, steel-mesh enclosure built to confine small puppies. It's essential equipment for a pint-sized companion. The pen should be her home within your home until she's big enough to stay out from under your feet. It's easily moved from room to room so Sprout will get the feeling of being with you.

SMALL SHARP TEETH

> A tiny dog sometimes chews objects that present serious hazards to her health.

Sprout experiences new objects in her environment by tasting. If she can't get an object in her mouth she'll lick it. Electrical cords that are in reach can burn or kill her with a single bite. Remove all electrical, telephone, and computer cords from within her domain. Don't forget non-electrical cords such as those controlling curtains and blinds.

Move all houseplants from Sprout's reach. Some are toxic and others may at least upset her digestive system. Even silk plants should be moved out of the range of her mischievous little mouth.

Be especially aware of pacifiers, sponge rubber balls, marbles, jacks, and other toys if your family includes children or if toddlers frequent your home. These items may be harmless to kids, but they present extreme liabilities to tiny pups. Yarn, string, and rubber bands are dangerous also and should be placed well out of Sprout's reach.

BACKYARD TRAPS

Fenced backyards are quite safe for most dogs but Sprout isn't just any dog. Spend some time in your yard before she comes home. Inspect every inch of the fence for

> A carrying case is as important as toys and other equipment you'll buy.

apertures that might allow escape. Some chain-link fencing fabric may permit a tiny puppy to stick her head between the wires and trap her there to strangle. Other fences may have a space of two or three inches where the fabric ends are clamped to the posts. Divots of grass are sometimes displaced when a fence is strung, creating ideal tunnels for a tiny puppy's use.

Gates are particularly dangerous when conventional backyard latches are employed. These latches allow a gate to swing open a couple of inches in each direction, which is just enough for Sprout to escape. If the space isn't wide enough to allow her body to squeeze through, she may push her head through, then try to back out, pulling the gate closed on her neck, resulting in serious injury or worse.

These hazards may be eliminated by running an 18-inch tall (46 cm) barrier of 1-inch aperture (2.54 cm) poultry wire along the bottom of the entire fence. Usually gates can be secured by installing a dead-bolt-type lock that doesn't allow them to swing. Pound a 2-foot length (61 cm) of steel reinforcing rod in the middle of the existing space between fence ends and posts.

Be aware of other yard hazards that are equally important to your little dog's health. Poisoning is an ever-present danger. Sprout can walk through a toxic substance, lick her feet, and become sick from that tiny amount of poison. Fertilizer and insecticide chemicals applied to lawns or gardens should be watered well into the soil before allowing Sprout's access to the backyard. Use fresh water to wash the sidewalk after chemicals are used, and dry up pools of chemical-containing water that form in low spots.

> **A seemingly safe yard may prove to be a minefield for your tiny pet.**

Soft plant shoots are fair game. Many plants and shrubs contain toxic substances and should therefore be fenced off from Sprout's access. Cacti and rosebushes are likewise dangerous to the thin skin of a tiny puppy.

Sprout may decide to chew on a bicycle tube, tire, or handlebar grip. The tiny pieces of rubber can be swallowed and create a serious hazard to her health.

A fishpond may be responsible for Sprout's death if you haven't fenced it off or provided for her escape. Your backyard swimming pool may be fenced to prevent children from drowning, but a child-proof fence won't stop a tiny puppy from falling into the pool. Even if Sprout is able to swim she can't keep it up indefinitely. Provide an escape ramp by anchoring a length of wood or Styrofoam to the pond or pool's edge and allow it to float where Sprout can reach it. It should be weighted so that the floating end remains just under the surface. The stable end should be securely fixed to dry land so that it can't flip over.

A Papillon about to escape from the yard.

You may find that your previously beautiful yard is transformed into a maze of boards, stakes, fences, and poultry wire when you're finished puppy-proofing it, but only when it's safe for your little pal can you relax. When you're finished you'll appreciate having Sprout follow you about your house and yard instead of being confined to a pen all the time. Your little pal deserves to be just as comfortable and safe in your yard as in your home. The major reason you bought her is for companionship, so knuckle down and fix the yard.

> **Make your garage and yard shed off-limits.**

SHEDS AND GARAGES

Cars, wheelbarrows, lawn mowers, Weed Eaters, rakes, and shovels are common items that kids usually can handle but present real dangers to a tiny dog. Imagine the effect of a shovel falling over and the heavy handle striking little Sprout squarely on the head. Imagine the wheel of a lawn mower passing over her foot. Just try to find Sprout in a congested garage and imagine the disaster that results if she isn't found when the car is backed out.

This Frenchie has found a wonderful pull-toy.

Toxic automobile chemicals may be licked up from spills on the floor. They're dangerous to children and may be fatal for a little dog. It's best to exclude the garage and shed from Sprout's access.

Make a checklist from the foregoing discussion and begin puppy-proofing and supplying your home with the essentials before Sprout arrives. You'll be glad you did.

NEIGHBORS

Tell your friends and neighbors about Sprout well before her arrival. Let them know why you're cleaning the yard, hanging up tools, staking down your fence, and making sure the gate is snugly fastened against the post. Then tell them of the tiny size of your new pet and point out some of the problems facing every small-dog owner.

> **Advance notice of your plans will prepare them for your new pet.**

Tell them that visiting her for the first couple of weeks won't be possible because of her lack of immunity and fragility. Let them know that tiny children and tiny pups shouldn't be allowed to play together. Put Sprout in her kennel anytime neighborhood toddlers visit your house, and advise their parents that Sprout is off-limits until she's a little older and stronger.

You'll probably suffer fewer sour remarks and unhappy encounters when Sprout arrives if you make these announcements in advance.

TEMPORARY CAREGIVERS

Americans today think nothing of being away from home for several days. Make advance preparations for such an eventuality. The best person to keep little Sprout for you is her breeder. Before you take her home ask this person if you can bring her back for a day or two if you're called away for an emergency. Of course you should expect to pay a boarding fee and should say so when you ask.

Don't rely on boarding kennels because most aren't properly equipped to care for a tiny young dog.

Have another possibility in mind in case the breeder is too far away or can't help you. Contact a good friend, relative, neighbor, or professional dog-sitter. Choose this person carefully after discussing caregiver qualifications. Furnish written instructions relative to Sprout's care, feeding, and exercise. Furnish your veterinarian's name, address, and telephone number, and notify that clinician of your intention to leave Sprout with a surrogate owner for a few days.

HEALTH INSURANCE

Routine veterinary care is often expensive but the worst-case scenario can't be imagined until you've faced it. Discuss health insurance with Sprout's breeders before she's taken from their home to yours. Then speak to your veterinarian about policies and contact a company that seems to offer what you're seeking. Take the policy to your veterinarian before your pay the first premium, and be sure the clinician thinks it will serve you both effectively in predictable situations and especially in emergencies.

Ask about coverage and cost, and get recommendations from several companies.

First Experiences

Most small puppies are quite content with their new family and aren't particularly interested in meeting all your friends and neighbors. Give Sprig a few days or better yet several weeks in his new home before allowing visitors. It's important for him to first acquaint himself with his family's routine, establish a feeding schedule, begin housebreaking, and feel comfortable with his surroundings. Don't hurry to exhibit your new little buddy and show him off to the neighborhood.

> **Little dogs need time to become acquainted with their surroundings.**

MEET THE FAMILY

Place Sprig's carrier on the floor as soon as you've arrived from the breeder and instruct everyone to sit or lie down on the carpet. Open the door to the carrier and allow Sprig to progress at his own pace. Your family won't be able to refrain from speaking to him, but try to keep everyone's voices low. He'll first sniff the rug, then run to the nearest face and begin licking. It's okay to pet him briefly as he greets you, but don't restrain him or pick him up. Be sure no one makes a sudden move or tries to evade his busy tongue. Face licking is a pup's natural way to greet his friends. If necessary, close your eyes and lips tightly, but don't squeal or pull back, and don't sit or stand up.

After he's finished greeting the first person, he'll make his way to the next until he's given each his personal salutation. Spend as much time as possible in this activity and don't hurry him. After a time, he'll signal you that he's satisfied everyone's had sufficient facial washing, and that he's ready to do something else. Then let him follow you to another room, then another, and finally pick him up and carry him to the already puppy-proofed backyard. Take him to the toilet area or place where you want him to defecate and urinate, and set him down.

He may surprise you by squatting for a minute to empty his bladder or bowel, but he may instead whine for your arms. Ignore his whining and stand in the toilet area until he's sniffed the grass and walked about for a few minutes. Pick him up and carry him back inside and place him in the X-pen, the floor of which has been covered with newspapers. Leave him in the pen, but stay in sight. He'll investigate his pen and the water bowl that's half full of fresh water. Let him sniff the unwashed sock that you've placed in his carrier that you've put at the other end of the pen.

> **A quiet, well-planned introduction to your home is best.**

You may perceive an oversight in the foregoing discussion. You weren't advised to pet and snuggle Sprig. Bonding is a natural event that takes time and it shouldn't be hurried. There's plenty of time for embracing and smooching after Sprig has investigated his new world. It's okay to speak his name and pet him briefly anytime he returns to your feet but don't pick him up or hold him. He needs to investigate his surroundings under his own power.

After an hour offer him a small portion of the food you've brought from the breeder. Don't be surprised if he just sniffs it and returns to you, but if you don't pick him up, he'll probably eat at least part of the small meal. After he's eaten, pick up little Sprig and carry him to the toilet area of the yard. Repeat your toilet routine and when you return to the house, ask another member of the family to sit on the floor. Take turns patting the floor, calling Sprig, and allowing him to run to first one, then another. This is the time to smooch, pet, and snuggle the puppy. Give him an opportunity to express his love with each family member and when he's on one person's lap, the remainder of the family shouldn't interrupt. Don't pass him from one person to the next and don't overwhelm him with laughter and baby talk. Sprig has a very limited understanding of your vocabulary at this time, and he'll appreciate hearing his name spoken frequently and quietly. Don't add to his confusion by using name variations or he will think his name is Little Spriglet or some other ridiculous-sounding words.

Impress on children the right way to handle your new little dog.

PICKING UP AND CARRYING

Pick up your tiny companion by sliding your hand under his chest, and as you lift him, bring his body up against yours so that he lies cradled on your arm next to your body, with his forelegs dangling between your fingers. Teach your family this technique, and don't allow any other method to be used. Little dogs' bones are quite fragile and easily injured by mishandling. Warn family members of Sprig's wriggling nature and caution them to hold him snugly so as not to drop him.

Grooming is an excellent tool to establish kinship. Accustom Sprig to being groomed shortly after the beginning of your relationship. Within a few days after he's arrived set him on the floor between your legs, hold him steady with one hand, and with the other, brush or comb him for a few minutes. Make grooming a happy time and always follow a grooming session with a treat and a game or walk. Soon, Sprig will look forward to grooming time that he shares with you.

BONDING AND SOCIALIZATION

A bond between a person and a dog is an attachment, an unstated pledge that's probably the single-most important feature of the human-canine relationship. Bonding can't be rushed but must be nurtured throughout the dog's life. Bonding doesn't mean feeding or giving treats. It's a mutual and reciprocal respect

The girl on the left has picked up the dog correctly. Avoid picking up your pup in the way the other girl has.

Walking on its hind legs is no problem for this Jack Russell.

with human standards. It's his manners, his conduct in the presence of humans, or the way he reacts to the humans in his domain.

His socialization began with the experienced breeder who handled Sprig from the time he was born. The breeder taught each puppy what to expect from humans, to trust them, to depend on them, and at the same time to respect them. A new owner's role in the socialization process begins where the breeder's role stopped. Sprig will never be shy or snippy if you consistently impress upon him the manner in which you wish him to behave in public. One caveat that will be repeated many times throughout this book needs to be inserted here. It pertains to tiny dogs and tiny children. Your place should always be in the middle of the group when Sprig is in the presence of preschoolers and toddlers. Maintain this safety edge so you can quickly pick up your little dog and remove him from grasping, probing hands.

that includes fairness, compassion, and consistency. Sprig will bond first and most strongly with the person who spends the most time with him, his teacher, caregiver, and most attentive companion. The little dog will respond to the person who teaches him manners, spends hours with obedience training, takes him for walks, and plays games with him. Bonds develop between the little dog and each family member, but the bond between Sprig and his favorite human will be more pronounced.

Bonding is different from human socialization, which is a learned trait. A well-socialized dog will be comfortable in any human gathering and won't embarrass his owner by behaving badly. Socialization is Sprig's adjustment to human society. It's his acceptance of and compliance

> Bonding is another name for becoming close and dependable friends. It must be experienced rather than taught.

SMALL DOG HOUSEBREAKING

Little dogs make little messes that are easily cleaned up and easily ignored. That's true. However, if that philosophy accurately describes your plan, you're selling short your little dog's intelligence and trainability. Tiny dogs are easily trained, but because of owners' laziness many little dogs are neglected. Another reason for dismissing housetraining is the owner's misplaced sympathy and reluctance to enforce the housebreaking rules. It seems so cruel to carry an 8-ounce puppy out in the yard and plunk him down on the cold ground.

To accomplish the housebreaking task you must accept your dominant role in Sprig's pack and you must discipline yourself to follow a set routine. Sprig should be confined to a small pen whenever he can't be with you. Take him outside to the toilet area first thing every morning, last thing every night, after each feeding, and any other time you see him circling and sniffing. If you hear him whine during the night, take him again to the toilet area. When he performs correctly, praise him, give him a yummy treat, pick him up, and return him to his pen. Within a week or so he'll be asking to go out whenever he feels the urge and will have very few indoor accidents. It's always best to begin housebreaking at eight weeks of age and persist until you can trust him. Don't give him the run of the house until he shows interest in getting to the toilet area several times daily. Always reward him with a treat when he does as he is asked.

Watch for signs that the pup needs to go out.

> **Patience and persistence produces a positive payoff.**

SANDBOX AND PAPER TRAINING

Begin sandbox training by confining Sprig to his pen when he's indoors. A short-sided plastic litter box should be placed at one end of the pen and his bed and food and water bowls at the opposite end. Place an inch of garden soil, cat litter, or sand in the box and shorten his expandable X-pen so that it doesn't allow much space between sandbox and bed. Usually a clean little dog will use the box quickly, especially if you clean it as soon as you discover that he's used it. Leave the pen gate open after Sprig routinely uses the sandbox and doesn't make many mistakes when given the run of the house.

> **Small dogs are quite willing to go outside but sometimes an inside toilet is handy.**

Paper training uses the same idea. Spread a dozen thicknesses of newspaper in place of the box of soil. Housebreaking to the backyard toilet area is far better, but either of these techniques can be substituted if circumstances demand.

CRATE AND PEN

Kenneling Sprig is one method of assuring his safety and comfort in a multitude of situations. Training is quite easy and should begin as soon as he arrives in your home. His fiberglass carrier is the kennel. It's his cave or refuge and is furnished with his blanket and one of your unwashed socks or T-shirts. Sprig is told "kennel" and is immediately placed in the cage and given a treat, rawhide chewy, or toy. Tell him "wait" and walk quickly away. Stay out of sight if he cries and remain in another room until he quiets. Return to the kennel several minutes later when he's stopped fussing and open the gate, but don't make a fuss over him or give him a treat. Don't play with him or pet him near the carrier. Walk into another room and busy yourself with some project until he's quiet. Then play a game or pet him but don't give him a treat.

He can be left in his kennel while you're away for an hour or two or when neighbors visit with their toddlers. The kennel can be used as a safe haven for nighttime sleep, naps, and any other time he chooses to separate himself from the family. It's a must for house-cleaning day, carpet-cleaning day, or when doors are open for service people.

> **The key to crate training is to reward his entry but ignore his exit from the kennel.**

The kennel is used instead of the larger X-pen for a tiny puppy that's difficult to housebreak, and an owner may choose to have the tiny pup sleep in his kennel beside the bed. The kennel is essential for automobile trips.

SMALL DOG'S FOOD

Special attention should be given to dietary consistency during Sprig's first days in your home. When you collected him from the breeder you should have received a precise formula, instructions about feeding frequency, and the amount to be fed. Continue this schedule without

This pup is enjoying his crate time.

change for a week. He's already undergoing many changes, including a new family, new house, housebreaking, new yard, new sleeping quarters, and a new routine. Don't add additional changes that could exacerbate the problems he has with leaving his dam and siblings. Keep his diet stable and consistent.

Many small dogs eat ravenously when competing with their siblings at mealtime, but when Sprig leaves his nest he misses the competition and his appetite wanes for a short time. If he passes up a meal, leave the food down for fifteen minutes, then toss it into the disposal. His next meal will probably be eaten with gusto, but if a portion is left for more than fifteen minutes, remove it.

Changing diets frequently during the first few weeks in your home can cause an upset stomach, diarrhea, or vomiting, but the most important long-term effect is initiating a finicky appetite. Sprig may refuse his first meal because he's not yet adjusted. He's a little frightened of his new surroundings and generally uncomfortable. That's natural

> **Feeding human food is a sure way to upset Sprig's stomach and will establish poor eating habits as well.**

and to be expected. However, if you offer him a piece of roast beef, he'll probably wolf it down. Next time he's hungry he'll expect steak and potatoes and so forth. Please read about nutrition in Chapter Nine if you feel he needs a new diet and make your changes accordingly.

EXERCISE

Watch for signs of fatigue when playing with Sprig. His diminutive size predisposes him to problems such as hypoglycemia and dehydration, but neither of these conditions is an excuse for neglecting needed play. Exercise is essential for bone and muscular development, and it's also critical for mental stimulation and human socialization. Begin elementary training and play games with him in the house while he's confined to his pen most of the time. Then as soon as possible begin collar and leash training and take him out frequently for a walk.

Owners are fooling themselves if they think they're providing satisfactory exercise for their tiny dogs by furnishing a big backyard. A yard will provide opportunity for exercise but it doesn't furnish a stimulus for activity. Exercise that involves you is necessary to be meaningful to your diminutive canine companion.

Mental exercise should be encouraged by giving Sprig problems to solve and rewarding him when the challenges are successfully met. Many little dogs will retrieve and some are proficient at scent work. Tie a knot in a small sock and toss it for him to bring back to you. Allow him to smell a favorite treat, hide it under a throw rug, and tell him to find it. As he matures, play chase and hide-and-seek with him in the house and yard. You'll be amazed at his ability to learn exercise activities and solve problems.

> **Tiny dogs' exercise is critically important to their growth and maintenance.**

IDENTIFICATION

Little dogs are often escape artists, yet few wear visible, positive identification. Tiny puppies have poor homing instincts, and when out of their house and yard they are especially at risk of being picked up by passersby. Little dogs on the street are out of the drivers' field of vision and may be hit and killed. Some little dogs are taken from their yards by dognappers who then contact the owner to claim a reward. Although visible identification doesn't protect Sprig from all these possibilities, it may help.

Tattoos may stop dognapping by unscrupulous characters who sell their booty on the open market. An ear can be tattooed without sedation to permanently imprint a set of numbers and letters of your choosing. Belly tattoos are also popular, but they usually require sedation. Tattooing costs very little compared with the loss of a wonderful companion.

Microchips can be implanted under Sprig's skin by veterinarians, rescue agencies, pounds, and shelters. The procedure requires no sedation, is permanent and positive, but requires a scanner to identify the owner. The microchip will prove ownership when he's found but it doesn't help to find him.

Soft, flexible, nylon collars can carry a name tag that's riveted tight against the collar. Even if Sprig is an ultratiny breed these visible identification tags can and should be worn perpetually, and owners should seriously consider the consequences of not carrying some identification.

A tattoo will make your tiny dog easily identified.

A Small Dog's Education

Many small dogs lead pampered lives that are completely devoid of challenges. This oversight isn't the dog's fault but is caused by owners who fail to see their pet as a functional companion. Such owners are missing half the fun of owning a tiny dog. Little dogs are intelligent, bright, keen learners, and many are skillful and logical in their approach to problem solving.

MANNERS

A well-mannered little dog is a joy to own, but everyone shuns an ill-mannered pooch of any size. If Sprout has ghastly manners it's your fault! She learned nothing from you and instinctive behavior governs her actions.

Owners often fail to discipline their small charges just because of their size. Let's examine that fallacy. A disciple is a pupil or follower of a teacher, and when you train your little dog, you are the teacher and she's your disciple. *Discipline* is a nearly identical word that implies leading, teaching, or training. Training promotes self-control, character, and orderliness of conduct. Dog discipline or training isn't about size, and it isn't about physical abuse, scolding, nagging, or striking your tiny dog to force compliance. It is about gently teaching commands to your companion, repeatedly demonstrating their meaning, and reinforcing compliance by ignoring failures and rewarding successes.

The benefit of teaching good manners should be obvious. For instance, housebreaking your tiny dog is evidence of good manners. Teaching Sprout to kennel is another discipline that's part of good manners. Come, walk on lead, sit, and stay are obedience exercises but are part of good manners training.

> **Training your little dog enhances the bond between you and increases your appreciation of your pet.**

> **When you speak Sprout's name she should focus on you immediately.**

TEACHING THE SMALL DOG ITS NAME

Every dog should have a call name regardless of its registered name. A call name is a short, preferably single-syllable word that doesn't rhyme with any command you're planning to teach. *Sprout* is an excellent example because it's easily pronounced and understood. From the first day Sprout's in your home you should use her name each time you see her, call her, reward her, or discourage her from doing something mischievous. Before long, each time you say "Sprout," you'll notice she'll look up and focus her attention on you.

Every command should be preceded by her name: "Sprout, *come*," or "Sprout, *sit*."

In that way you're notifying her that you wish her to comply and aren't directing your command to anyone else.

TEACHING *COME*

The easiest method of training a dog to come is to watch her closely when you arrive on the scene. Every time she looks up and sees you across the room, immediately command her, "Sprout, *come*." The last thing she'll remember as she runs to you is your voice, her name, and your command to come. Reward her with a treat when she arrives, pet her, and give her a quick snuggle to seal her success. She'll never forget if she's consistently rewarded.

Fix her meal and as soon as she smells it and begins to run toward you, say, "Sprout, *come*." Always make her response a positive event; never call her to you to scold.

COLLAR AND LEASH

Why are so few small dogs seen on a leash? The reason certainly isn't that small dogs are untrainable or too vain for this training. I suspect one reason the little dogs of the neighborhood aren't taken on walks is because owners haven't taken the time to train their little companions.

From a pet store choose a tiny nylon buckle collar to match a lightweight nylon leash. Pick up an ounce of little treats, and you're on the way to success. Buckle Sprout's new collar in place and allow her to wear it a few days when you're with her, then attach a shoestring to the collar and let her drag it around the house while you're present.

Next snap on her leash and stoop over to let her smell the small treat in your left hand. While you're still bent over say, "Sprout, *walk on*." Simultaneously begin walking forward,

> **Whenever possible, teach as she does.**

continually tempting her with the treat and inviting her along with gentle tugs on the leash when she balks. After a dozen steps and verbal encouragement, stop, give her the treat, and praise her. Repeat this exercise three times, then wait a few hours and try it again.

Soon she'll be looking forward to the appearance of the collar and leash and will surprise you by wagging her tail joyfully when she sees them. Take her for a short walk on the sidewalk in front of your home as soon as she's obediently walking on lead. As she gains confidence she'll begin to invite you to take her for a walk.

Always watch for big dogs that may approach Sprout aggressively, and quickly pick up and protect your little dog from the big dogs' feet and teeth. One injury will intimidate her, ruin her poise and bravery, and may cause her to decline to walk on lead.

TEACHING *SIT*

Begin this training by holding a treat an inch above her head and moving it back over her eyes. She will sit to keep the treat in sight and when you see her beginning to sit, say, "Sprout, *sit*." As soon as she's seated, praise her and give her the treat. Release her from the sit command a few seconds later by telling her *"okay."* Soon each time she sees a treat approaching her from above, you'll have to hurry to give the command before she's sitting.

> **Sitting on command is less important than other exercises, but it will really impress your friends.**

CANINE GOOD CITIZEN (CGC)

CGC training is an AKC-sponsored program that's overseen by an individual dog club. It's a practical type of informal obedience work that results in a disciplined little dog. Contact your local all-breed club to get started in a CGC class. The various lessons will teach her good manners, and the safe exposure to other dogs in the class will increase her self-confidence. CGC training involves ten different tasks such as walking through a crowd, meeting other owners and their dogs, and walking in congested places where shopping carts, wheelchairs, or crutches abound. CGC isn't a game or contest, no points are awarded, and there's no competition between dogs. An officer of an AKC-approved dog club will administer and evaluate her performance, and when she passes she'll be awarded an AKC Canine Good Citizen Certificate.

> **Formal obedience training involves joining a club and working with other owners and their dogs.**

> **CGC is a more structured type of training but it's just an extension of simple manners.**

OBEDIENCE

Obedience trials are judged on Sprout's ability to follow your commands, and the training serves several important functions. It strengthens the bond between you and Sprout and increases your enjoyment of your companion. Obedience training for tiny breeds is problematic because dogs of all sizes are trained together. However, it's an excellent way to improve Sprout's canine socialization and reduce her timidity.

Obedience competition is formal training that goes far beyond CGC exercises and includes heeling on and off lead, broad jumps, bar jumps, and retrieval of objects. Tiny dogs aren't famous for obedience work but they can hold their own if given proper schooling. For more information, contact your all-breed club or the AKC.

Small dogs are quite competitive in obedience trials.

TERRIER TRIALS

Numerous clubs have devised earth-dog tests in which terriers prove their ability to scent and follow their quarries, and Sprout's tenacity and working ability is exhibited and judged. A trial course consists of man-made tunnels complete with bends, scents, and dens

> **Trials are intended to exhibit a working dog's ability to do what she was bred to do.**

containing protected quarry. The various terrier and all-breed organizations have rules governing the participants as well as providing for the protection of prey used in the event. Titles may be won in progressive fashion, depending upon the sponsoring club. Get on the Internet and find the time and place of a terrier trial near you. If you've never seen one, it's well worth the time and trouble to attend.

AGILITY TRIALS

An agility trial is a contest in which the dog is timed as it runs through and over various obstacles. The various obstacles are set according to the height of the participant, and often small dogs have a distinct advantage. A penalty is assigned for refusal or an incorrect approach to or exit from an obstacle. Agility trials are sponsored by several different organizations and can be found by contacting an all-breed club or by scanning the Internet. You can begin training for agility work when Sprout is just a pup. Home schooling is simple and easy, using homemade tunnels, weave poles, boardwalks, and such. If you haven't decided on a specific breed and are interested in such

events, it's logical to watch small dogs perform in agility trial.

FLYBALL

Flyball is another timed event that might interest you. Many competitors are small dogs although the winners are often bigger dogs. It is a contest in which each dog in a team takes turns running and jumping hurdles until it reaches a small box fitted with a pedal. When the competitor reaches the pedal, she steps on it, it flies open, and a ball pops out. She catches the ball and returns to the starting place as fast as possible. The hurdles are set according to the height of the smallest dog on the team so the teams often include a little breed. If Sprout is athletic and ball-happy, she may be a winner.

THERAPY DOGS

It's been proven that well-mannered dogs are good therapy for patients in nursing homes, hospitals, hospices, or care centers. Residents often miss their own dogs, and in a small dog's soft eyes they recall their favorite pal and relive good times of their past. Sprout's busy tongue brings pleasant memories of the devoted response they received from their own dogs.

In the role of therapy dog, Sprout may sit quietly beside an elderly woman, loving the petting she's receiving, or she may fetch a ball for a disabled child. Sprout's gentleness makes the day a little brighter for shut-ins, lifts their spirits, and motivates interaction.

Your little dog may bridge the gap between reality and the incognizant minds of dementia patients. A small therapy dog can charm and amuse an Alzheimer's patient or restore the sparkle to the staring eyes of a senile nursing home patient.

> Unquestionably one of the most gratifying jobs for your little dog is visiting the infirm.

Therapy dogs must have an even temperament, be more than one year old, healthy, well groomed, up-to-date on immunizations, and responsive to fundamental obedience commands. Sprout should be certified by an agency such as the Delta Society or Therapy Dogs International, both of which also provide liability insurance and temperament testing.

A Scottish Terrier showing his "jumping up" vice.

CORRECTING A SMALL DOG'S BAD HABITS

Jumping Up

Jumping up is a vice that's often ignored in small breeds. Physical injury rarely results from a little dog's jumping up on someone, but the nuisance value of the vice is significant. Damage by Sprout may be confined to snagging women's nylons or inflicting a few shin scratches on a friend's bare legs, but the vice is still one that shouldn't be ignored.

Correction is easy. When Sprout jumps up, her intention is to reach your face and lick it. To deal with this habit you should kneel down when you see her running toward you. Offer her your face at her level and after she's greeted you and you've petted her, tell her sharply "okay" and immediately rise, turn around, and begin walking. This release word usually works and lets her know greeting time's over.

If you have a school-age child in the family, ask him to act out a little skit. When Sprout jumps up on him, he should immediately fall over and begin crying. This action will startle your little dog, and after it's happened a few times Sprout will probably rethink her greeting. Repetition is important with either technique, and persistence will pay off.

Begging

Begging at the dining table is a vice that leads to obesity and is often ignored. Sometimes it's purposefully perpetuated in a tiny dog because her owners think it's cute. Please skip the next paragraphs if bad manners seem cute to you.

Begging may allow the little dog to obtain most of its daily nutrition from a human table, which is recognized as the world's worst source of dog food. Begging stimulates meal skipping, malnutrition, weight loss, dental caries, loose teeth, gingivitis, and pancreatitis, and is a terrible nuisance behavior.

Correction is simpler than you ever imagined. Save your breath: stop repeating "no" till everyone's patience is gone. Simply get up from your chair, pick up Sprout, and walk to another room. Put her in her kennel or bed and provide her with a toy or a rawhide chewy. Return to your seat at the table, closing the door behind you. From that day on see that she's in the other room behind closed doors when you eat. The same therapy proves equally effective when human meals are being prepared, because kitchen begging is probably worse than dining table begging.

Mouthing or Chewing

Mouthing is a pup's method of investigating its environment. Sprout will quite naturally taste any object that will fit into her little mouth, including hands, fingers, and clothes. Mouthing progresses to chewing, which is another vice that must be squelched when Sprout is very young. No one needs to tell you that her teeth are sharp and may cause serious damage to human tissues as well as fancy woodwork, books, and table scarves.

Prevention rather than correction should be the goal. Don't try to reason with her. Remove every item that's at risk and place it above her reach for the first few months she's in your home. Anything that you can't move should be treated with bitter apple or another foul-tasting preparation that's designed to discourage chewing. Never let her chew your fingers but don't make a big issue of it. Simply remove the finger and hand her a chew toy instead. If she chews your clothes, gruffly tell her no and divert her attention to some attractive toy.

> **Little breeds' vices often are ignored or misunderstood and sometimes ruin relationships.**

Running Away

Running away from home is rarely a vice without excellent motive. A terrier is especially prone to take off at any opportunity to pursue the tracks or signs of quarry. Sprout's hereditary propensity is deeply engraved on her brain, and you can't blame her when she smells an interesting track to follow, find, and dig out. The best correction is to keep her busy at other endeavors and keep your fence in good repair.

Running away when not in pursuit of quarry usually indicates overdiscipline on your part. Sprout's attempt to abandon your home is often the result of a flaring temper or scolding, both of which will frighten a little dog and encourage timidity traits.

Biting

Biting is a vice that often results from poor early socialization or repeated teasing. If a puppy is kept from birth in a kennel apart from human contact it will be socialized only with its siblings and dam. The amount of mental damage done is relative to the duration of isolation time, and when Sprout is kept away from human interaction for several months, a potential fear biter is born.

Small dogs are often teased by their owners who don't realize the harm that's caused. Sprout's only defense is an offense and, because her teeth are her only tools, she'll occasionally use them when being teased. Many little dogs have a terrific sense of humor, but they see nothing funny about being teased. Why would anyone offer a tidbit or toy and, before it's accepted, jerk it away? Why would a friend pretend to toss a ball, then hide the ball and tell their trusting buddy to fetch? Sprout may submit to teasing for a time, but sooner or later she catches on, her trust vanishes, and she retaliates.

If you find yourself with a fear biter, spend as much time as possible with her. Don't rush the program but gradually earn Sprout's trust with repeated games, training, petting, grooming, and handling. Soon your love and attention will overcome her biting problem.

Separation Anxiety

Separation anxiety or Canine Compulsive Disorder (CCD) is sometimes associated with overbonding and is quite important in little dog ownership. It can occur at any time of life but frequently is seen when Sprout bonds too tightly with you. You're heading for trouble if you let her become overly dependent on you. This is especially true if she decides that you've deserted her every time you go to the store for a bottle of milk or decide to go bowling for the evening. Shortly after being left alone she'll become nervous and anxious, and this anxiety feeds upon itself until she's in a panicky frenzy.

Her housetraining is lost and her normal good manners go with it. She may destroy anything that she's capable of destroying. The damage is usually focused on the area of a window or door where you pass by or enter. She may dig and chew on rugs, nearby coats, hats, furniture, or any other object. She follows no particular pattern and may urinate or defecate on your possessions in the immediate area or elsewhere.

CCD is a very serious affliction and often requires the help of a canine behavioral specialist. If you notice any such pattern beginning, nip it in the bud.

- Don't make a big issue out of leaving. Just spontaneously go out the door.
- Leave home, wait several minutes, then return. Continue this in a stepwise pattern, being gone longer each time.
- Before you leave give her a chewy that normally occupies her for half a day.
- Leave your car keys in your pocket when you prepare to leave. Seeing or hearing them jingle before you leave may trigger the anxiety attack.
- Vary your leaving times when possible.
- Ask a neighbor or friend to drop in at irregular times to check on her and give her a pat on the head and a little tidbit.
- Put her morning meal in a cube from which it takes a significant amount of time to get the food. These cubes are available from pet supply stores.
- If necessary, crate her during the day and come home every noon to allow her out for half an hour.
- Never show excitement, make a fuss over her, or give her a treat when you return. Instead ignore her for a short while, then play a game or take her for a walk.

Your Small Dog's Health

AN EARLY BLOOMER

Precocious maturation brings many health considerations to little dogs. For example, Sprig's skeletal structure reaches maturity very early. He may act like a puppy all his life, but his adult height and weight will be attained at a relatively young age. The same applies to reproductive organ maturity, which presents another consideration.

If you've invested in a pair of little dogs, both will probably reach sexual maturity before you're ready. Many little females show very little bloody discharge during the initial phases of heat, and often you won't realize she's in season until you find the pair tied together, rump to rump. At first you're in shock, then you're concerned, then you begin wondering what to do about the potential pregnancy. Pregnancy in a canine can't be positively diagnosed before about three weeks gestation, at which time it may be considered dangerous to spay her.

Genetic problems arise if your promiscuous adolescents are closely related. Perhaps they're of different breeds; sometimes that's worse, because you haven't the slightest idea how the offspring will look. The tiny female's sexual maturity often precedes her physical maturity, and your puppy is now preparing to have a litter. Successful delivery before maturity is possible but it's a definite stress on her

> **Small dogs mature rather quickly.**

young system. Genetic deformities interplay because an immature female and her mate haven't been proven to be free from hereditary weaknesses.

So what do you do? First, you must decide whether or not you want the responsibility of raising a litter. If you don't want to raise puppies but are a high-stakes gambler, you might pursue the first option, which is to wait and see. If she's proven not to be pregnant, you're home free—this time.

If she's proven pregnant by digital palpation, ultrasound, or X-ray imaging, and you don't want to allow the pregnancy to advance, she can be spayed. A veterinary surgeon can successfully remove the uterus and ovaries, but the operation at that stage of pregnancy on a very small dog may present considerable risk. The larger the bitch, the easier the surgery.

Please don't rely on so-called morning-after or abortive injections. Many of the female hormones that are used bring significant risks to a pint-sized female. The injection may successfully cause expulsion of embryos, but the side effects of it can be multiple and life threatening, and the injection generally isn't advised.

Depending on your veterinarian's advice, another option is to spay your little female as soon as possible after she's been bred. The surgery should be scheduled before significant uterine enlargement is apparent. Very little increased risk accompanies this surgery if the veterinarian is fully aware of the situation.

A better option is to decide whether or not you are planning to start your own breeding kennel at the time you buy your little dog. If not, consider early neutering. Spaying or castration can safely be done before sexual maturity.

> **Select Sprig's veterinarian with the same thoughtfulness as you would choose your own doctor.**

YOUR VETERINARIAN

You've accepted the responsibility to care for Sprig's routine, everyday needs. The professional who will advise you and provide his health care stands beside you. Sprig's veterinarian is a valuable resource who should be chosen for compatibility with you and knowledge of small dog idiosyncrasies. A few veterinarians try to handle small dogs with the same techniques that are used for large breeds. Dogs are all canines but their attitudes and attributes are quite different. The small-dog veterinarian receives no special education in college but must be sympathetic to a little dog's frailties and strengths and be particularly mindful of its personality.

Sprig's doctor must be gentle and understand his peculiar needs and should possess an excellent tableside manner. The clinician should know the proper way to hold and examine a cat-sized dog and should have the necessary equipment and trained staff to provide special anesthetic needs and monitoring.

A veterinarian's examining ability and diagnostic skill can be of greater value if Sprig's normal vital signs are recognized and recorded

repeatedly when he is presented for routine visits. Sometimes little dogs are poorly served by a veterinarian not because that professional lacks canine medical knowledge but because the practitioner lacks tiny dog experience.

Take your time selecting Sprig's veterinarian. Visit more than one, tour several animal hospitals, talk to staff, and meet the clinicians. If possible, observe the veterinarians as they examine a toy breed or small terrier. See if the clinician is gentle but firm, calm, relaxed, and at one with the patient. Watch the dog while it's being examined. If it continually squirms and whines, see how the veterinarian reacts.

Ask questions. If answered thoughtfully, with the size of the dog being considered in each response, you're probably in the right hospital. If the examination is rushed, an assistant is needed to calm the little dog and keep it on the table, and questions are answered in a general way that indicate that "all dogs are cookie cutter creations," you'd better leave at once.

Ask to see a fee schedule if one is available and if not, ask if fees are itemized. Inquire about the cost of a routine well-dog examination. Ask about neutering and vaccination charges, how heartworms, ticks, and fleas are controlled, and the cost of a fecal examination. Return with Sprig only if you're sure this is the place to be and this veterinarian can be trusted with his health care.

HISTORY AND PHYSICAL EXAM

On Sprig's first trip to his doctor, watch the technique used. His heart and lungs should be auscultated using an infant stethoscope. His temperature should be taken rectally and his mucous membrane color and brightness should be noted. Teeth and palate should be quickly examined and perhaps a remark added about his bite and future attention to double teeth. His ears should be examined for moisture, excess wax, odor, and foreign bodies or mites. His extremities, including pads and toenails, should be checked for abnormalities, and comments may be made about dewclaws and the importance of nail care.

Sprig should be weighed to evaluate future growth rate, and his joints should be palpated for pain or swelling. See how many notes are taken as the examination progresses or as soon as it's finished.

Thoughtful answers to your questions enhance your confidence in the veterinarian.

ASK AND UNDERSTAND

After the examination ask if Sprig's heart and lung sounds are normal, not to see if the doctor was paying attention but to indicate your interest in your pet. Let the clinician realize that you want to be included and are concerned about Sprig's health. The doctor should relax with you for a few minutes and discuss Sprig's health with you. Probably at this point the veterinarian will ask for your questions. If you're never given the opportunity to ask questions, you're in the wrong practice.

DIAGNOSTIC AIDS

Small dogs' medical and diagnostic challenges are somewhat unique. Sprig's 5- or 10-pound body simply doesn't have the reserves of a bigger dog. His skeleton is more fragile, he retains less body heat, his metabolism is in perpetual high gear, and if he contracts a disease, it's likely to progress rapidly. For these and other reasons laboratory tests often are used to aid the clinician. The operative word in that statement is aid, because abnormal test results may be misleading unless those test results are supported by discernible signs, a thorough physical examination, and history.

All diagnostic procedures, their costs, and their influence on recovery should be discussed with your veterinarian. Always ask questions. An informed owner shouldn't be surprised when the time comes to settle the veterinary fee. Not only the dollar amount of each procedure, but the specific reason behind each one should be understood. This is one reason for itemization of your bill.

A blood test can support a presumptive diagnosis or a diagnostic panel may indicate needed individual tests.

Examples of diagnostic blood tests that may be necessary:

Complete blood count (CBC). This is often the first screening test included in any blood work. The results of a CBC may indicate the place to begin more sophisticated blood tests.

– Abnormal numbers or appearance of erythrocytes (red blood cells)

– Erythrocytes deficient in hemoglobin or oxygen-carrying capacity

– Abnormal packed red cell volume in the blood sample when centrifuged

– Abnormal numbers or appearance of neutrophils, lymphocytes, monocytes, or eosinophils (types of white blood cells)

– Abnormal quantities of plasma proteins

– Presence of fat in plasma

– Abnormal coagulation time

Alanine aminotransferase test helps understand liver health.

Alkaline phosphatase is another liver test that also screens for Cushing's disease.

Amylase values survey pancreatic and kidney health.

Bilirubin level increase may indicate bile duct obstruction.

Blood Urea Nitrogen (BUN) is an old standby to survey kidney health.

Calcium levels indicate kidney and parathyroid gland health.

Cholesterol values may indicate liver and kidney compromise.

Creatinine is another kidney function test.

Glucose values, if reduced, can indicate liver disease and, if elevated, may indicate diabetes.

Phosphorus levels are used to support a kidney disease diagnosis.

Total protein is a general test that can indicate compromised liver, kidney, or gastrointestinal tract.

These and other blood tests are used to aid or confirm the diagnosis and understanding of Sprig's illness, to help predict a probable outcome, and assist in the establishment of appropriate therapy. In addition to blood tests, X-ray, ultrasonic, or MRI imaging may be necessary as well as biopsy. In some cases, laparoscopy or exploratory surgery is employed to obtain a positive diagnosis.

PROGNOSIS

Sprig's doctor should offer a thoughtful prediction of the illness's course and Sprig's recovery potential. This prognosis helps you arrive at a decision about what to do and how to do it. Once a diagnosis is reached, a prognosis

> **Prognosis is an estimation of the disease's duration and outcome.**

should be made before therapy is begun. If you understand the veterinarian's expectations you'll be prepared for the best or the worst. Either way the prognosis should prevent surprises.

Beware of a clinician who always offers a poor prognosis even when excellent results are really expected. This is a ploy used by inexperienced practitioners to make themselves look good in every case they handle.

THERAPY

The diagnostic phase can't be rushed but must progress to the treatment phase without undue hesitation. Once the illness is diagnosed and evaluated and prognosis is made, therapy options should be cited and choices made with your concurrence. Sprig's veterinarian is responsible for providing diagnosis, prognosis, advice, and recommendations, but ultimately, therapy decisions are your responsibility.

Often IV fluids can be used to supply energy and electrolyte balance to enhance Sprig's response. Ask if supportive therapy will influence the eventual recovery. Ask if one medicine is more effective than another and if any have potentially dangerous side effects. Consider recurrence of the problem and be ready for that eventuality. Ask about dietary changes and if exercise will influence recovery.

Finally, if Sprig's veterinarian hesitates or seems unsure of the diagnosis or therapy, ask about referral to a specialist. If

> **Successful small dog practice won't tolerate procrastination.**

specialists aren't available in your immediate area, veterinary colleges often can help. Sometimes a telephone conference is needed and other times the specialist may ask to examine the little dog. In any case, proceed with haste; your diminutive companion has no time to waste.

Normal values for a large dog aren't necessarily the same for a small dog.

NORMAL ISN'T NECESSARILY NORMAL

Enroll in a first aid course for dog owners. Learn techniques and bandaging procedures, as well as cardiopulmonary resuscitation and canine artificial respiration. Learn how to apply a muzzle, where and how pressure bandages are used, when a tourniquet is employed, and the proper way to carry Sprig when he has suffered an accident or serious injury.

A first aid course will teach you to count Sprig's respiratory and pulse rates and judge their character. You'll learn how to recognize normal and abnormal mucous membrane colors. Taking his body temperature, capillary filling time, and other vital signs are taught as well.

Knowing the normal and recognizing abnormalities may be the difference between life and death. In very tiny dogs these signs take on even greater importance because of Sprig's increased metabolic rate and skimpy energy reserves.

Average 20-Pound Dog's Normal Vital Signs

Pulse Rate	70 to 90 per minute taken by pressing your finger inside the thigh, slightly above stifle. Pulse usually is more rapid in tinier dogs.
Pulse Character	A strong and steady pulse is easily felt by decreasing digital pressure on the pulsating artery. A weak and thready pulse is a serious sign.
Temperature	101.5°F (38.5°C) is the average rectal temperature when a dog is at rest. Sprig's normal temperature may be one or two degrees higher.
Respiration	10 to 30 per minute, taken when dog is resting. A tiny dog's respiration rate will be faster than the average.
Respiratory Character	Even and deep, taken when dog is resting, not when panting.
Mucous Membranes	Gums, underside of lips, and tongue's surface should be bright pink and moist.
Capillary Filling Time	Two seconds. Evaluated by pressing your finger against his gums then releasing quickly and recording the time lapse required for the white pressure-dimple to return to normal pink.
Eye Appearance	Bright, clear, and moist cornea without notable blood vessel enlargement or yellowish discoloration of sclera (white).

Sprig's Normal Vital Signs

Record these values in pencil when Sprig is a puppy, then erase and record them again when he is past a year in age. You'll find that his normals will vary slightly as he matures.

At Rest		Immediately After Exercise
_____	Pulse Rate	_____
_____	Pulse Character	_____
_____	Temperature	_____
_____	Respiratory Rate	_____
_____	Respiratory Character	_____
_____	Mucous Membrane	_____
_____	Capillary Filling Time	_____
_____	Eye Appearance	_____

The next time you see Sprig's veterinarian, have her review the average vital signs given, and Sprig's normal values that you've recorded. Anytime your little buddy appears to be feeling unwell or is acting strangely, compare each of his vital signs with his recorded normal signs. If a difference is noted, call the veterinarian.

MEDICAL KIT

When away from home you should carry a first aid kit for your little dog. If you have a kit for yourself it will suffice with a few additions.

> **Emergencies may never occur, but don't bet the farm on it.**

Your cell phone is important if Sprig suffers an injury when you're away from home. Write your veterinarian's emergency number on the phone or enter it in your telephone's directory, because 911 won't help you reach an animal doctor.

- Antibiotic cream
- 1- or 2-inch-wide bandage roll
- Small package of cotton balls
- Eyewash or a bottle of artificial tears to flush foreign material from his eyes
- Small bottle of 3 percent hydrogen peroxide
- Pad and pencil
- Pair of blunt-tipped or bandage scissors
- Small bottle of organic-iodine liquid soap for cleaning skin wounds
- 6-cc syringe for flushing wounds
- Styptic stick for minor torn nails
- 1-inch roll of adhesive plastic tape
- Plastic digital thermometer
- Muzzle cord (2-foot piece of light cotton rope)
- Tourniquet or a foot of latex tubing

Tweezers or a pair of inexpensive hemostatic forceps

Sprig's vital signs chart

SHOCK

Shock may result from an injury that causes internal or external hemorrhage such as a blow to the body or an animal bite. It may be associated with chemical poisoning or acute allergic reaction to vaccines, antibiotics, or other drugs. Anaphylactic shock may be associated with wasp or bee stings, especially multiple stings caused by Africanized bees. Shock occurs in many different situations, involves various serious and sometimes fatal factors, and may develop suddenly.

> One of an emergency veterinarian's nightmares is a tiny dog in shock.

Tiny dogs often incur trauma that would be nothing more than an inconsequential bump or a short fall for a larger dog. Such an apparently minor injury can be fatal for a small dog unless the signs of shock are recognized and reversed quickly. Shock is a common cause of death even when help is obtained immediately.

One of the most significant shock signs is a sudden decline in blood pressure, but that symptom is difficult to ascertain in tiny dogs. Other important signs of shock are pale or bluish mucous membranes, including gums and tongue, prolonged capillary filling time, rapid and shallow respiration, weak and thready pulse, rapid heart rate, and coma.

To evaluate shock you should know your little partner's normal vital signs and act quickly to stabilize abnormalities. Sprig may be alert or unconscious, anxious and frightened, or depressed. Lowered blood pressure causes a drop in body temperature, and he may shiver and become progressively quieter.

When handling a small dog in shock always take precautions to protect yourself from being bitten by a panicky little dog that's gasping for breath. You can't help Sprig with bleeding, torn fingers.

When shock is suspected and bleeding is seen, control the hemorrhage and try to maintain Sprig's body temperature by wrapping him in a coat or blanket. Obtain emergency treatment immediately. Antishock injections such as steroids, epinephrine, and intravenous infusions of whole blood, plasma expanders, and electrolytes may be used to combat shock and, it is hoped, prevent death.

ARTIFICIAL RESPIRATION (AR)

Apply AR before CPR in the case of a fall or other blunt trauma where hemorrhage isn't apparent. If Sprig has suffered external wounds, first control bleeding with digital (finger) pressure over the source of hemorrhage or apply a pressure bandage, then proceed with the following treatment.

Open Sprig's mouth and quickly clear his throat by wiping away mucus with the corner of a pocket handkerchief, necktie, shirttail, or other cloth.

Straighten his neck for easier air passage to and from his lungs.

Close his mouth and take a moderately deep breath.

Place your lips tightly over his muzzle and blow gently

> Ask your veterinarian to suggest a canine first aid course that demonstrates CPR and AR.

into his nostrils until his chest rises slightly. Take care not to overinflate his lungs, and remember, your lung capacity is many times greater than that of tiny Sprig.

⊙ Remove your mouth and allow the air to escape from his lungs.

⊙ Repeat this procedure about ten or fifteen times per minute until he breathes on his own.

CARDIOPULMONARY RESUSCITATION (CPR)

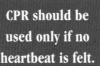

CPR should be used only if no heartbeat is felt.

When examining and recording Sprig's vital signs, find the exact location of his heart by laying him on his right side and noticing where his left elbow is positioned. Move his elbow slightly forward, and with your other hand, gently press your fingers over his rib cage. His heartbeat will be quite apparent. Make a mental note of this spot for future reference.

CPR technique uses your hand to manually compress Sprig's heart and when properly applied should cause blood to flow to vital tissues. Position Sprig on his right side and place the heel of your hand on his rib cage over his heart. Gently compress the rib cage to about half its normal thickness, then quickly lift your hand to release the pressure suddenly. Repeat this chest compression-massage once every second until a heartbeat is detected.

CPR is a one-person job when the patient is tiny. There just isn't enough dog for two people to work simultaneously, but if help is available, ask your friend to perform CPR while you apply AR. Once Sprig's respiration and heartbeat has returned, wrap him in a warm coat or blanket, and hastily transport him to an emergency veterinary clinic.

Protective Care

Ideally you'll be present throughout Sprout's life to attend to her health needs. Your plans are to keep her under your arm and out of harm's way, but that's not good enough.

A big-dog puppy often is given the usual vaccinations and from puppyhood onward lives in a big yard and comes into frequent contact with neighborhood and stray dogs through a chain-link fence. It's exercised in the park and plays Frisbee and romps with other big dogs. It takes walks in the country where other dogs have been and the sniffing is good, and sometimes goes swimming in the lake with strange dogs. These regular exposures to dogs and their excretions are almost as good as booster vaccinations. In the course of a year a big dog can come into contact with literally hundreds of well and sick dogs.

Sprout shouldn't be turned out to fend for herself, but you should remember that your tiny companion is a canine with canine susceptibilities. Follow your veterinarian's advice about vaccinations and, after she's been properly immunized, find a small-dog kindergarten where she can go for interaction with other small dogs. This dog-to-dog experience promotes mental soundness and provides canine socialization and physical exposure to other tiny pooches.

> Little dogs can't be isolated from the world and its evils even if Sprout is always kept in the house.

PREVENTIVE MEDICINE

Preventive medicine is commonplace in America and is well documented in canine breed manuals and health books. The following discussions are brief and are limited mostly to little dog situations.

Discussion of small dog parasite control isn't accidentally omitted. This subject is vitally important to preventive medicine but isn't addressed because parasites aren't universally distributed. Internal and external parasites' incidence depends on the supply of host animals, the habits and care of those host animals, and the friendliness of the environment. The wide variety of parasite control measures, the products available today, and the introduction of new systems every year also preclude such a discussion. Never treat Sprout for parasites without being certain. If you suspect the presence of parasites, discuss the matter with your local veterinarian and don't take any cracker-barrel advice or universal thesis as absolute law.

Most canine parasites and their eggs or larvae are nearly invisible. If you travel with Sprout you'll probably let her out at highway rest stops where her leash does nothing to

43

This Papillon enjoys out-of-yard walks but can be exposed to ticks.

prevent her exposure to diseases and parasites. However, roadside exercise areas may be heavily contaminated with parasite eggs and larvae from all over the world. Sprout will gratefully sniff around, explore, and investigate, and at the same time may expose herself to various diseases and a plethora of internal and external parasites.

An imperceptible tick may attach itself, and before you find it, Sprout could be infected with Lyme disease. A flea hops on and hides in her coat. A few weeks later she may pass tapeworm segments, and your house and yard could be infested with fleas. Only a couple of sniffs of a pool of dog feces and she's exposed to parvovirus or corona virus. She may be exposed to hookworm larvae by simply walking a sandy trail, and when you camp by a beautiful lake to fish, the mosquitoes may be loaded with heartworm larvae.

Don't leave your little pal at home, but before starting on your trip show your route to your veterinarian and ask about parasites that are endemic to the areas you plan to visit. The veterinarian may recommend heartworm tablets, Lyme vaccination, or other preventive procedures. Ask about flea and tick control for the trip even if Sprout doesn't encounter them in your backyard. A few weeks after your return from your trip take a stool sample to your veterinarian for intestinal parasite evaluation. If Sprout begins scratching or is uncomfortable while on the trip or shortly after, examine her coat and skin for evidence of external parasites. Above all else, be absolutely certain that she is up to date on all her vaccinations.

ACTIVE IMMUNITY

You just enrolled Sprout in kindergarten, where she loves to play with other small dogs, and the resultant socialization is resolving her timid disposition. It's gratifying to see her running circles around other pups. However, Sprout should remain in her house, backyard, or in your arms until she is immunized. Even playing with healthy-appearing neighbor dogs may be risky. It could be disastrous for this tiny dog to be exposed to parasites, virulent bacteria, or viruses at an early age and before she has developed a protective immunity.

Active immunity results from natural exposure to and recovery from a disease or from receiving a vaccination. In either case, contact with an antigen (virus or bacteria) stimulates the production of protein molecules called antibodies. These antibodies live only for a period of months or possibly years, and as their numbers wane they must be renewed by a booster vaccination.

Antigenicity refers to the relative potency of a bacterium, virus, or vaccine and its relative

> **Preventive measures are always cheaper than therapy.**

ability to stimulate antibody production. The degree of immunity produced may be high or low, depending on the age and health of the puppy and the antigenicity of the virus.

Vaccinations are injections of modified, attenuated, or inactivated viruses, which if administered to healthy puppies will confer active immunity. Ideally when Sprout is vaccinated she'll be old enough to produce antibodies in great numbers. She'll be in good condition and in excellent nutritional status. If the antigenicity of the vaccine is high, the result will be complete immunity from the disease.

> **Prevent Sprout's exposure to other dogs until she's properly immunized.**

Conversely if Sprout is immature, weak, under stress, in marginal nutritional status, parasitized, or if her health is in any way compromised, the same vaccination will confer inadequate immunity. As you can see, the words *vaccination* and *immunization* aren't necessarily synonymous.

VACCINES

Vaccines are becoming more complex every year. Some are now made from portions of the capsule that surrounds a virus. Others are made from killed or modified live viruses. Some vaccines aren't made from viruses but are killed bacterial products called bacterins. Immunizing agents have one thing in common: their injection into a normal, healthy dog stimulates antibody production. These products are tested for concentration and uniformity in a laboratory but they haven't been tested in Sprout. Each tiny dog is a unique individual

that may establish long-term immunity after a single vaccination—or not.

Passive Immunity

Antibodies circulate in the bloodstream, and when blood fluids are taken from one animal and given to another, antibodies from the first animal are transplanted into the second. In this case, the antibodies can't stimulate production of antibodies in the recipient, and over a period of time the transfused antibodies are lost by natural attrition.

A similar situation occurs in a newborn animal. Antibodies are passed through the dam's placenta and to a greater degree in her colostral milk, which is produced the first few days after whelping. By these means, Sprout borrows a portion of her mother's immunity. Because the dam provides the pups with antibodies, but doesn't provide the stimulus for producing more antibodies, this temporary protection is called passive immunity.

A neonatal puppy has only a very slight ability to produce antibodies. By three or four weeks of age the antibodies Sprout borrowed from her mother begin to die off, and when the antibody number falls below a protective level, her health is at risk. That's the time to vaccinate. Not earlier, because Sprout's borrowed antibodies will destroy the vaccine agents, and not later because with each passing day, immunity drops lower and her health is at risk.

Veterinary research has studied this phenomenon extensively to try to

> **A vaccine is worse than nothing if it isn't shipped and stored at the proper temperature and administered appropriately.**

> **Antibodies that are passed from one animal to another confer temporary or passive immunity.**

determine the best time to vaccinate a puppy. Unfortunately, the life span of antibodies varies from one disease to another and each dam-and-pup pair is unique unto itself. Sprout's breed, her nutritional condition, and health status influences her immunity as well. Consequently you're never precisely sure when to vaccinate and must rely on your veterinarian's estimation.

How Much?

Little puppies are given the same doses of vaccines as large puppies. Vaccinations are given only after health and nutritional factors are considered. Then if all factors are equal, a Maltese and a Great Pyrenees receive identical vaccine doses.

A veterinarian may administer a combination vaccine that protects against several diseases or a series of monovalent (single-disease) vaccines a week apart. The monovalent product allows your veterinarian to determine the specific cause if any vaccination causes a dangerous reaction. The downside of that technique is that Sprout will need to see her veterinarian frequently and five or six monovalent vaccines cost more than a single dose of combination vaccination. In any case, booster vaccinations are scheduled to assure that Sprout continues to produce a safe level of active immunity.

Orphan puppies have antibody deficit if they received no colostral milk. They are at risk and should be isolated from exposure

> **Small dogs receive smaller doses of vaccine, right? Sorry, but that's wrong!**

until they are sufficiently mature to produce active immunity.

When?

Vaccination schedules that fail to consider each influencing factor are obsolescent. All pups should be vaccinated but the age, size, and frequency at which the vaccines are given should be structured to fit the individual puppy. Vaccines should be considered according to the region of the world in which Sprout resides and diseases that are prevalent there.

Knowledge and experience of veterinarians vary but extreme caution must prevail when contemplating a vaccination schedule for a puppy that lives in a shoe box instead of a doghouse. Ask questions, and if you're not satisfied with the answers, find a veterinarian with more small-breed experience.

Diseases are more prevalent in certain areas than in others, and natural disease exposure potential is never the same in two situations.

Recently reports of adverse tissue reactions to various combination vaccines have stopped their use. The question about use of Leptospira vaccine is an example because of the adverse reactions documented. Ask if the species of Leptospira included in the vaccine differs from the species that occur in your region. Is cross-immunity between Lepto species a factor? Is Leptospirosis prevalent in your locality? Compare disease risk to vaccination risk. Ask if Sprout should be vaccinated for Lepto, because a consensus among veterinarians isn't apt to be reached soon.

Don't vaccinate Sprout yourself—or if you must, be sure you've had experience and training with the products being used. Consider the size of your dog and thoroughly study the diseases, the vaccines, and their potential reactions. Purchase the best and freshest products available, don't buy from mail order catalogs, follow product directions to the letter, begin vaccinations sooner than you believe necessary, and keep your fingers crossed. You might get lucky.

Effectiveness of early vaccination programs (before eight weeks of age) was proven in the 1980s when parvovirus was running rampant in America. Early vaccinates suffered much lower mortality rates than other pups. If you're committed to early vaccination, boosters need to be repeated at regular intervals and only the highest-quality vaccines should be given. The best advice is to rely on your veterinarian's counsel and expertise, and don't gamble with your little buddy's life.

Boosters

Canine vaccine manufacturers often combine products, making them less expensive than the sum of individual vaccines. Vaccine combinations are available that protect against Canine Distemper, Hepatitis, Leptospirosis, Parainfluenza, Parvovirus, and other diseases. However, Tracheobronchitis *(Bordetella)*, Lyme, and Rabies vaccines usually are packaged individually.

Some vaccines confer longer immunity than others. For example, the Lepto immunizing agent confers shorter immunity than distemper vaccine; therefore Lepto vaccine (if used) should be injected more often than distemper vaccine. However, a single dose of Lepto vaccine may cost more than a dose of a combination product. It's your choice whether you pay the price for Lepto by itself or use a combination vaccine.

Some veterinarians use blood tests to determine which vaccine is actually needed. Then they base their preventive program on these analyses. Unfortunately, the tests often cost significantly more than a combined-product booster. Consider your veterinarian's experience, risk, and cost, but please immunize Sprout before she's exposed to other dogs.

> Sprout should have a vaccination schedule designed for her after considering her age, condition, exposure potential, and nutritional status.

VACCINATABLE DISEASES

The following information is superficial except where it pertains specifically to little dogs. Remember that Sprout will be exposed to numerous other dogs on your walks, through the fabric of the yard fence, and by aerosol transmission.

Canine Distemper (CD)

This disease is as devastating now as it was forty years ago, although it's seen less frequently now. Sometimes known as hard pad or dog plague, distemper infection usually causes death because there is no reliable cure. It's spread by physical contact with infected animals or airborne sneezes and coughs. Its signs include cough, lack of appetite, high temperature, ocular discharge, greenish nasal drainage, convulsions or nervous twitching, paralysis, and death. Tiny puppies may die suddenly without displaying any signs.

Canine Hepatitis (CAV-1)

This virus also is more rare than it previously was and also can cause sudden death of small dogs without symptoms. Hepatitis is manifested as a liver disease but blood vessels and other organs are injured as well. Its signs are similar to those seen with CD. One of the telltale signs of this disease is corneal edema or the blue eye syndrome.

Leptospirosis

Lepto is principally a disease of the kidneys that thrives in wet regions. Muskrats and other water-loving rodents may act as reservoirs for lepto and spread the disease through their urine. Signs in the dog are kidney pain, bloody or orange-colored urine, loss of appetite, and fever.

Kennel Cough

Bordetella bronchiseptica bacteria and a host of other pathogens cause this croupy cough that often lasts for several weeks but usually isn't fatal. Exposure is by aerosol or airborne particles that include *Bordetella,* parainfluenza virus, distemper, CAV-2, and other viruses.

Parvovirus

Canine parvovirus was first recorded in the United States in 1978. It's possibly a mutant strain of the feline distemper virus (FPV) and is an aggressive, easily transmitted virus that's often fatal to unimmunized tiny pups. Watery diarrhea, vomiting, dehydration, high temperature, and heart disease are the usual signs. Parvovirus can affect the heart and cause sudden failure in small dogs without other signs. Parvo is spread by stepping in or sniffing an affected dog's stool, even one that's several months old. Parvo is resistant to common disinfectants and is one of the major reasons for not taking Sprout out of her yard until she's well immunized. Passive parvo immunity from colostral milk is weak and often is insufficient

to protect puppies. Mortality rate is high in the absence of quick treatment, and even when aggressive therapy is initiated, many affected small dogs die because there is no effective antiviral agent.

Corona Virus

Corona virus appears quite similar to parvo. Blood testing can differentiate one from the other but usually they are treated similarly. The prognosis is guarded in every case and the mortality rate often is high.

Lyme Disease

Borrelia burgdorferi is the causative agent of Lyme disease, which was named for a county in Connecticut. Lyme disease is now the most common tick-borne disease in America. Tiny deer ticks act as vectors (transmitters) of Lyme disease. These parasites also are seen on cattle, horses, elk, moose, dogs, cats, and man. In veterinary medicine Lyme is known to be transmitted by other bloodsucking insects as well. The disease was first seen in eastern regions but is now recognized in nearly every part of the United States. Lyme disease signs are fever, sluggishness, joint pain and lameness, lymph node swelling, and loss of appetite. A specific blood test is available that will aid your veterinarian in diagnosing Lyme, and a vaccine is available.

Treatment is possible using a wide range of antibiotics, but early diagnosis is critical to success. Don't forget to minimize exposure by maximizing Sprout's tick prevention program!

Rabies

Terriers are more likely to come in contact with wild animals than other tiny breeds. In

> Vaccines are dynamic entities that are injected into a living body, and their effectiveness varies.

1997, the American Veterinary Medical Association reported 126 confirmed cases of rabies in dogs. Rabies reservoirs are virtually any warm-blooded animals, especially coyotes, foxes, raccoons, bats, ferrets, skunks, and wolves. This fatal disease remains present across North America, and the Centers for Disease Control reported 6,280 cases of animal rabies in the United States during the first ten months of 1999.

Rabies virus travels by nerve trunks to the salivary glands and thence to the brain, and an infected animal soon dies. One sign of canine rabies infection is paralysis of the throat, which results in copious stringy saliva drooling from the mouth. With dumb rabies, the dog staggers about until death. In furious rabies, the infected dog takes offense at the slightest provocation, attacking and biting anything in its path, whether animate or inanimate.

This is a zoonotic disease (transmittable to humans) for which excellent vaccines are available. Regardless of your dog's size, canine vaccination is mandated by local and federal ordinances.

Nosodes

If you are a homeopathic follower you'll see nosodes advertised in canine literature. These tissue preparations that are taken from diseased animals are given instead of vaccinations. Canine immunology experts warn against use of this approach because it isn't effective and will fail if challenged by virulent disease-causing agents.

Small Dogs' Hereditary Problems

Conditions discussed are typical of one or more little dog breeds but these diseases rarely occur in all small breeds.

ATOPY

Atopy is an allergic skin condition that's believed to have a hereditary predisposition and most often is seen in short haired or hairless breeds. It's manifested as a non-parasitic skin itch, redness, or inflammation that affects young adults more often than older dogs. It may be caused by physical contact or inhalation but the allergen can also be ingested. Often the trauma caused by relentless scratching is more difficult to treat than the original allergic problem.

> **Atopy is difficult to diagnose and often more challenging to treat.**

Atopy signs are pruritus (itching), inflammation (redness), papules (blisters), and pustules (infected blisters). You might suspect grass or weed contact to be the problem if Sprig licks and chews at his feet, and that assumption might lead you to treat the condition with over-the-counter topical lotions that are ineffective because the source is an inhaled or ingested allergen.

DENTAL DISORDERS

Missing teeth are relatively common in many little breeds and sometimes the official breed standard excuses these shortcomings. A reduced number of teeth may be hereditary but the same isn't true of loose teeth accompanied by gingivitis (gum disease). Gingivitis, plaque, and tartar afflict many little dogs primarily as a result of their diet and dental care throughout life. Gingivitis is a disease that can cause teeth to loosen and fall out. It also can be the underlying cause for heart disease and kidney infections. Soft, reddened gums accompanied by halitosis should be ample reason for a trip to your veterinarian. Toothbrushing and regular inspections can help prevent gingivitis.

Malocclusion (over- or underbite) often is inherited in small dogs. These jaw problems can be disastrous for a show dog but shouldn't shorten Sprig's life if his dental care isn't neglected.

> **Halitosis is a sign that's hard to miss but it's sometimes neglected.**

DIABETES MELLITUS

A fat female little dog that's past middle age presents a significant risk for diabetes. Signs of diabetes include polydipsia (excessive water consumption), polyuria (increased urination), and weight gain. A warning flag should go up when these signs are seen, and you should schedule a trip to the veterinarian. Diagnosis is based on elevated blood sugar, and glucosuria (sugar in the urine) and other laboratory tests.

Diabetes mellitus is caused by an insufficiency of insulin production. Insulin is a hormone secreted by the pancreas that is necessary for glucose utilization by all body tissues. Diabetes sometimes is identified as an autoimmune disease and its hereditary predisposition is well documented. Consult your veterinarian if you suspect diabetes in Sprig. Successful treatment of this disease depends on early diagnosis and regular monitoring.

CIRCULATORY DISEASES

Mitral valve defect, patent ductus arteriosus, congenital right heart failure, and pulmonic stenosis are circulatory diseases that may be hereditary. Your veterinarian might suspect these outwardly invisible conditions when Sprig's heart is first examined with a stethoscope. These diseases may sound alike, but their effects are quite different and they must be diagnosed by X-ray or ultrasound imaging. Each has a different set of symptoms but all either restrict or interfere with normal circulation or with heart function. Some can be corrected surgically; in a very small breed the success rate depends on when surgery is performed and the skill of the surgeon.

CLEFT PALATE

This disease is prevalent in small brachycephalic (short-nosed) breeds such as the Pug, Boston Terrier, and Shih Tzu, but cleft palate can occur in any breed. Cleft palate is a genetic disease that's manifested by partial or total lack of fusion of the two bones that form the fetus's palate. It's possible to correct a cleft palate in small breeds but it requires microsurgery by a specially trained and skilled veterinarian.

ELBOW DYSPLASIA

Elbow dysplasia is a developmental, degenerative joint disease of the elbow. Foreleg lameness is the first outward sign, and diagnosis is based upon X-ray and other bone-imaging techniques. In this condition the anconeus (upper end) of the ulna (elbow bone) fails to unite with the lower portion. This results in severe, progressive pain and lameness. Several surgical treatments are possible to relieve the pain and effect relief for the condition.

EPILEPSY

Unpredictable and cyclic activity of neurons (nerve cells) initiates a seizure focus within the brain. Seizures occur more frequently as the disease progresses because the overactivity of damaged cells extends to other nerve cells in other areas of the brain. Dogs rarely die during an early and mild epileptic seizure, but severe and prolonged seizures can result in paralysis and death.

Epilepsy may be caused by brain injury but more often it's diagnosed as idiopathic epilepsy, which means the specific cause of seizures is unknown. Many authorities believe idiopathic epilepsy is hereditary. It's usually a disease of youths and the earliest sign is disorientation or confusion. Mild seizures pass quickly and afterward the dog appears quite normal. A few weeks or months later the epileptic dog acts bewildered for a minute, then staggers and falls, shakes and pants. In the next stage the prostrate dog throws its head back and its legs paddle furiously. If uncontrolled, seizure frequency and severity increases until the dog lapses into a coma and dies.

> **This serious but controllable neurological disease is often hereditary.**

Sprig isn't apt to hurt himself in mild seizures, but because he may strike immovable objects, you should place him on a thick rug or soft pad. Sprig's first seizure probably won't last longer than a few minutes; wait it out, keep calm, and protect him from self-injury. Don't stick your finger in his mouth to prevent him from swallowing his tongue because that's physically impossible and highly deleterious to your finger. Don't try to hold a stick between his teeth because mouth injury may result or if he bites it in two the result could be worse than the seizure.

Record the duration of the seizure and his actions and report these to your veterinarian when you call for advice. Medications may be prescribed that will reduce the severity and frequency of future seizures or halt them altogether, although there is no cure for idiopathic epilepsy.

HYDROCEPHALUS

Hydrocephalus is a dangerous condition wherein the fluid that's normally found in the cranial vault is increased in quantity. As it accumulates it exerts pressure on brain cells and these cells are damaged as they are forced against the walls of the skull. Infections, tumors, or blows to the skull may cause hydrocephalus, but when it's discovered in newborn puppies it's probably hereditary.

Brain cell damage causes incoordination, loss of balance, vision impairment, dizziness, and convulsions. Often a puppy with hydrocephalus has a bubblelike or highly domed skull but this single sign can be misleading. A domed skull is a breed characteristic of some tiny breeds and if no evidence of brain damage is seen, the puppy may be absolutely normal.

Hydrocephalus may be treated by surgical means if diagnosed early in its course.

HYPOGLYCEMIA

Fat, carbohydrate, and other energy sources are converted to glucose in the liver before this energy is available to body cells. A conversion failure results in hypoglycemia or reduced blood sugar. Low blood glucose is manifested by decreased body temperature, shivering, lethargy, fatigue, reduced mental alertness, and eventual loss of ability to move.

> **The predisposition for hypoglycemia is almost universal in tiny dog puppies, and owners are always cautioned to watch for this disease.**

If glucose is not supplied promptly, the pup's organs and tissues starve. The puppy may convulse, become comatose, and in severe cases, die.

At home, oral administration of honey, sugar syrup, or liquefied glucose will often restore the pup to normal activity. A veterinarian can administer intravenous glucose to bring about remarkable recovery if the pup is comatose or in danger of choking on oral fluids.

HYPOTHYROIDISM

Endocrine organs manufacture complex chemical compounds known as hormones and secrete them into the blood system to make them available to all tissues of the body. Thyroid glands are endocrine organs and are located in the throat region. Thyroid hormones called thyroxine (T-3) and triiodothyronine (T-4) are responsible for regulating many body functions. Tissue utilization of these hormones stabilizes the metabolic rate, which governs normal hair growth, energy conservation, activity levels, and other vital functions. If the thyroid glands are destroyed or their function is impaired by hereditary autoimmune disease, hypothyroidism results.

> **This long-recognized metabolic disease sometimes is caused by an immune system failure that's believed to be hereditary.**

Hypothyroidism may cause lethargy, inactivity, obesity, weakness of tendons and ligaments, dullness of mental faculties, and excessive sleeping. Ask your veterinarian about testing if any of these signs are seen.

This hereditary disease is seen in some small dog breeds and is treatable but not curable. Hypothyroidism usually can be controlled with oral medication.

INTERVERTEBRAL DISC DISEASE

A dog's skeletal characteristics may predispose it to intervertebral disc disease. Several small breeds' conformation includes an elongated spine, and in those breeds intervertebral disc disease is prevalent. The chondrodystrophic (short-legged) breeds are more likely to be affected than breeds that have stronger, more uniform balance between body mass and leg strength. Disc disease can occur anywhere along the spine and is sometimes precipitated by a twisting, minor traumatic injury, such as simply jumping from the sofa to the floor.

> **Conformational faults may predispose to spinal pain, paresis, and paralysis.**

In predisposed dogs the shock-absorbing, gelatinlike intervertebral disc becomes calcified and loses its elasticity. The calcified disc protrudes and infringes on the space already occupied by spinal nerves. Inflammatory swelling follows and pain results from pressure on sensory nerves. Pressure exerted on motor nerves causes paresis (partial paralysis) or total paralysis of the hind legs. Irreversible paralysis may occur if the pressure causes necrosis (death) of the motor nerves.

Conservative therapy may prove useful when pain is the total problem or when very minor paresis is seen. Many drugs are available to reduce inflammation and swelling of the calcified disc. Surgical correction to relieve the paralysis has an excellent success rate when used early in the course of disc disease. Some susceptible dogs require several operations in the course of their lives because the syndrome may recur between any two of the spinal vertebrae.

FACIAL DEFORMITIES

Undershot jaw or underbite is normal in a few breeds and prevalent in a few others in which it is considered a hereditary deformity. The lower jaw is longer than the upper, and lower incisor teeth protrude in front of the upper incisors (prognathism). This situation is normal in a few small breeds but is a recognized fault in others.

Overshot jaw is the opposite to the above and means the upper jaw is abnormally long and the upper incisors fail to touch the lowers in a scissor bite. This condition is a fault in literally every purebred.

CMO is recognized as a hereditary developmental deformity of some small terriers.

> **Undershot jaw, overshot jaw, and craniomandibular osteopathy (CMO) are believed to be hereditary.**

It's a proliferative bone growth along the lower aspect of the mandibles and other bones of the skull. It's a serious but treatable genetically transmitted disease. Its onset usually occurs between three months and one year of age and causes drooling, difficulty opening the mouth, pain when eating, and often a slight fever. It's suspected when a veterinarian palpates the jaw, and X rays confirm the diagnosis. CMO may be self-limiting and progress stops when the dog is physically mature but sometimes the bony change interferes with eating and may cause death if it progresses without intervention.

Anti-inflammatory drugs usually are successful in treating this disease that must be regularly monitored, with therapy continued until bone growth is complete. The bony swelling often recedes when it's treated, but some enlargement and impaired chewing may be permanent.

KNEECAP LUXATION OR SLIPPED STIFLE

Patellar luxation means kneecap dislocation, a condition quite common among little dogs. It's more prevalent in some breeds than others and many authorities believe it to have hereditary predisposition or genetic transmission.

> **Predisposition to patellar luxation is sometimes genetic.**

Patellar luxation is a complex disease that may include deformities of the lower end of the femur (thighbone) and the upper end of the tibia (shinbone), as well as ligaments of the stifle (knee) joint.

The femoral groove in which the patella slides is quite shallow and deformed in affected dogs. Often the ligaments holding the patella in place are weak, and poor angulation exists between the femur and tibia. The result is a patella that may pop out of its track when the small dog jumps or pivots. The first episode of luxation usually occurs in a young adult sometime before maturity, but occasionally it's seen in a four- or five-year-old.

Luxation causes pain and lameness. Sometimes the dog hops on three legs for a time; then gradual leg use returns. The patella may spontaneously return to its normal position and lameness is intermittent thereafter.

Anti-inflammatory drugs are sometimes prescribed to reduce pain, but surgical intervention is indicated to stop arthritis complications and return the little dog to its normal frisky state.

LEGG-CALVÉ-PERTHES DISEASE

The technical term that's used to describe the spontaneous degeneration of the uppermost portion of a puppy's thighbone (femoral head) is *avascular (or aseptic) necrosis*. That hereditary condition is known as Legg-Calvé-Perthes Disease and its occurrence in small dogs is significant. The syndrome usually begins at about six months of age and is most easily recognized when the little dog is running or trotting and suddenly begins to limp on one hind leg with no apparent injury. The insidious onset of this chronic, intermittent lameness masks the problem for a time, and owners often believe it to be the result of a simple problem such as a broken toenail.

> **Small dog hind-leg lameness that's unrelated to injury is always suspicious.**

Be alert for grouchiness with children, snippiness when picked up, and other signs of discomfort. When temperament changes and physical signs become more frequent, owners realize this is more important than first believed.

Veterinary examination reveals pain when the hip joint is manipulated and shrinking of the upper thigh muscles. Diagnostic X-ray images will show femoral head degeneration. An affected dog may respond to several months of forced rest in a mild case, but surgical removal of the femoral head and subsequent formation of a false joint is reparative even though some lameness is seen throughout life.

OCULAR DISEASES

Anytime Sprig's eyes appear red or inflamed or if he squints or paws at his face or rubs on furniture, floor, or grass, call for a veterinary appointment.

Keratitis Sicca

A normal eyeball is constantly bathed with tears flowing from the lacrimal glands through the lacrimal ducts, emptying through tiny openings in the conjunctival sac that surrounds the eye. Tears wash away microscopic dust and debris that's found its way into the conjunctiva.

Keratitis means corneal inflammation and *sicca* means dryness. Keratitis sicca refers to a hereditarily impaired tear secretion and inflammation of the cornea that's associated with drying. If the condition isn't diagnosed and promptly treated, Sprig may rub his eyes on furniture or a rug and ulcerate the cornea or even rupture it. Keratitis sicca can begin at any age but is commonly seen before one year.

A few simple tests will help your veterinarian diagnose keratitis sicca. Treatment is begun with artificial tears combined with antibiotics or steroids to combat corneal inflammation. The tear ducts may be flushed periodically, and sometimes surgery is required to eliminate a specific cause of keratitis sicca.

> **Several conditions involving the eyes are genetically transmitted and you should be aware of their signs.**

Progressive Retinal Atrophy (PRA)

The posterior internal eye membrane is the retina. It's the cell

Double-dapple Dachshund color is relatively rare, but beautiful to behold.

layer on which visual images form and is made of very delicate and highly specialized nerve cells. In progressive retinal atrophy, the light-sensitive retina begins to deteriorate and the central portion dies. That means the dog's ability to see fixed objects is lost but moving objects are still visualized by the peripheral (outer) portion of the retina. PRA may not be evident until the dog reaches about five years of age when you first notice Sprig becoming cautious or afraid when in darkened rooms and refusing to use the stairs. He may bump into furniture and fail to see his toys that are immediately in front of him. His pupils often remain dilated as the disease progresses.

Although no treatment or cure is known, PRA is preventable by having all potential dams and sires examined prior to breeding. A national organization called CERF offers help in identifying affected dogs, and when CERF certifies a dog free from PRA, a certificate number can be annotated to his or her registration.

Glaucoma

Glaucoma refers to increased fluid pressure within the eyeball. It may be the result of injury or old age but in small dogs it can be hereditary. Aqueous humor is the fluid in the eye's foremost chamber between the cornea and the lens. This fluid is constantly produced, circulated throughout, and continuously drained from the eye. When drainage is impaired for any reason the fluid pressure increases and intraocular tissues are damaged. Pain and eventually blindness follows. Irreversible damage to the retina may occur rather suddenly when the pressure reaches a critical level.

Outward signs include eyeball enlargement but this is sometimes difficult to evaluate. Other signs include corneal cloudiness, rubbing the eyes, excessive blinking, and obvious discomfort.

Glaucoma is treatable with drugs but they don't cure it. In some cases surgical procedures help stabilize the problem but usually eyedrops, oral medication, and frequent monitoring are required to control this painful disease.

Distichiasis

Distichiasis is the hereditary presence of a double row of eyelashes that emerge from the lid margin. These hairs irritate the cornea, cause increased tearing and inflammation, predispose to infection, and sometimes result in loss of vision. The double lashes often are visible without magnification. If the extra lashes are few, they can be epilated with an electrosurgical needle but if numerous they may require removal through a surgical eyelid-splitting technique.

Trichiasis

Another hereditary ocular condition is trichiasis, which often occurs in small longhaired breeds. Trichiasis means aberrant or ectopic (abnormally positioned) lashes growing from the conjunctival surface of the upper lid. Signs and consequences are similar to those mentioned above.

Epiphora

True epiphora is defined as excessive tear production. Apparent epiphora may be caused by plugged nasolacrimal ducts that normally carry tears from the eye's conjunctival sac and empty inside the nostrils. In either case the tears flow over the cheek and discolor the facial hair, causing a rusty appearance.

Several small breeds inherit the predisposition for either of these unsightly conditions. If the tears keep Sprig's cheeks soaked most of the time the wet hair will attract flies, collect dust, and make the wet skin subject to infection. He may rub the irritated lesions and cause eye injury.

Specific diagnosis must precede any efforts to treat this situation. Your veterinarian can flush the nasolacrimal ducts if they are plugged and prescribe drops that will help maintain their patency. If true epiphora is diagnosed, the cause must be ascertained and treated.

Microphthalmia

Abnormally small eyeballs aren't terribly common but when they occur, they're often hereditary. The degree of smallness of the eyeball varies and, in some little dogs, it's hardly noticeable. In other cases, the eyeball is so small that its physical structures can't be identified. In extreme cases the eye is blind, but in slight microphthalmia normal vision may persist. This condition may exist in one or both eyes and there is no treatment.

Cataract

The lens of the eye lies behind the cornea at the rear of the aqueous humor and is a gelatinous, refractive organ that's enclosed in a capsule. Cataract is defined as opacity of one or both lens and may include the entire lens or a portion thereof. Congenital or developmental or hereditary cataracts occur in several small breeds.

Surgical cataract extraction is possible but the technique isn't the same as human cataract surgery because of lens structural differences. Dog's lenses are larger and more difficult to extract, and the tissue is quite sensitive to surgery. Often cataract surgery is reserved for dogs that are blind in both eyes and those that have undergone careful medical evaluation and are expected to be good anesthetic risks. Surgery is sometimes futile because of other internal ocular structural damage.

Entropion

A genetic fault, entropion exists in the skin surrounding the eyes and is more common in small breeds with wrinkled facial skin. Entropion is an inversion or inward turning of the eyelid. Signs may begin at any time of life but more often occur in young adulthood. Often this condition affects the lower lid, but it can occur in both upper and lower lids and involve one or both eyes. Entropion usually causes epiphora and irritation of the periorbital skin that surrounds the eye. Diagnosis is reached by visual and ophthalmoscopic evaluation. It's surgically correctable but needs early treatment to prevent complications.

TRACHEAL COLLAPSE

The trachea or windpipe is the hollow tube that extends between the pharynx (throat) to the bronchi in the lungs. The normal trachea is quite flexible because it's made up of thin, elastic tissue membranes that fasten the many rigid cartilage rings together. The rings maintain patency and accommodate airflow from top to bottom.

Softened cartilage rings and elongated elastic membranes combine to cause tracheal collapse. The soft rings lack rigidity and flatten, causing the windpipe to collapse and the air supply to the lungs to be compromised. All degrees of tracheal collapse are observed. Some are minor and involve only a few rings, but other cases involve the entire trachea and are life threatening. Tracheal collapse may be present at birth or developmental.

Palpation, history, signs, X-ray or ultrasound imaging, tracheoscopy, and dye studies confirm the diagnosis. Treatment is often futile but several new surgical techniques have been developed that are promising. Specialist surgeons in larger cities or at veterinary universities may be able to correct the condition and lengthen the life of affected little dogs.

REPRODUCTIVE DISORDERS

Some tiny dogs simply can't breed or whelp naturally. They require human help, either by supporting the female or assisting the male to mount and penetrate. Tiny dogs may require assistance during whelping as well and without human help the bloodline or even the entire breed could become extinct. By careful selection of brood stock these traits could disappear within several generations, but that selection could also eliminate many of the important characteristics of the breed or strain. Therefore owners must supply the help needed or ask their veterinarians to intervene.

Dystocia

Dystocia means difficult birth and may be caused by a plethora of factors such as uterine fatigue, uterine inertia, malpositioned fetuses, and puppies that are too large. The solution to these problems lies in the help of an expert midwife. The pregnant female is closely monitored throughout gestation and never left for a moment during the whelping process. Assistance is given when needed and veterinary help is called for when home delivery is impossible. Cesarean sections are common among little dog breeds.

Testicular Retention

Testicular retention is also common to many small breeds and is believed to be hereditary. The dog is monorchid if only one testicle is retained in the abdomen. He's referred to as cryptorchid if both testicles are retained. Both conditions are unhealthy because retained testicles often become cancerous later in life. Cryptorchids usually are sterile but monorchids are fertile and can propagate the condition. Castration is indicated for both monorchids and cryptorchids. Careful selection of brood stock can be used to eliminate this trait.

Eclampsia

Adequate calcium must be present to support life but sometimes calcium reserves are lost when a dam's milk production begins. Less than normal amounts may precipitate convulsions in a lactating bitch about the time of whelping. Call your veterinarian immediately if you see your little bitch displaying incoordination, shivering, staggering, falling, or convulsions. Eclampsia may be fatal if it isn't properly treated. The hereditability of eclampsia is debated, but it does occur primarily in small, heavily lactating dogs, and usually in those with a large litter that requires large quantities of milk.

> **Sunburn presents a real challenge to little dogs' owners.**

SUNBURN

Sunburn is seen in dogs with insufficient natural protection from ultraviolet sun rays. Protection from the sun is normally afforded by skin pigment and by the dogs' hair covering. When a combination of coat scarcity and reduced skin pigment occurs, sunburn won't be far behind. Hereditary predisposition is proposed because certain individuals, strains, or breeds frequently produce sunburn-susceptible offspring.

When sunburn is confined to the muzzle or ear rims, various types of protection have been devised, but when the entire skin is involved, therapy becomes more challenging. Light-colored and extremely shorthaired or hairless dogs are most susceptible to sunburn and are treated with sunscreen lotions. Some hairless dogs must be exercised inside, before sunrise, or after sunset. Shade trees and awnings can be provided in yards, but many susceptible dogs won't lie in the shade and prefer the warm sunshine.

UMBILICAL HERNIA

An umbilical hernia is sometimes considered to be hereditary. A hernia is a fault in the muscular abdominal wall that allows fat or internal organs to protrude and take a position immediately below the skin. Umbilical hernias occur at the navel and usually appear as an enlargement about the size and shape of a marble. Sometimes umbilical hernias will close as the puppy matures and will capture a small bit of fat within the pocket of skin. In such cases the hernia poses no danger to the puppy.

Surgical repair is warranted if the hernial ring doesn't close and its contents can move back and forth through the ring. Failure to repair the hernia may allow a loop of intestine to be trapped within the hernial sac. As ingesta travels through the intestine, the captured loop swells and effectively strangulates the intestine. The gut's blood supply is cut off and, if it is not corrected promptly, the patient may die.

> **A strangulated hernia may become a life-or-death surgical emergency within hours.**

Urgent Care

Urgencies include trauma, wounds, poisoning, and rapidly progressing diseases. Life-threatening emergencies are rarely seen in tiny house dogs but you should always be prepared. Sprout may weigh a few ounces or she may be a 20-pound adult, but the precise dosage of medications that are mentioned in this section should be calculated by your veterinarian according to Sprout's weight and breed.

> Health threats often are inversely proportional to the size of the dog.

POISONING

If you have any reason to suspect poisoning of your little pal, take her immediately to your veterinarian or the nearest emergency pet clinic. If unable to make this trip immediately, try to ascertain the name of the toxic substance ingested and call the National Animal Poison Control Center at 1-900-680-0000. A fee is charged for this service but it could save Sprout's life.

> One lick of a toxin by a tiny dog could be fatal.

It's possible for Sprout to be poisoned every time she sneaks into a cupboard. Check your kitchen chemicals and be sure each has a spill-proof, clean lid. Licking a can of oven cleaner can be disastrous for a tiny dog. Read all labels. If containers have accessible contents, fix the problem before it happens. If she contacts any dangerous household chemicals call your veterinarian immediately and watch her carefully for signs of illness such as lethargy, vomiting, or diarrhea.

VOMITING AND DIARRHEA

Vomiting and diarrhea may not be urgent in larger dogs with more reserve but are indications of digestive illnesses that could be emergent in Sprout. You can safely assume that any tiny dog that's vomiting or has diarrhea is also becoming dehydrated.

Tiny puppies may swallow any number of things that can cause vomiting, including virtually anything they find on the floor or lawn. Call your veterinarian immediately if blood or foreign material such as bits of sponge rubber or steel wool is seen in the vomitus.

Consult your veterinarian about the dosage of medicines named here because it varies according to the size and age of your little dog. If you have any doubt about Sprout's fluid balance or energy level, seek professional advice because small dogs are very susceptible to dehydration and hypoglycemia when they're not eating regularly.

When Sprout vomits, withhold all food and water for twelve to twenty-four hours, during which time she should be closely monitored. If vomiting has subsided or stopped within a few hours, allow her to lick a couple of ice cubes and watch her closely. If vomiting doesn't resume after another hour, administer a dose of bismuth subsalicylate (Pepto-Bismol).

After several more hours begin feeding the bland diet described below.

Unformed or liquid feces is common to all pups at one time or another. Diarrhea is one of the principal signs of overeating or consumption of an unnatural food. Rich foods such as milk or table scraps can cause diarrhea. Her appetite may not be affected and she may be playful and active but her feces are watery, her control is faulty, and she's dehydrating.

Withhold all food after reviewing the dehydration and hypoglycemia precaution. Allow small amounts of drinking water but feed nothing for twelve hours and keep Sprout confined to her pen or crate. Watch for lethargy, vomiting, bloody stool, or other complicating signs while she's confined. If you see none of these signs by the end of the twelve-hour fast, start her on a bland diet.

Boil rice in an overabundance of water. Then let the water reach room temperature and allow Sprout to drink it. Mix one part cooked rice, one part fat-free cottage cheese, and one part broiled and drained hamburger. Give her about one-third of her usual total daily quantity divided into three meals. Feed no other food for at least two days. Tofu or tapioca may be substituted for the cooked rice.

> Sprout is quite susceptible to dehydration because her body surface area is large compared with her weight.

If the bland diet and rice water corrects the problem, continue to feed it for three days, then gradually mix it with her regular diet. Give her oral Kaopectate or bismuth subsalicylate three times daily. Gradually return to her regular diet if her digestive problem is resolved within two days, but if she isn't improving daily or other problems or signs are observed, call your veterinarian.

CHOCOLATE POISONING

If significant chocolate consumption is discovered, immediately rush tiny Sprout to the veterinarian. Baking chocolate contains 400 mg of alkaloid per ounce and poses a greater danger of poisoning than any other chocolate form. Although a 20-pound dog would need to consume 25 ounces of baking chocolate for it to be fatal, a lesser amount will cause dramatic illness. Dark chocolate has 150 mg alkaloid per ounce, and milk chocolate contains 50 mg per ounce. These products are less toxic than baking chocolate but they're more readily available. Signs of chocolate poisoning include nervousness, vomiting, diarrhea, and urinary incontinence.

> It's cute to see Sprout beg for a piece of chocolate, but it's a dangerous trick to teach!

For home treatment, induce vomiting by administration of oral hydrogen peroxide or by placing a pinch of table salt on the back of Sprout's tongue. Activated charcoal also may be given to absorb the toxin. Administer 0.45 to 1.8 grams of charcoal per pound of body

Small dogs can suffer heatstroke and must be cooled off.

weight mixed with 2 to 4 ounces of water. Repeat this dosage every two to four hours.

HEATSTROKE

The term *heatstroke* relates to brain damage brought about by abnormally high temperature. A small dog has a large surface area per ounce of body mass and will therefore dissipate heat more quickly than a larger dog, but she is still susceptible to heatstroke. If she's overweight or her coat is heavy, her risk is higher.

Heatstroke is manifested by body temperature that's elevated to 105° to 110°F. Signs include panting, production of thick, stringy saliva, and bright red mucous membranes. Within a few minutes the dog staggers, falls, and eventually becomes comatose. A precipitous drop in blood pressure occurs, membranes blanch, and death follows if the condition isn't reversed.

> The temperature inside a closed automobile in a parking lot on a cloudy day often reaches 150 degrees!

Reduce her body temperature by applying plenty of cool water. Run water from a garden hose over Sprout's body, or immerse her in a sink or tub of water and fan her. Don't use ice cold water because it will cause superficial blood vessels to constrict, which slows cooling and exacerbates the condition. Encourage her to drink plenty of cool, fresh water, but don't pour it down her throat. Monitor her body temperature and stop the cooling process when it reaches about 103°F.

Always carry Sprout into stores with you and never leave her in a car. She'll probably jump out if you open the windows for circulation and she's at risk for heatstroke if you close them.

AUTO INJURIES

If an automobile injures little Sprout, don't panic but observe her carefully before you touch her. Look for bleeding wounds, legs that

> **Nothing appears as hopeless as a 9-pound dog lying in the street.**

aren't normally positioned, and eyes that aren't focused or have a blank appearance. Then rapidly formulate a plan to treat her. Prepare to carry her to an animal hospital as soon as possible, but do a thorough visual exam or you won't know how to pick her up, hold, and carry her.

MUZZLE

Gentle little Sprout may snap or bite viciously when in shock, frightened, or in pain. She'll need your reassurance when she's injured so keep your voice calm and speak in low, soothing tones. Extend the back of your hand to her but don't grab at her. If she's obviously afraid, avoid direct eye contact and quickly apply a muzzle.

Many small dogs' muzzles are too short or too tiny to safely apply a muzzle. In such cases, the key word is caution. Don't risk a serious bite by a panicky little dog, but don't take chances on injuring your diminutive Pekingese or Chihuahua by trying to muzzle it.

> **Your little dog can present some pretty big teeth when she's hurt!**

Tie a loose single knot in the center of a necktie, shoestring, or strip of rolled bandage. Slip the loop over her closed jaws and pull the knot snugly on top of the middle of her muzzle. Take the ends of the cord beneath her lower jaw and tie another single knot, then wrap both ends of the cord behind her ears and tie a slipknot.

You must act quickly to determine whether your best course of action is an immediate trip to the veterinarian or if she should first be treated at the scene to control hemorrhage. If she's bleeding, apply a pressure bandage to any visible wound, then wrap her up and keep her quiet and warm. Use a shirt, jacket, or blanket as a stretcher on which to transport your little dog. Time is critical because shock is almost assured when a tiny dog is hit by a couple of tons of steel.

> **Extensive muscle wounds are extremely dangerous to tiny dogs.**

BODY WOUNDS

If Sprout has been bitten or otherwise injured and is bleeding profusely, you must quell the hemorrhage immediately. Remember that little dogs have no surplus. Find the source of the spurting blood and apply a snug bandage directly over the wound. Tie or tape the bandage securely in place and keep Sprout quiet. Wrap her in your shirt, jacket, or blanket and get her to the veterinarian quickly.

PAD WOUNDS

If Sprout steps on a broken bottle or a sharp tin can, first evaluate her foot injuries. Lacerations or punctures involving only the pad leather may not require veterinary care but should be bandaged to prevent further injury and contamination.

> **Pad lacerations are accompanied by extreme pain, so handle carefully.**

Clean the wound with water and apply antibiotic cream, then place a snug but nonrestrictive bandage on the wounded foot. If the wound is extensive or is bleeding profusely, immediately apply a pressure bandage and get her to a veterinarian.

A pressure bandage is formed by placing a pad or clean cloth directly over the hemorrhaging wound. Hold it tightly in place with your hand or bind it to the body part by any means to apply pressure and stop the hemorrhage. Leave it in place for at least two minutes, then slowly release the pressure. If the bleeding hasn't stopped, repeat the procedure for three minutes, and so forth.

TOURNIQUET

> **Apply a tourniquet only if absolutely necessary.**

A tourniquet is the last resort for hemorrhage control and should be used only when there is no other way to stop bleeding. Use the muzzle cord or rubber tubing from your first aid kit or fashion a tourniquet from a strip of gauze, a shoelace, a necktie, or any similar fabric. When a tourniquet is properly applied, it will slow the flow of arterial blood from the heart to the injured body part. Place a tourniquet just above her ankle if hemorrhage from Sprout's foot wound can't be stopped with a pressure bandage. Don't use a tourniquet if the wound is on the trunk of her body, head, or upper leg. In such situations, a pressure bandage or finger pressure should be used to stop the hemorrhage.

When a tourniquet is used, tighten it only enough to stop the hemorrhage and release it for a few seconds every fifteen minutes.

FRACTURES

Broken bones are another cause for quick action but they require

> **All fractures are painful and shouldn't be handled unless absolutely necessary.**

extreme care to avoid increasing the pain and shock to the little dog. If a leg is in a crooked or strange position, don't handle it and don't attempt to straighten or splint it.

If you suspect a broken leg, first evaluate Sprout's shock, control hemorrhage, then transport her to a veterinarian as quickly as possible. Carry her on a board or makeshift stretcher if possible to minimize movement of the broken bones.

EAR WOUNDS

Bleeding may be profuse from an ear wound and will be worsened by Sprout's constant head shaking. Steady her head firmly and bandage the torn ear snugly to the side of her head with gauze. Wrap the gauze with tape that overlaps the bandage and extend the tape onto the skin of her cheek. The actual wound may be minor, but bandaging a torn ear will save blood spatters on clothing and upholstery while on the trip to the veterinarian.

> **A bleeding ear wound is a problem to the little dog and everyone around her.**

NOSEBLEEDS

> **Trauma and foreign bodies are the most common causes of nosebleeds.**

First try to determine the reason for the nosebleed. If caused by minor trauma the hemorrhage usually will stop if Sprout is kept quiet for half an hour. If more copious bleeding is seen, apply ice packs or cool compresses to her muzzle for several minutes and keep her quiet for half an hour after the bleeding stops.

If unsure of the cause, keep her quiet and call your veterinarian. Such cases usually are associated with foreign objects such as foxtails or cheat-grass seeds lodged in the nasal cavity.

DEEP PUNCTURES

If Sprout should run into a sharp stick or nail, or if the cause of a bleeding puncture isn't known,

> **A small skin wound accompanied by copious hemorrhage is cause for alarm.**

apply a pressure bandage or digital pressure. If you see a stick in her flesh, leave it alone. Carry Sprout to your car, keep her quiet, and transport her to your veterinarian. If you attempt to remove the stick, you might cause increased hemorrhage or you might leave a tiny piece of the stick lodged deep in the tissues where it's difficult to find. Deep punctures should always be examined to determine whether or not the wound contains foreign material. Always inquire about tetanus antitoxin.

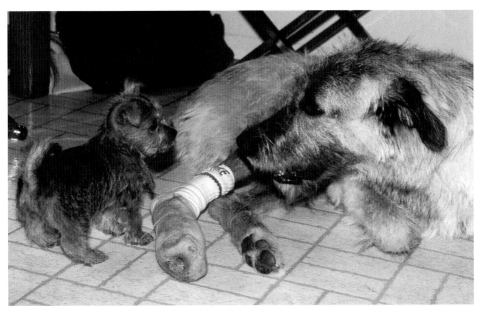

Comparing injuries and bandages in a veterinary office.

Small Dog Nutrition

Ancient canine progenitors commonly gorged on their quarry, then fasted a few days till another conquest was made. Big dogs probably can follow a similar feast-and-fast nutritional intake but small dogs are unable to survive on that regime.

> **A little dog's diet should be formulated from canine, not human, food.**

All stages of nutrition must be monitored closely because of tiny breeds' lack of energy reserve, and sensitivity to caloric intake and fluid balance. Hypoglycemia and dehydration have been discussed previously, and in those respects small dogs do have special needs. However, a common misconception is that small dogs should be fed a special diet, often composed of human food. But canine basic nutritional requirements are the same regardless of the size of the dog.

Sprig's diet should consider his high rate of metabolism, the small size of kibble that he's able to chew, and his limited digestive and energy storage capacity. He should be fed a premium-quality dog food as frequently as necessary. His need for human food doesn't exist and if fed will harm his health.

WATER

Water is a critical part of Sprig's diet. A century ago when humans traveled they carried canteens and barrels filled from rivers along the way. This isn't very different from today's travelers who carry designer bottles of pure spring drinking water from place to place. Share this convenient resource with your little dog and encourage him to drink frequently from his own pocket-size stainless steel bowl, because he probably will refuse to drink directly from a sipper bottle or Styrofoam cup.

> **Water is as important for a tiny dog as it is for his owner.**

FREE-CHOICE FEEDING

You may find it convenient to leave a quantity of dry food in a self-feeder for Sprig's occasional snacking. This technique is advantageous for small dogs with light appetites. Free-choice feeding should be started when he's still a puppy and is nearly as interested in food as in play. The free-choice plan works best if he eats a few mouthfuls periodically throughout the day. Frequent small meals are excellent for tiny dogs but monitoring food intake may be problematic.

> **Don't leave food of any kind on the floor if it attracts flies and other insects.**

MEALS FOR A SMALL DOG

When Sprig first comes to your home, feed him exactly as the breeder did. Use the same food mixture, the same frequency, and the same quantities. Then after considering his dietary needs and getting the advice of your veterinarian you can make gradual changes.

A great advantage of acquiring a small breed is the cost of dog food. You can splurge when visiting the dog food store because you'll always buy the smallest package available, and the best-quality food is affordable. When making changes do so by mixing a fourth new food with three-fourths old food. After a few days, mix half new food with half old and so forth.

If you find that free-choice feeding doesn't work for you, feed Sprig premium dry puppy food four times daily until he's six months old and three times daily from six months onward. At a year of age, his diet can be changed to a premium adult ration. Continue feeding Sprig at least twice daily, regardless of the manufacturer's recommendations.

If Sprig has a finicky appetite, experiment with his diet. Soak his dry food with warm water and combine it with a little bit of premium canned food if you like. However, feeding a softened diet after adulthood usually means his teeth will need regular professional scaling.

Buy an infant scale when Sprig is a tiny pup. Record his weight daily for several weeks and weekly during his growth phase. If he fails to maintain a normal growth pattern or if he loses weight, increase the quantity of each meal slightly. If he begins to look pudgy and

> **Dogs rarely have gourmet appetites, but their owners can't believe that one food is sufficient for their tiny dog.**

his weight climbs, decrease the quantity of each meal accordingly. If he's an ultrasmall dog, continue to check his weight regularly throughout life, and if you aren't sure of his nutritional needs, contact your veterinarian.

Never buy large quantities of dog food. Antioxidant stabilizers have been added but they aren't perfect. Deterioration rate is increased when food is exposed to warm air, fat may become rancid, vitamins A, D, E, and K deteriorate, and B complex may be lost.

DOG FOOD TERMINOLOGY

The National Research Council (NRC) of the National Academy of Sciences establishes minimum nutritional requirements of dogs of all ages under varying circumstances.

American Association of Feed Control Officials (AAFCO) is the agency that regulates dog food label statements such as *Complete* and *Balanced,* which is AAFCO's designation for a food that contains all nutrients according to feeding trials.

Anabolism is the process by which Sprig changes food into living tissue, and *catabolism* is the process by which that tissue is converted into energy and waste products. *Metabolism* refers to both of these processes and is used to describe the ongoing physical methods

> **It's easier to read canine nutrition pamphlets and shop intelligently for dog foods if you understand the terms that appear on boxes, bags, and cans.**

within a dog by which foods are digested, energy is produced, and tissue is renewed.

Bioavailability refers to the quantity of a food that's actually used for energy. A dog food containing indigestible elements may offer a colorful label but lack good nutrition.

ENERGY REQUIREMENTS

Growing puppies require twice as much energy-producing food as adults of the same body weight. Little dogs need more calories per pound than big dogs because of their higher metabolic rate. Therefore a rapidly growing, healthy, and active tiny-breed puppy is at the top of this energy-need pyramid.

Sprig's smooth weight gain is an indication of optimal energy intake. His ribs should be palpable but not seen. He should be active, his coat shiny, and his skin supple and movable because of a thin fat layer over his skeleton. If in doubt about any of these factors a quick trip to your veterinarian should answer your question.

READING LABELS

A label must identify its ingredients and list them in order of quantity. If soy flour is listed first, the product contains more soy flour than any other ingredient.

A dog food that meets the recommendations of the NRC may apply only to maintenance requirements. Such a food is adequate for adult little dogs but is inadequate for growing puppies, dogs in training, or those under breeding stress.

Labels may specify the total quantities of various elements and never mention their bioavailability. If in doubt, call or write the manufacturer or select another product.

> A dog food label is a legal document that tells you a great deal—providing you know what you're reading.

Protein comes from many sources. The sources of protein are found in the ingredient list.

CALORIES

Food produces energy when it is oxidized or digested in Sprig's body. This energy is measured in *Kcal*, which is the abbreviation for kilocalories or large calories. One Kcal is the amount of heat energy required to bring 1 kg of water from 15° to 16°C.

FAT

Fat is a calorie-dense nutrient containing 9 Kcal per gram. The difference between various fats is their palatability, and those derived from animals taste better to dogs than those extracted from vegetables. However, either animal or vegetable fats provide adequate fatty acids for your little dog. Adult maintenance diets should contain a minimum of 5 percent fat but slightly more may be desirable to improve food palatability.

PROTEIN

Protein elements are called amino acids. Vegetable protein has lower bioavailability than animal protein and is less palatable. Adult maintenance diets should contain about 18 percent protein, including specific amounts of ten essential amino acids. Excessive quantities of amino acids are dangerous, and total protein should always be balanced with the total Kcal of the diet.

Twenty percent dietary protein usually is adequate for growing puppies, and generally 15 percent is considered too little. Increased protein demands are seen during heavy exercise and training times, but these levels gradually decrease as the dog ages. As a senior citizen, Sprig will require a lower quantity of a higher-quality protein.

STARCH

Carbohydrates or starches are often the cause of obesity. Little dogs have an almost insignificant requirement for starches, but some manufacturers use this cheap source of calories to increase the energy content of their foods.

MINERALS AND VITAMINS

Dogs require twelve essential dietary minerals. Canine diets should contain a ratio of 1.2 to 1.4 parts calcium to 1 part phosphorus, according to the NRC's *Nutrient Requirements of Dogs.*

Canine diets must supply eleven vitamins. Vitamin C isn't required because dogs adequately manufacture it. Vitamin A can be toxic in high doses and vitamins D and E requirements are interrelated with other nutrients. Dangers of excess or insufficient intake are covered in the NRC book mentioned above.

SUPPLEMENTS

Premium dog foods need no supplementation. Sprig's coat sheen may be improved by adding vegetable oil, fish oil, lecithin, or fatty acids, but usually such products aren't needed when he's fed a premium-food diet. Ask Sprig's veterinarian about his needs before using over-the-counter supplements.

Never feed milk, meat, or whole eggs, either raw or cooked. Meat product supplements have been proven unnecessary and sometimes are dangerous.

FEEDING TRIALS

Premium-brand foods will include on their labels an AAFCO feeding-trial statement. These products will contain the right amount of bioavailable food elements for puppies, youths, and working adults that have been proven by testing the food in colonies of dogs. If such a statement isn't included in the label, call or write to the manufacturer and ask for feeding trial results.

DOG FOOD TYPES

Canned

A canned food stores well and is quite palatable. It may not supply Sprig enough vegetable fiber and it may predispose him to urinary frequency because of the diuretic effect of preservatives and seasoning. Canned food contains about 60 percent water.

Each type of food has advantages and drawbacks.

Meat quality in a canned food may not be the best and some canned foods contain virtually no meat. Read each label carefully!

Semi-Moist

Semi-moist foods rarely contain any appreciable amount of animal protein. They cost more and may contain sugars and chemical preservatives that constitute health risks. Semi-moist products promote excessive water consumption and frequent urination and are sometimes incriminated as the cause for certain allergic reactions.

Dry Food

Kibble or dry dog food usually is the least expensive and best diet for Sprig. All dry foods aren't the same, so read carefully before you buy.

Premium Quality

The most costly foods available are premium foods, but biologically they're the most economical. High nutritional content means you feed less quantity, and high bioavailability means less waste. No great advantage is gained by mixing dry foods with canned products. If you decide to increase palatability by mixing one with the other, choose premium, balanced canned foods to mix with premium dry food.

Other Commercial Foods

Brand name foods have earned their places in the nutrition market by providing sound nutrition for modest prices. Quality varies from one to another and if in doubt, call or write to the manufacturer and ask for the bioavailability of the nutritional elements, feeding trial results, analysis, and the sources of the ingredients.

Give pea-sized treats to your pint-sized pal.

Homemade Diets

Formulating Sprig's diet in your kitchen is a disservice to him. Please leave dog food production to companies that use analytical laboratories, research facilities, and feeding trials to test their products. Homemade mixtures may promote vitamin and mineral deficiencies, protein excesses, fiber deficiencies, gum disease, obesity, and even pancreatic disease.

Puppy Rations

Puppy foods are formulated specifically for growing dogs and should furnish adequate nutrition for normal development of small-dog puppies. A label designating a product as puppy food doesn't mean you can accept it without question. Constituent quality and sources are critical, puppy feeding trials are conducted as well, and the AAFCO label should be found on puppy rations.

Special Diets

Foods are available both by prescription and over the counter to support geriatric nutrition, aid treatment of kidney disease, assist in treating diabetes, gastritis, flatulence, and other health problems. Consult your veterinarian before you use these foods.

Treats

Treats are part of your dog's daily diet and may not be balanced. Measure the quantity of his daily treats and deduct that amount from his daily dog food ration to be sure you're not overfeeding him. Another possibility you might try is to offer him a bit of his regular kibble as a training treat. If you buy commercial treats, check the ingredients the same as if they were his regular food.

Human Foods

Never feed the following foods to your little dog:

- Milk will usually cause diarrhea.
- Meats often cause diarrhea and will upset dietary balance. This includes all animal muscle and organ flesh.
- Chicken or chop bones, steak bones, ribs, and some roast bones may splinter when Sprig chews them. Bone shards may lodge in his mouth, throat, or gastrointestinal tract and cause serious medical problems.
- Ice cream, candy, pizza, potato chips, peanuts, and a host of other human junk foods are difficult for Sprig to digest and should be avoided.
- Table scraps are equally dangerous and are reported to be the most important cause of canine pancreatitis.

Put human food on the dining table and dog food on the floor.

OVERFEEDING AND OBESITY

You're probably overfeeding Sprig if his weight is climbing and he's past his growing phase. If using a free-choice method, discontinue it at once and begin individual meals. If he's a beggar, stop this vice. If you have two or more pets in the house, feed the dogs individually in separate rooms and put the cat's food out of Sprig's reach.

Overfeeding often is a training problem for a tiny dog. Treats work so well that you lose count of the number he receives, and suddenly he's plumper than he should be.

Although obesity usually isn't considered a disease it's a serious threat to small older dogs and may be an important side effect of several serious metabolic diseases, including diabetes, hypothyroidism, Cushing's disease, and others. Even

> **Accidental or unintentional overfeeding is just as dangerous as stuffing Sprig on purpose.**

when not associated with disease, obesity shouldn't be ignored. It will shorten Sprig's life by stressing leg joints and internal organ function. Schedule an appointment with your veterinarian for a laboratory workup to rule out diseases. If Sprig is simply overweight, begin a careful reducing plan, one that won't cause undue physical and mental stress. Your veterinarian can prescribe a special dog food to help him reduce, and others are commercially available. Use low-calorie dog foods that contain a complete nutritional balance. Don't subscribe to a crash diet but with your veterinarian's advice plan to reduce his weight over a period of months. Slow down his eating with little plastic cubes and balls that are constructed to dispense dry food one kibble at a time. Sprig will push the cube around his crate, pen, or backyard for an extended

Well-mannered group of Corgis out for a walk.

period of time to get a meal. These feeding devices are available in most pet supply stores and catalogs.

Gradually begin an exercise program by taking Sprig for short walks several times daily. Take him to new places where he'll find new smells to stimulate his interest and increase his desire to exercise. Sometimes years may be added to an obese little dog's life by weight reduction and appropriate exercise.

SUDDEN WEIGHT LOSS

Regular monitoring of your tiny companion's weight throughout life is extremely important, but it becomes even more critical in Sprig's geriatric years. If you've discontinued examining and weighing him regularly, begin again and check for the following clues:

- Is he eating a normal amount of food?
- Does he have halitosis?
- Are his stools normal in color and consistency?
- Does he vomit occasionally?
- Is he consuming the usual amount of food?
- Is he drinking the usual amount of water?
- Is he normally active?
- Has he any visible swellings or nodules?

Your veterinarian may suggest laboratory tests to check organ function and to help diagnose obscure diseases.

> Sudden weight loss is cause for alarm and should be addressed immediately with your veterinarian's help.

Small Dog Reproduction

Anthropomorphic thinking is quite common among tiny-dog owners. Many consider their small companions to be equivalent to children. Maybe they're eager to see grandchildren bouncing around their feet and are so wrapped up in their tiny pals that they lose sight of reality. Little dogs aren't disposable, and breeding them is a science in itself and one that can't be taken lightly.

Just wanting to see Sprout's puppies isn't enough. The question isn't, Can Sprout be bred? but rather, Should she be bred? If so, which person is best qualified to accomplish this feat?

Regardless of your superficial reasoning, search your subconscious mind and discover your true motives.

> **The science of dog breeding requires extensive thought, study, and practical experience.**

QUESTIONABLE MOTIVES FOR BREEDING

I didn't pay for a breeding-quality puppy, but my neighbor says Sprout is show dog material.

She's never been in competition, but I'm sure I could train her if I had time.

My groomer says she's a wonderful little dog that should be bred!

She's about to come in heat, and I can't bear to put her in a boarding kennel.

All my friends want a cute little puppy like Sprout.

A friend said a breeder told her Sprout will be a much better pet if she has a litter.

I read somewhere that she'll get fat if she isn't bred once.

Our children want to watch the miracle of birth!

You love your little dog and want to share her loving personality with friends. That's an admirable goal, but please consider your pet first. Consider the problems encountered when producing a litter of exceptional puppies and finding exceptional homes for them. Producing puppies is an obligation that requires commitment!

The world is overrun with dogs that once were cute little puppies. More than five million innocent pets are euthanized annually and others manage to avoid capture to survive in the alleys of urban America. If they avoid being killed by traffic, they live by their wits, scavenge from Dumpsters, and serve as disease reservoirs for our pets.

Greed often is the underlying motive for breeding pets, proof of which

> **Are my motives logical and above reproach?**

is easily found in the dozens of newspaper ads for pet-quality pups. In small dogs, profit expectations are reduced because tiny dogs whelp tiny litters. Profits are further diminished when one considers the cost of veterinary fees, your time spent properly caring for a tiny brood bitch, dealing with tiny-dog whelping problems, raising healthy pups, and finding good homes for your puppies.

> **You can afford the time and money to produce a valuable litter of puppies.**

RIGHT REASONS

* You invested in an exhibition and breeding-quality pup and Sprout has proven her merits in competition.
* She's been certified free of hereditary diseases.
* You've studied pedigrees and found a proven, high-quality stud dog to complement Sprout's minimal faults.
* You can afford the costs associated with breeding and raising puppies.
* Your facilities are adequate for whelping and raising a litter.
* You have the time and are prepared to properly care for Sprout and her litter.
* You've found and assured good homes for the puppies.

PLAN, PLAN, PLAN

* Study the canine estrous cycle and make notes about Sprout's individual cycle, its various stages, duration, and her attitude while in each stage.

> **You've read the best book and have your veterinarian's commitment to help.**

* Be certain Sprout is receiving the finest nutrition, is up to date on all vaccinations, and is not parasitized.
* Investigate the cost of a cesarean section and discuss with your veterinarian the best way to monitor her pregnancy and predict the need for help.
* Study whelping procedures, dewclaw amputation, tail docking, monitoring puppies' weight, weaning, vaccinating, and finding good homes.
* Breed her at a convenient time, after her second birthday, and after she's been certified free from hereditary diseases.

> **Reproductive knowledge alone may not prepare an owner for breeding small dogs.**

SMALL DOGS HAVE BIG PROBLEMS

* Many females must be held in position for the male to mount.
* Males often require encouragement or physical help to accomplish intromission (penetration) during copulation.
* Many little dogs are bred by artificial insemination because natural breeding is impossible.
* Little dogs sometimes require help during whelping.
* Small females that are tightly bonded to their owner occasionally abandon their litter and take their place on the owner's lap.

A FULL-TIME COMMITMENT

You must accept a nearly full-time job for about four months to cover the involvement in preparing Sprout, monitoring her pregnancy, attending the whelping, caring for the dam and litter till weaning time, and placing the puppies in good homes.

You undoubtedly will enjoy this process if the commitment doesn't bother you. Will you make money at this endeavor? Don't bet the farm!

LIFE AFTER WHELPING

After Sprout has made her contributions to her breed's gene pool, she should be retired and spayed. Earlier retirement is prudent if breeding, pregnancy, or whelping complications occurred.

Little bitches' reproductive lives end earlier than males', and by six years of age most dams have passed their productive peaks. After that age, smaller litters can be expected and reproductive problems and health risks are likely to increase. Spay operations in older females are somewhat difficult to perform and pose slightly higher risks than for young animals. Those risks are minor compared with the risks of pyometra, tumors, and mammary cancer, all of which are too commonly seen in unspayed middle-aged bitches.

> **My little pal has given me a couple of litters and now I want her to enjoy life to the fullest.**

SPAY BENEFITS

Spaying Sprout isn't just an arbitrary birth control program. The surgical procedure is performed under general anesthesia, and both ovaries and the uterus are

> **Puppies are fun but delivering and raising puppies is tedious work.**

removed (ovariohysterectomy). Her age and the number of pregnancies and cesarean sections performed influences the risk. Short hospitalization is required and within a few days she should act and eat normally.

* She no longer has three-week heat cycles twice a year.

* She doesn't become pregnant.

* If spayed early before her first heat, breast cancer rarely occurs.

* Spaying precludes development of hormone-related diseases such as pyometra and endometritis.

* Spaying at any age doesn't change Sprout's personality, ambition, trainability, growth, or development rate.

CASTRATION BENEFITS

Castrating a male entails the surgical removal of both testicles. Recovery should be uneventful and rapid and within a day of two he'll be playful and hungry.

> **What are the advantages of castration?**

* Aggressiveness toward other males is reduced.

* Testicular tumors, prostatitis, and prostatic cancer are averted.

* Castration curbs the desire to escape from your yard to search for females in heat.

> **One reason for spaying your little dog is to make her a more stable pet.**

AGE TO SPAY OR CASTRATE

Many veterinarians recommend spaying females at five to six months of age because, if done before the first heat, the threat of breast cancer is virtually nonexistent. Male pets usually are castrated at eight to twelve months. However, it's quite feasible to spay or castrate a much younger dog and the technique is reported to be safe, effective, and without personality problems. In recent years thousands of shelter and pound puppies have been sterilized as early as twelve weeks of age without complication. This has led to rethinking of formerly recommended canine

Is early castration dangerous?

reproductive control measures in our cities and has changed the opinions of some breeders and ethologists (behavior scientists).

It's too soon to unequivocally recommend young-age sterilization, but recent experience and documented research indicates no significant negative effect on either the physical development or personality, and the practice has greatly reduced canine euthanasia in American shelters and pounds.

Small Dog Geriatrics

With good care a small dog inherits a longer life than his large cousin. As always, this general rule has exceptions which include the following:

   The tiniest of small breeds often live shortened lives because of their increased susceptibility to accidents and illnesses.

   Inbreeding to produce extremely small dogs often is accompanied by genetic weaknesses.

   Nutritional stresses and deadly dental diseases may be increased by owners of pocket-sized dogs who believe their pet can't survive on dog food and must eat human food. Some of these owners even chew the food for their pet.

   Small dogs' vaccinations are sometimes neglected because microsize pups aren't considered strong enough to withstand vaccinations, but unfortunately these tiny canines are susceptible to aerosol-transmitted diseases.

   A recent British survey reports that life expectancy of all breeds averages eleven years and one month. For dogs dying of old age without influencing factors, expectancy was twelve years and eight months. Similar studies in the United States haven't been reported to the best of my knowledge, but because British dogs' care is similar to ours, their report should be significant.

> **Little dogs live longer than big ones.**

Miniature Poodles were at the top of the UK's life expectancy list at 14.8 years. The British figures are averages for all breeds and all causes of death. Cancer caused nearly 16 percent of all deaths, and heart disease caused half as many. Only 8 percent of dogs reported lived more than 15 years, and disease or euthanasia caused 64 percent of all deaths. Little mutts usually lived longer than purebreds, although Whippets, Miniature Poodles, and Jack Russell Terriers outlived mixed breeds.

According to Professor Michell, president of the Royal College of Veterinary Surgeons, dog owners should abandon the belief that one year of a dog's life is equal to six or seven years of a human's life. No such arbitrary formula works when all factors affecting longevity are considered.

One calculation for life expectancy says that the first year of a dog's life is equal to 21 years of human life and that each year following the first is equal to four human years. By this calculation a healthy 8-year-old dog would be $21 + 28 = 49$ years old or equal to a 49-year-old human. This formula may be more logical than the 1-to-7 calculations but it may err when extraneous factors are thrown into the formula, such as exercise, nutrition, the dog's size, and its metabolic rate.

A Toy Manchester all dressed up for a stroll on the strand.

GENERIC DRUGS FOR GERIATRIC DOGS

Many old dogs depend on over-the-counter pain-relieving compounds to see them through their golden years. These drugs may be quite important to old Sprig's comfort, but consult your veterinarian about the proper dose and the safety of the drug before a treatment is administered.

> **Old dogs may not tolerate pain-relieving drugs.**

MAKING A SMALL OLD DOG'S LIFE EASIER

Providing physical comfort is perhaps the most important and easiest part of taking care of a geriatric pal.

 Don't lift him to places where he may try to jump down, and don't hug him.

 Provide soft, thick plastic-backed rugs or bath mats to sleep on and wash them frequently.

 Rub emollient creams into Sprig's calluses to prevent decubital ulcers or bedsores.

 Trim his nails frequently to prevent them from growing into his pads and interfering with walking.

 Consider shearing off his long coat in summertime because grooming may be painful.

 Don't awaken him by a sudden touch, but make a noise when you approach your sleeping pal.

 Alleviate stress on his old joints by gently helping him to his feet.

 Provide ramps to reduce the stress of climbing up and down steps.

> **When old age approaches, avoid picking him up and putting him down.**

 Don't move furniture frequently. Leave items in their time-honored positions.

 Take him on frequent short walks and never urge him to continue when he prefers to rest.

 Let him choose the pace when you take him on walks.

 Buy a coat or knit a sweater for him to wear on walks in cool weather.

 Give him small quantities of food three or four times daily.

 He probably can't chew as well as he once could. Soak and soften his food.

 He may have lost some taste sensations. Mix his food with nonfat broth to add palatability.

 Be sure he always has plenty of fresh water in a clean bowl.

 Take care not to overfeed him.

- Prevent feces from collecting in the hair around his anus by clipping regularly.
- Use his pen or carrier to protect him from rowdy visitors.

GROUCHY OLD DOGS

Sprig has been a model pet for fifteen years but lately he resists being lifted and carried. He whines when you stroke his back, and combing him is out of the question. He no longer goes to see who rang the doorbell and he snapped at your neighbor who reached out his hand to pet him. What evil is at work in your graying old pal?

ARTHRITIS

He may limp on one leg or simply slow down altogether. His hip joints might be affected the worst, but virtually every joint of his body may be a source of pain.

Arthritic pain may limit Sprig's activity and alter his playful happy-go-lucky atti- tude. Maybe he'll take a minute or

more to find a comfortable position when lying down. He'll take as much or more time when getting up to start his engine and shift to drive. He may become notably lame in one leg or all his joints may creak and groan as he moves about.

DENTAL DISEASE

Neglected dental plaque and gum disease may contribute to loose teeth, reduced appetite, kidney dis-

ease, heart disease, and other health problems. Any of these conditions cause grouchiness but it's never too late to correct them.

DEAFNESS

Sprig's deafness may be real or it may fall under the category of selective hearing. Some hearing loss occurs in practically all old dogs of any size. When Sprig's hearing fails, he'll be easily startled when sleeping and may be accidentally stepped on or kicked. His pain tolerance is reduced as he ages and his attitude may be grouchy and irritable. Some small dogs find low- traffic areas in which to nap; others hide in closets or behind furniture.

LUMPS AND BUMPS

Tiny dogs' faces and legs sometimes develop wartlike tumors or skin cysts. Occa- sionally round, fatty tumors are evident on Sprig's abdomen or chest immediately under his skin. None of these old-timer conditions are terribly dangerous, but your veterinarian should check them on his next visit. Treatment depends on the size and position of these lumps as well as Sprig's age and general health and the tumor's potential growth and ulceration. Your veterinarian may elect to leave them alone and monitor them if Sprig is quite old and the lumps aren't causing pain.

NUCLEAR SCLEROSIS AND BLINDNESS

Nuclear sclerosis is the hardening and clouding of an old dog's lens that's similar to a cataract formation. Rarely does this opaque lens cause total blindness although low-light vision usually is impaired. When Sprig's vision decreases he may bump into chair legs or furniture that's been moved and, when he becomes unsure of his surroundings, he may undergo a personality change. He'll avoid stairs because of his impaired depth perception, may resent being picked up, and often will panic if he isn't given total body support when he's lifted.

Nuclear sclerosis usually proceeds gradually and your little buddy will deal with it on his own. Total gradual blindness is acceptable to most little dogs, providing objects in their environment remain stable. Successful lens extraction can be performed by a veterinary ophthalmologist, but the operation is different and the risk is greater than in the human operation.

CANINE COGNITIVE DYSFUNCTION (CCD)

Memory loss associated with CCD is a well-documented old-dog problem in which Sprig may forget his housetraining as well as other habits. He may urinate or defecate in unlikely new places or begin sleeping on cold tile or in the middle of the floor because he can't remember where his bed is located. Some CCD patients display loss of appetite, pacing, or barking for no reason.

CCD is a little like Alzheimer's disease in humans in that faulty training doesn't cause the problem and therefore correction usually is futile. Your old pal's habits and personality are so well established that you will probably quickly recognize his confusion. Don't add to his confusion by scolding or deriding him because Sprig may withdraw from society and become melancholy if he's scolded for these indiscretions.

It won't hurt to frequently take him to the yard's toilet area in hope of success. Just be sure to praise and pet him when he remembers why he's there. Take him for frequent short walks if feasible because new odors and experiences may stimulate his eliminations.

Make an appointment for a physical exam to rule out other diseases. Sometimes a new memory drug will be of value.

INCONTINENCE

Sometimes it's difficult to determine whether Sprig's inappropriate urination is caused by some specific disease or cognitive dysfunction, and it's often simply the result of tired old muscles. Sprig can't control his sphincter muscles when nerves that control those bladder muscles degenerate. He'll leak urine when asleep and sometimes even when he's walking across the room. Females seem to be affected more frequently than males.

Monitor his water intake closely for a few days by measuring the daily amount you put in his bowl. Check the odor of his urine and then take Sprig to his doctor. Urinalysis and blood tests should rule out conditions such as cystitis (bladder infection), nephritis (kidney inflammation), and metabolic diseases such as diabetes or Cushing's disease. Sometimes drug therapy will help and occasionally dietary change will also give some relief, but in case nothing works don't be discouraged. Providing him with several plastic-backed, washable rugs will help control odors, and frequent trips to the toilet area of the yard may bring some measure of success.

> **Old-dog obesity is a problem in itself.**

METABOLIC WEIGHT GAIN

Obesity and its accompanying stresses may be caused by overfeeding, or it may be a sign of serious metabolic diseases such as diabetes, hypothyroidism, or Cushing's disease. Schedule a veterinary examination to rule out systemic diseases. If Sprig is simply overweight, begin anew your old habit of weighing him every week. With veterinary help begin a careful reducing plan using a special low-calorie dog food that contains complete and balanced nutrition. Sometimes months or years may be added to his life by weight reduction.

WHEN TO GIVE UP

Sprig's life can be maximized by your care throughout his life. Take the advice offered at each stage of his life. Keep him in good nutritional condition, properly exercised, and attend to his vaccinations and veterinary examinations. Treat minor and major illnesses aggressively, and above all treat Sprig as a wonderful pal, but as a dog, not a child.

> **The best time to assure your tiny pal's longevity is when he's still a pup.**

It'll be a stormy day when it's time to give up your little pal. It will break your heart when the veterinarian tells you that Sprig's problems are extremely serious, painful, and irreversible and are the result of old age. Then and only then is the time to consider a painless end to Sprig's life.

WHY EUTHANASIA?

One of the toughest veterinary jobs is to take responsibility for ending a pet's life. To simply accept an animal and a signed euthanasia release isn't enough, yet that's often considered sufficient by less concerned pet owners. Throughout this text owners are advised to treat their little dogs like canines and not like children, but that doesn't mean that they should be treated like inorganic chattel. Here are a few typical owner reasons and veterinary responses to unjustifiable euthanasia.

He's a pest. He can't be housebroken, he's always underfoot, he won't eat dog food but begs for ice cream, potato chips, and candy.

> **Some inappropriate reasons for euthanasia.**

Truth: Lack of training is never a legitimate excuse for euthanasia. Sprig can learn, but he needs a teacher. You didn't make an effort to train him when he was a puppy. You've treated him like a tiny spoiled child instead of a dog. His bad manners are easily corrected but you must take your pack leadership role seriously. He's not too old to learn, but are you able to teach? If you're planning to give up on Sprig, find him another home with a patient and experienced family but don't consider euthanasia.

He's so small and delicate. My three-year-old son dropped the little pup off the porch and he broke his pelvis and one hind leg and suffered a brain concussion. The bill to fix him is enormous; it's more than he's worth. I'm only human. I can't watch him every minute.

Truth: Small children and small dogs present problems. You should have thought of these possibilities before you acquired the little dog. Where was his X-pen? Why was a young child allowed to play with a tiny puppy? Did you buy insurance? Don't end his life but instead ask about monthly payments. Contact a rescue agency and ask for help in paying his veterinary bills and finding him a new home.

I lost my job and recently suffered extensive financial setbacks. Now Sprig is sick and I can't afford the mounting medical bills. I want to cut my losses and get out from under this financial obligation.

Truth: You have options. Explore every possibility. No-kill shelters and animal aid institutions are out there. Veterinary colleges and philanthropic organizations may provide low-cost veterinary care. Don't give up or neglect your best friend; fight for him.

I don't know why it happened but suddenly he's toothless. He's only about six years old. His teeth began falling out a year or so ago and now there's only one or two remaining. He can't eat kibble and just rolls it around in his mouth. He drools all the time and lately his tongue is always hanging out. His breath is horrible and I know he's in pain.

Truth: Tartar and plaque caused his teeth to loosen and fall and this situation didn't occur suddenly. Weekly toothbrushing when he was younger would have helped. Annual dental exams would also have deterred this condition. Your neglect is the reason for his present condition, and the infected gums may have injured his heart, liver, and kidneys as well. First, spend an office call for your veterinarian's advice. Perhaps your little dog will benefit from cleaning or extraction of the remaining teeth. Then select an appropriate diet and mix his kibble with hot water to soften it or feed him a canned food. The odds are he'll live a normal life span if his internal organs haven't been too severely damaged.

We're moving to Europe and can't take our tiny dog with us, and we can't bear to see him adopted by another family where he might not be treated well.

Truth: Animal or specific-breed rescue organizations will help. Get on the Internet and contact one near you. They have foster homes for an immediate fix and can find him another permanent, loving home. Ask your local breed or all-breed club to help. Veterinarians often can put you in touch with potential owners who may have recently lost a similar little dog. Sprig is a friend. Treat him like one.

> Sprig's time has run out. He's never comfortable and his discomfort is killing me.

WHEN EUTHANASIA IS REALLY NECESSARY

Those who have never watched an old dog wither away and suffer can't imagine how pitiful old age can be. Your little pal's been losing weight for several months, his vision is gone, and he hears only shouts. Sprig was for years your active little buddy, but now he can barely rise and stagger forth to get a drink of water. Several times recently you've stepped over him and he didn't even acknowledge your presence.

He eats sparingly of the geriatric food, you buy him, and he frequently doesn't make it to the back door when he needs to urinate or defecate. He bumps into chairs when he walks and he sleeps twenty-three hours a day. He doesn't tolerate grooming anymore and whines when you pick him up. His nails are long but you can't bring yourself to handle his sore feet. It's obvious that his old joints are stiff and painful and that every step is a chore.

Sprig is never comfortable and is probably always in pain. You know that it's time to give him up, but he's been such a wonderful companion, you can't bear the thought of taking him to the clinic for the last time.

Pleading little eyes dimly seek comfort, and how you wish you could give him relief from his pain. You've discussed this with your veterinarian, but there's little he can prescribe for Sprig at this point. The last lab tests indicated that his liver and kidneys were working overtime and most pain medication is contraindicated. When he can no longer get to his feet you realize it's past time.

Euthanasia is the final act of love and kindness you can give your well-loved little buddy. He'll suffer no fear or apprehension when your trusted veterinarian administers the lethal injection. Stay with your old friend so he will know he isn't being abandoned and that he's still your best friend. That's the best comfort you can give him.

> **Painless death is a blessing for the pain and suffering Sprig has endured these last days.**

AN ACT OF KINDNESS

A good friend deserves the best. Your decision is the only option open to you. Call your veterinarian and ask to take Sprig to the clinic before regular office hours so there will be no wait, or, if the veterinarian is open to your suggestion, ask her to come to your house to perform this humanitarian procedure.

Give Sprig an abundance of gentle petting and love before the veterinarian comes. Hold him on your lap or put him in his favorite chair. The veterinarian will prepare the injection in advance and, while speaking to Sprig quietly, will administer the lethal dose. Death follows instantly and painlessly and without struggle.

> **He lived a long, happy life, and that's the best any of us can hope for.**

FINALIZE A SMALL DOG'S LIFE

Bury his body at home, in a pet cemetery, or arrange for cremation, then plant a tree or decorative shrub as a memorial to his life. Don't give in to perpetual grieving and despair. Instead remember that Sprig's life was filled with happiness and that he brought you many years of great joy.

GRIEF SUPPORT

Join an established grief support group or, if none are readily available, start one. Consult your veterinarian for information pamphlets or books. Search the Internet for contacts. Loss of a little companion of many years causes severe grief, anxiety, and

> **Talking with others about your old friend will help you understand his loss more clearly.**

depression. Many little-dog owners say this devastating loss is second only to the anguish of losing spouses, friends, and relatives.

Share your loss with others to make the process easier. You've just lost a friend, a little buddy that you loved a great deal. Don't be afraid to shed some tears; go through the natural grieving period, but keep your mind open to another little pal in the future when you're sure the time is right for you.

STARTING OVER

Some people find that immediate action frees their mind and allows them to live without depression or self-pity. They can best remember their little old pal in his youth by beginning again with a new puppy.

Others who had their pal with them for thirteen or fourteen years prefer not to experience all the joys of a puppy again and want to find an adolescent or adult.

To attempt to find a substitution for Sprig would be folly.

Regardless of how long you decide to wait, keep Sprig's photograph on the mantelpiece in a place of honor and begin shopping for his successor.

Don't search for a clone. No other dog will have Sprig's personality; none will be identical. If you acquire one that looks just like Sprig, you'll find yourself comparing every trait with Sprig's. You'll expect the new pup to duplicate all of Sprig's lovable traits and will be disappointed when he doesn't, and the new dog will suffer because of your disappointment. You may never realize just how great your new dog is. Try a similar but different breed or acquire a female. Get a larger or smaller size if possible or find another color or one that has different characteristics. Play fair. Don't make your new dog live in Sprig's shadow or you'll never fully appreciate its true value.

Purebred
Small Dogs

Affenpinscher

This dog's German name means Monkey-Terrier and refers to the breed's comical, bewhiskered face and slightly undershot jaw. It's also called Monkey Pinscher and in France it's known as Diablotin Moustachu, which translates to Moustached Little Devil.

Its dense, rough, harsh, flyaway coat puts one in mind of a little boy immediately after he gets out of bed in the morning. The Affenpinscher's shaggy plumage requires little combing and brushing, and after grooming this little dog shakes and looks about the same as he did before brushing.

Unlike other terrier types, the sturdy and hearty little Affenpinscher will get by on a minimal amount of exercise but will enjoy regular romps in the yard and play with its owners. Leashed walks are a bonus for this active little dog.

CURRENT FUNCTION

Affenpinschers of today are mostly companions and house pets. This little dog is classed as a toy by the AKC, is a fine playmate for larger children, and is a clever and alert companion for adults and kids alike.

ATTITUDE

An Affenpinscher is a naturally alert and vigilant alarm dog that's lively, cheerful, and entertaining. It's affectionate with its family and bonds quickly. It may challenge strangers who knock at your door but makes friends easily after they've been properly introduced.

APTITUDE

The Affenpinscher takes consistent training in stride and learn commands quickly. It's anxious to please its handler but becomes bored easily, so training should be varied and sessions should be kept short. This intelligent and curious little dog likes to learn new tasks, so be inventive when training.

APPEARANCE

The Affenpinscher stands 9 to 11.5 inches tall (23 to 30 cm) and weighs 7 to 8 pounds (3 to

3.5 kg). Its medium bone structure is sturdy and never delicate. Its domed skull is not pronounced but refined and it has a curious, almost comical facial expression. Its unkempt tufts of facial hair add to its impish, clownlike appearance. Ears are either cropped or uncropped, erect or dropped, but they must be symmetrical. It has a straight, blunt muzzle and its bite is slightly undershot, with the lower incisors touching the uppers.

Its coat is harsh, dense, and about 1 inch long but may be shorter on the rear and tail and shaggier on the head, neck, chest, stomach, and legs. Mature adults often grow longer coats on the chest and neck in the form of a cape. Its tail is either docked to approximately 1 inch or left natural to curve up and over the back when moving.

Origin

Germany claims origin of the Affenpinscher, but the little dog was probably bred elsewhere in Europe as well. The breed originated in the seventeenth century and descended from terriers that inhabited farms and shops of central Europe, where it was an undauntedly confident and sharp-witted little hunter.

The Affenpinscher is believed by some to be a descendant of the Miniature Pinscher, possibly crossed with some of the German wirehaired breeds or the Skye Terrier. It may be one progenitor of the Brussels Griffon and is possibly related to the Miniature Schnauzer as well.

Its color is usually black but it is sometimes seen in gray, silver, or black and tan. A small white spot or fine line of white hairs on the chest isn't penalized but larger white patches are undesirable. Overall color is not a major consideration.

Original Design

The Affenpinscher's original purpose was vermin hunter, alarm dog, and companion. It first made its way to America in the 1930s and was entered in the AKC studbook in 1936. Its first appearances in American show dog rings were in the Chicago and New York regions.

Australian Terrier

This little Aussie Terrier is among the smallest of the AKC-recognized working terriers and has been known in various period development as the Blue and Tan, Toy Terrier, Blue Terrier, and Rough-Coated Terrier.

Show-dog Aussies require combing and brushing about once a week and plucking to remove dead hair about every three or four months. Shedding usually isn't a problem with this terrier. A pet Aussie's hair is often clipped with electric clippers, but doing so will cause the coat to become softer and will impede or ruin the dog's chances in the show ring. Minimal washing of this dog's hard, dense coat is better than too much.

It's a hardy, active working terrier that requires greater-than-average amounts of exercise, but most will adapt to long walks and backyard romps with children.

CURRENT FUNCTION

The Australian Terrier of today is an excellent indoor-outdoor family dog and a biddable little sporting terrier that possesses a strong kinship for his owners. It's esteemed for its outdoor hardiness and willingness to spend the night in the rough Australian weather or indoors by the hearth with its family.

ATTITUDE

The Australian Terrier has a propensity to bark in keeping with its guarding and warning characteristics, and this quality readily fits its role as family companion.

It's a tireless and spirited little dog that possesses a great deal of confidence and determination and is an intensely curious pet that's quick to socialize with other dogs.

It is quite affectionate and bonds with its human family readily, although it's said to choose one particular person as a favorite. Its good humor and playful attitude is well known and is marred only by a little stubborn streak and an independent temperament.

APTITUDE

The Australian Terrier retains all of its original hunting and vermin-destroying propensities in its new role as a companion. Its ratting ability qualifies this terrier for sporting trials and ridding vermin from its owner's property, but a major problem sometimes develops when its family includes pet rats, mice, gerbils, guinea pigs, and other rodents. It's an intelligent and trainable pet when consistent control is used to curb its independence. Learning comes easily to the young Aussie and it has a propensity to accept feline members of the household when they are appropriately introduced. Agility trial work and flyball might be considered for this little dog's enjoyment.

Origin

As its name implies, the Aussie was originally bred and developed in Australia or Tasmania by the early white settlers. Its background includes a number of British terriers including dogs that were also progenitors of the Black and Tan or Manchester, Irish, Skye, Dandie Dinmont, Yorkshire, and possibly the Cairn. It was the very first Australian breed to be recognized in that country and was first exhibited in Melbourne in 1868 under the name of Rough Coated Australian Terrier.

Original Design

The Aussie was developed for ratting, hunting, and companionship, and its visual and auditory acuity made it perfect for sounding an alarm to announce strangers. It is an excellent vermin destroyer and has doubled at times as a herd-tending dog. Settlers prized this little dog for its protective attitude and ability to tackle and kill poisonous snakes in its native land.

APPEARANCE

This little terrier stands about 10 to 11 inches tall (25.5 to 26 cm) and weighs 12 to 14 pounds (4 to 7 kg). It's a medium-boned dog and a sturdy companion. The Australian Terrier has erect, high-set ears and a body that's longer than its height. Its tail is docked and it sports a distinctive ruff and apron and a soft, silky topknot.

Its coat is of medium length and over its back is often colored deep blue-black, but blue and tan, solid sandy, or solid red is equally permissible.

Basset Fauve de Bretagne

This sturdy little hound is also known as the Tawny Brittany Basset. It's a hunting dog that requires a great amount of exercise, the lack of which may dispose it to illness as well as promote obesity.

Its hard, dense, and relatively short coat is easily cared for by regular combing and twice-annual plucking, but it is spoiled with electric clippers and shouldn't be trimmed or sheared.

CURRENT FUNCTION

In its native France, and to a lesser degree in other countries, this gentle and loving little basset is popular as a companion dog and pet. Its friendly disposition makes it a fine family dog that's very good with children who are properly instructed in the fine art of handling a small dog.

In spite of its personable disposition the Basset Fauve de Bretagne is an aggressive gundog that's never reluctant to jump into brambles for its quarry.

ATTITUDE

This little basset is an intelligent and jovial hound that's always cheerful but it definitely has a mind of its own. That fact alone might render this dog more difficult to train than many other breeds. Like most pack hounds it gets along well with other dogs, but care should be taken when introducing smaller household pets such as cats and rodents. The little dog is a hound through and through, and like other hounds its value as a watchdog is suspect.

APTITUDE

The Basset Fauve de Bretagne is easily trained for its hunting function and learns pack etiquette quickly. The breed is not recognized by the AKC and is uncommon in American obedience rings, so little is known about its adaptability to classic training. Remember that most dogs must be trained at an early age to respond to commands, and without fundamental obedience training the Basset Fauve

This little hound was first used in packs of four to hunt rabbits and other small game. It's a fine family dog as well and is a happy little hound with a little stubborn streak and a big voice. Like other hunting dogs, it has a strong sense of smell and an inborn desire for following a wide range of quarry in the field.

de Bretagne may quickly lose favor with novice owners.

APPEARANCE

The Basset Fauve de Bretagne stands 12 to 15 inches tall (30 to 38 cm) and weighs between 30 and 40 pounds (16 to 18 kg). It has typical basset conformation with a long thick body, crooked legs, and a long-faced, soulful expression. Its thick body is longer than it is tall, and its tail is tapered and carried in a hanging sickle fashion. Its ample hound ears hang in a typical manner and its nose is dark brown or black. Its short legs often are crooked but may be straight and its breastbone is prominent.

Its coat is hard, dense, and straight but not very long. Its color is a uniform golden pink or slightly darker shades of tan. White patches are sometimes seen on the chest and belly, but any white is considered a fault and is strongly discouraged.

Origin

France is the home of the Basset Fauve de Bretagne where it was developed during the nineteenth century. The breed was probably developed from the larger Grand Griffon Fauve de Bretagne by crossing that dog with smaller bassets or perhaps by selective breeding.

Bichon Frisé

Tenerife Dog, Bichon Tenerife, and Bichon a poil Frisé are other names for this pint-sized white fur ball that slightly resembles a miniature poodle. The name *Bichon* probably came from its Barbet ancestors called Barbichons. *Bichon* may well be a contraction of *Barbichon*.

Frisé means curly-haired and this is quite fitting because the Bichon's coat is very curly and requires at least daily combing to keep it looking plush and soft. Bathing usually is an essential monthly chore, and frequent brushing is necessary between baths to remove the dead hairs from the coat.

The Bichon's exercise requirements aren't as great as those of its water-dog ancestors, and usually its inclusion in family fun will make this cheerful little dog even happier.

CURRENT FUNCTION

This charming little dog bonds quickly with its owner and is considered one of the best all-round family companions in the world. The Bichon is a wonderful pet for larger children but only those who are well taught the proper way to handle this tiny dog.

ATTITUDE

The sociable little Bichon is clever, entertaining, and is a clean house dog with few faults unless its need for grooming is considered a problem. Scarcely anyone can refrain from tossing a ball or playing a game of hide-and-seek with the frisky little powder puff. It's an active dog that loves to entertain everyone. The Bichon is a proud breed that's gentle, cheerful, and active under practically any circumstances and is always ready to play games. It's a sensitive, biddable little dog with a quick mind and body and an unmistakable desire to please. Its positive attitude and friendly nature captures the hearts of most owners who quickly look beyond the Bichon's grooming needs. It is sociable with other pets and makes an honest effort to meet everyone with mutual respect.

APTITUDE

The Bichon is probably best suited for family companionship, but its trainability renders it an excellent candidate for obedience work. Circuses occasionally employ dogs of this breed in the dignified capacities of star performers. A Bichon enjoys applause and is at its glory when entertaining, whether at a family gathering, on the stage, or under the big top. Another vocation for which it is suited is freestyle because this breed will catch on to about anything it's introduced to and is at its best when in the spotlight. Its intelligence and owner-focus should equip it well for sports such as flyball or agility.

APPEARANCE

The Bichon stands 9½ to 11½ inches (24 to 30 cm) and weighs about 7 to 12 pounds (3 to 6 kg). Its body is longer than tall and it's a compact, medium-boned little dog that's described as a small, sturdy, white powder puff. Its tail is plumed and is carried proudly over the back. The expression peering from under its copious wooly exterior is one of

Origin

The Bichon was developed in Belgium or France and on the Canary Island called Tenerife. The Bichon is thought to be a descendant of the Barbet, a French water retriever that has a coat type similar to the Bichon's. The Barbet is twice as tall as the Bichon and is black, white, gray, or chestnut. The Bichon type was common in fourteenth-century France and was one of four small lapdogs that are individually known as the Bichon Maltais, Bichon Bolognais, Bichon Havanais, and Bichon Tenerife (Bichon Frisé). This gay little dog probably found its way to Tenerife via French trading ships on which it was kept as a favorite trading stock.

The Bichon Frisé returned from Tenerife Island to Europe to become the pampered pet of French, Spanish, and Italian royalty. The breed's popularity rose and fell with the fortunes of the countries in which it resided for many years.

happiness, inquisitiveness, and intelligence. Its eyes are round and dark and set in black rims and the nose rubber is always black, as are the lips. Ears are down and are also covered with long, flowing hair.

The Bichon's 2-inch outer coat consists of coarse corkscrew spiral curls that stand away from its short, soft undercoat, both of which are always pure white. Serious faults are discouraged and one of the worst is a limp coat or one that lies flat because of lack of sufficient undercoat.

Border Terrier

At one period of development this breed was associated with the Border Hunt Club and was known as the Coquetdale Terrier

The Border Terrier's harsh and dense coat is easily cared for by weekly brushing and combing and rare baths. Show dogs' coats are plucked occasionally, but never trimmed with electric clippers.

Exercise requirements can be met by vigorous play and leashed walks, although the dog would probably prefer to spend its energy in more productive endeavors.

CURRENT FUNCTION

This sometimes stubborn and independent little dog fits in nicely with American families. It will likely never lose its desire to hunt and dispatch its quarry, but it has adjusted remarkably well to backyard living. Care should be taken to provide the Border with sufficient mental challenges and physical exercise. It has a strong independent streak and a bit of wanderlust that will cause it to dig to escape and pursue its quarry. If left alone in a yard, it is bound to become melancholy and adopt various vices.

The Border Terrier gets along well with children but, in spite of its hardiness, it can be inadvertently injured by preschoolers and toddlers.

ATTITUDE

A typical Border Terrier is brave and biddable with a willful streak. It's sociable with children and other dogs, but remember its instincts and introduce it to smaller household pets with extreme caution. Affectionate and assertive, this little dog is a bundle of overflowing energy.

APTITUDE

The Border is tireless when pursuing quarry and its willingness and desire to play is equally insatiable. It's said to lose its zest for living when overly restricted and may become bored if its talents aren't put to regular use. Its body

Origin

The Border Terrier was named for the region in which it was developed in the Cheviot Hills that was known as the Border country between Scotland and England. It is among the oldest type of small British terriers and was developed by farmers to hunt down the bold and destructive hill foxes, run them to ground, and kill them. This breed was carefully bred for many years and was worked and exhibited at agricultural shows in the Border region long before it received significant attention from the English Kennel Club.

The Border Terrier existed as a specific breed type as early as the first quarter of the nineteenth century, and a picture taken in 1826 is clearly a Border Terrier type. Its progenitors possibly include those of the Lakeland, Bedlington, and Dandie Dinmont. This terrier may have been standardized by the now extinct Border Hunt Club that used a similar type of dog to follow the foxes to ground.

is hard and muscular, and its gameness is one of its principal features.

It's inherently comfortable in most climatic conditions if provided with shelter from the elements and will work anytime in virtually any weather. This little dog has the necessary endurance and persistence to thrive in flyball contests and agility trials. It's trainable and well focused and therefore a prime candidate for obedience work.

The Border Terrier was designed with legs of sufficient length to follow horses on the hunt, yet short enough to invade the fox's lair. It was a tough, tenacious little dog that would spend whatever time and energy necessary to bolt or kill its quarry. The original Border was a versatile and industrious terrier that hunted any animal that infringed on its owners' domicile. Quarries included badgers, otters, and foxes, and this little dog was also quite adept at ridding farms of small rodents of every description, including mice and rats.

The Border Terrier was developed as an all-round farm dog with guarding abilities as well as a superior hunting prowess, whether running with a pack or as an individual. Although its uniformity was established in the Border country for many years, its formal breed standard was adopted by Great Britain's Border Terrier Club in 1920, and the breed was recognized by the AKC in 1930.

APPEARANCE

The Border Terrier stands about 10 inches (25.4 cm) and weighs 11 to 15½ pounds (5 to 7 kg). Its appearance is quite natural and blessed with no artificial, man-made looks. It has a strong, solid working body that's not flashy. A Border Terrier is well built and sturdy, and is an ambitious sporting dog or companion. It is medium boned with straight legs, and its forequarters are rather narrow as befits a hunting terrier.

Its coat is hard and thick with a dense undercoat. Colors include red, grizzle and tan, blue and tan, and wheaten, and its dark muzzle is a desirable feature of the breed.

Boston Terrier

Early in the Boston Terrier's history it was sometimes referred to as Round Head or the Round Head Terrier. This was followed by the name American Bull Terrier that was shortened to Bull Terrier, which was soon after changed to Boston Terrier. It has a terrierlike build that's dissimilar to that of a Bulldog and its clean head is also terrier-like; thus the bull designation wasn't pursued.

The Boston's coat is quite short and easily cared for by brushing with a rubber slicker brush or grooming glove.

Exercise requirements are easily met because this little dog adapts well to its owner's activities and likes to accompany them everywhere.

Its desire to take longish walks is not strong, especially in hot or cold weather, when the Boston prefers to be carried.

CURRENT FUNCTION

Nothing much has changed since this breed was established. Today it's a low-maintenance companion dog with a built-in watchdog ability. It's content to live with its family in a small apartment or large country house. A yard to play in is appreciated, however, and this little dog's fixation on games or playing ball is second to few.

The Boston is a wonderfully clean play-mate for older children and adults.

ATTITUDE

A sweet temperament and lively disposition characterizes the Boston Terrier. It exudes a self-confident sense of humor and the intelligence to work out challenges in a short time. It's a pretty fair watchdog but is rarely yappy. Very sociable with other family pets, the affectionate Boston is patient but enthusiastic and sometimes even boisterous in play. It's no couch potato, but because of its short, smooth coat it doesn't tolerate hot or cold weather without protection from the summer sun and it likes a coat in the winter.

APTITUDE

Born and bred to be a family companion, the Boston is good at what it does. It may be the epitome of companion dogs. It's small enough to pick up and carry but is very focused and trainable and has a strong desire to please. It does well in obedience classes, usually responds to voice modulations, and rarely requires correction or repetition. The Boston is subject to heatstroke and its tolerance to long training sessions or work in hot weather is problematic.

APPEARANCE

The Boston's smallest weight class stands about 10 inches tall (25.4 cm) and weighs less than 15 pounds (6.5 kg), usually about 11 or

Original Design

Although descended from bull-baiting ancestors, the Boston isn't much of a fighter, but this little dog puts up a brave front when challenged. It was conceived to be a good friend, fine companion, family pet, and at odd times a ratter and alarm dog. The AKC recognized the Boston Terrier in 1893 after an amazingly short period of development and standardization.

12 pounds (5 to 5.5 kg). This small breed has a good overall balance with a compact body, short head, and short tail. The naturally short,

Origin

This is truly an American breed that was developed in the 1870s from its well-documented ancestors, which were an imported English Bulldog named Hooper's Judge and a small white English Terrier bitch. Many crosses followed with other small terriers and bulldogs, and considerable inbreeding took place before the Boston type was attained. Continued concentrated selective breeding eventually produced a uniform type that's shown today in three separate weight varieties.

sometimes crooked tail is not docked and is never carried above the back. Its alacrity, curiosity, and intelligence are obvious in its facial expression and its soft, dark eyes.

The Boston has a smooth coat of brindle, seal, or black, evenly marked with white, and the brindle coloring is preferred if all other conformational points are equal.

Brussels Griffon

This little dog has an abundance of monikers, among which are the Griffon Bruxellois, Belgian Griffon, Petite Brabançon, and Griffon Belge. The nomenclature puzzle is solved when you realize that in Europe the Brussels Griffon (Griffon Bruxellois) is reddish-pink in color and rough coated. The Belgian Griffon (Griffon Belge) is black, black and tan, or red and is also rough coated. The Petite Brabançon is accepted in the same colors as the other griffons, but is shorthaired. This brings up a paradox that's related to the smooth-coated variety (Petite Brabançon) because the term *griffon* means a thick or wiry coat. Just remember that all varieties are shown in common classes in the United States and in the UK, but that on the European continent they are differentiated by color and coat type.

Coat care depends on whether the Griffon is rough or smooth coated. Rough coats require regular combing and every few months their facial hair needs plucking to give the dog its typical appearance.

A Brussels Griffon's exercise requirements are minimal and are usually fulfilled in a backyard or even within the house if regular games are initiated. It's quite at home in an apartment or suburban dwelling, but this athletic and energetic little dog has an affinity for walks in the country whenever possible.

CURRENT FUNCTION

The Brussels Griffon retains some of its genetic ratting quality and expresses this quality when occasion demands. Generally it serves as a lovable, funny, active, and intelligent family companion. It socializes well with adults and children but may be wary of toddlers if they aren't introduced properly.

ATTITUDE

The Brussels Griffon is classed as a toy breed, but it's a no-nonsense little dog with a giant personality and sturdy build. Its saucy looks and carriage endear it to everyone it meets.

Origin

This humorous-appearing breed was developed in Belgium from crosses between the Affenpinscher and the Griffon D'Ecurie or Stable Griffons that were sometimes called *chiens barbus.* Perhaps proof of this breed's origin is shown in Jan Van Eyck's 1434 painting of Arnolfini that shows a typical small rough-coated Griffon type with sharp eyes and cropped ears. Other paintings from the sixteenth and seventeenth centuries depict similar types, and certainly by the late 1800s the Brussels Griffon was here to stay.

This popular and common peasant's dog was developed in and around farms and stables to control rodent populations. Various authors speculate that the Yorkshire Terrier, Black and Tan Terrier, and Ruby Spaniel were included in the Affenpinscher-Stable Griffon gene pool that produced the Brussels Griffon. Another writer traces the Brussels progenitors to include the Barbet and Hollandsche Smoushound. Pugs were developed next door in the Netherlands and were crossed into the mixture. Such a cross might account for the smooth variety or Petite Brabançon that so strongly resembles the Pug.

Its attitude is described as curious and mischievous but it's calm, eager to please, quite trainable, and just a little bit stubborn. The breed is self-confident and lively and sometimes resists leash training, so this phase of schooling should be undertaken while it is still a puppy. Small household pets, especially rodents, are at risk unless guarded against the Brussels Griffon's terrier instincts. This little dog bonds tightly with its principal handler but is loved by every family member.

APTITUDE

The Brussels is an exceptionally intelligent dog and can be put to any task that its small size allows. It's sufficiently athletic to participate in obedience and agility trials, and because of its easy training propensity should be a great therapy dog. It's usually quite sensitive to cold weather and should be furnished with a coat when going outside in the winter.

APPEARANCE

This small breed stands 7 to 8 inches (18 to 20 cm) tall and weighs 8 to 12 pounds (3.5 to 5 kg). Because of its whiskers and almost human expression the Brussels shows its Affenpinscher heritage as well. Its body is thick and short and somewhat square in appearance, and its legs

Original Design

This little dog originated from dogs belonging to peasant farmers. One can assume it also was used as a ratter and probably lived in close contact with its human family. Farm dogs were prized for their alarm or watchdog quality, and this was the case with the Brussels Griffon. The breed was recognized by the Belgium Kennel Club in 1883 and was transported to America and the United Kingdom sometime in the late 1800s.

are straight. Its head is large and round with a domed forehead and a short, black muzzle with its nose rubber set back deeply between the eyes. In Germany and sometimes in America its ears are cropped, but in other countries the natural semierect ear is preferred. It has an undershot jaw but lower teeth do not show when the mouth is closed.

The Brussels's coat is thick, rough, and wiry in some cases. In others it's smooth, straight, tight, and glossy with no trace of wiry hair. Colors are red, which is reddish brown with black tones; beige, which is black and reddish brown; black and tan, which is black with uniform brown markings; or black, which means solid black without any trace of white.

Cairn Terrier

Past names for the Cairn are the Shorthaired Skye Terrier and Cairn Terrier of Skye.

Its coat needs regular combing and brushing, and several times a year it should be hand plucked. Electric trimmers usually aren't used on the Cairn's coat except in the case of a pet.

Backyard running and playing with other dogs or family members usually provides sufficient exercise for the Cairn, but it thrives when taken for long walks, especially in the country or forest. This is an energetic, active little companion that wants plenty of opportunity to run.

CURRENT FUNCTION

The Cairn is a wonderful companion and pet, but any Cairn worth its salt is still ready to scent, follow, and dispatch a rodent or any other perceived quarry. In spite of its energetic and athletic capacity the Cairn is nevertheless a small dog and the same warnings apply when buying a Cairn puppy for a young child. Always teach children to respect the diminutive size of

their playmate and take great care when picking up and carrying the little dog.

ATTITUDE

The Cairn's attitude is that of an affectionate and independent extrovert. For this reason its schooling at an early age should include introduction to cats and other small pets. Even when the Cairn is solidly trained, the old terrier instincts rise to the surface if it's exercised off lead in the country. It's an energetic, highly intelligent, brave, lively, and cheerful playmate. It welcomes tug-of-war games and will chase a ball endlessly, but it should always be reminded when the game is over. Its ancestor's tenacity when digging in rock piles has carried over into today's Cairn and is displayed in its tireless play. Its hallmark is a fearlessness and never-say-quit attitude.

APTITUDE

This dog is easily trained, eager to please, and ready to go at any moment. The Cairn needs consistent training. It catches on to most

Original Design

Cairns are cone-shaped heaps of rocks that were erected as memorials or landmarks. These gigantic rock piles were located on farm ground and served as lairs for many agricultural pests. The little dog bred to hunt in the hundreds of cairns that dotted the Scottish countryside was naturally named for them. The Cairn Terrier was developed to kill or bolt (put to flight) otters, badgers, foxes, and other pests from their rocky lairs. It was a formidable hunting dog that was tenacious and ready to meet any serious opponent regardless of the circumstances.

Its quarry diminished over the years but the little Cairn Terrier slipped unnoticed into an equally important role in the community and proved itself a loyal companion, playmate, and pal.

The Cairn developed on Scotland's misty isle of Skye. This spunky little dog is one of several Scottish terriers that were developed during the fifteenth century on the island of Skye and perhaps on the Scottish mainland. The origin of the Cairn is tangled with that of the Scottish Terrier, Skye Terrier, West Highland White Terrier, and the now-extinct Kyle Terrier. Experts speculate about which breed came first and whether each type originated on the Scottish mainland or one of Scotland's islands.

It's well known that Scotland was the breeding ground for a number of small, compact, interrelated terriers, the smallest of which is the Cairn. All Scottish terriers were exhibited and classed together in shows until 1873, when the Dandie Dinmont and Skye Terriers were separated. The Scottish Terrier, the West Highland White Terrier, and the Cairn Terrier were included in the Skye Terrier class.

In about 1881 breeders decided to form a class for Hard Haired Terriers that included the Westie, the Scottie, and the Cairn. By 1909 shows included classes for Short-Haired Skyes (Cairn Terriers). In 1910 this name confusion led to the suggestion that it be further changed to the Cairn Terrier of Skye, but within a year or so the breed completed its split from the former Skye classification and its name was changed to Cairn.

commands quickly and is obedient unless its terrier instincts rule otherwise. It's an alert and attentive watchdog, and little training is necessary to stimulate guarding instincts. It retains all its ancestors' ill feelings toward varmints and a Cairn will go far afield to find a viable quarry. Its focus and intelligence make it a fine competitor in timed contests such as flyball and agility. Obedience should also be a vocation for which this little terrier is well suited.

APPEARANCE

A Cairn stands about 10 inches tall (25.4 cm) and weighs about 14 pounds (6 kg). It's a muscular little dog with short, straight legs and a well-proportioned athletic body. Its broad head is equipped with strong jaws that were needed to pull its quarry from the rocks.

The Cairn's coat is double and straight and is made of a topcoat that's hard, thick,

and weather resistant. The undercoat is soft and short. Acceptable colors include any except white and the coat is often shaded darker on ear tips and tail.

Cardigan Welsh Corgi

Cardigan Welsh Corgi is known by no other name. This is the long-tailed Corgi that with its plumed tail and in its red and white coat looks like a thicker-than-usual fox. The name *Corgi* may have been named for the contraction of two Celtic words: *cor* (to gather) and *gi* (dog).

Its coat is easily cared for by combing or brushing whenever shedding demands. A thorough grooming session is needed toward the end of the semiannual shedding season.

An adult Cardigan Corgi will plead many excuses for exercise. A herding dog needs lots of outdoor activity such as long walks, play, and training. However, a growing pup's exercise must be limited to prevent bone disorders.

CURRENT FUNCTION

Herds became smaller and open land was fenced. The Cardigan Corgi neared extinction, but when the going got tough, the breed took to other duties such as guard dog, companion, and family pet. Today's Cardigan Welsh Corgi is considered to be an exceptional companion for active families. It's sometimes a bit short tempered in its treatment of other dogs and should be socialized at a very young age with other canines, family pets, and children.

ATTITUDE

This little cattle dog is intelligent and eager to learn. It focuses on and responds to its handler and wants to please everyone. It's an affectionate dog that's usually calm, adaptable, and loyal, and has a superb sense of humor. It's a clean house dog, but needs daily mental challenges and physical exercise. It's a better-than-average watchdog that's quite alert and responsive to noises and is usually very cautious toward strangers.

APTITUDE

If you happen to live on a ranch, this dog's instinctive nature will probably get it into trouble when it tries to drive your cattle or sheep. If none are available it'll settle for a flock of

Original Design

This short-legged and courageous little cattle dog is long on ambition. Its close-to-the-ground stature made it ideal for driving cattle because, unlike shepherd dogs, the Cardigan Corgi dives into a herd and bites the heel of the lagging bovine. Then the little dog quickly drops to the ground (a short trip) to avoid the indignant cow's well-aimed kick. That sounds like a recipe for disaster, but the Cardigan is adept at performing its trick hundreds of times a day without taking a single direct hit. Its astonishing bursts of speed are related to its powerfully muscular legs rather than to their length.

In bygone days driving cattle was its life. It lived in close association with its owners, was handled by them daily, and developed a bond or rapport that today stands it in good stead as a loyal companion. Later in its history this little dog was used to flush out game and other small animals such as weasels, foxes, and mice.

This breed was admitted to AKC registry in 1935.

The Cardigan Welsh Corgi stands 10½ inches to 12½ inches tall (25 cm to 30 cm) and 36 inches to 43 inches (86 to 110 cm) long measured from tip of nose to tip of tail. It weighs 30 to 38 pounds (13.5 to 17 kg). It's quite muscular and sturdy as the height to weight ratio indicates, and has heavy bone structure and a deep chest. Its long tail is set low and is finished with a foxlike brush. Its relatively long muzzle is refined and balanced with other head features. Ears are erect, slightly rounded, and prominent.

Its coat is short and weather resistant. Admissible colors include all shades of red, sable and brindle, black with or without brindle points, and blue merle. White flashings are usual but white is limited on the Corgi's head.

ducks, turkeys, or chickens. Nowadays farm animals usually are worked slowly, behind fences, and biting the livestock's fetlocks (ankles) is quite undesirable.

The Cardigan Corgi is an intelligent and ambitious dog that should shine in agility and flyball trials, and its trainability makes it a good candidate for obedience training. This breed prefers an outdoor life, but many live in apartments and take their exercise on the leash and in training. Guarding and herding children is inherent to this breed.

Origin

The Cardigan is the most ancient of the two Corgis (Pembroke Welsh Corgi is the other) and dates to the time of invasion of Wales by the Central European Celtic tribes in about 1200 B.C. This breed therefore claims residence in the Welsh countryside for more than 3000 years. Speculation about the progenitors of this breed often names the Dachshund family as probable genetic sources but there are no records or proof of this premise. Popularity of the breed began when King George VI kept many Cardigan Welsh Corgis on his palatial estate. This Corgi was interbred with the Pembroke Welsh Corgi at one time but that practice has long since been discontinued.

Cavalier King Charles Spaniel

This breed that's affectionately shortened to Cav is distinguished from the King Charles Spaniel by its longer muzzle and heavier build. It was named for the Cavalier King, who ruled Great Britain in the 1700s.

The Cav's coat requires frequent brushing and careful combing to prevent matting. Its coat care is perhaps the only drawback to ownership of this friendly little dog.

This usually pampered house dog usually finds plenty of exercise opportunities in daily household activities because its needs are not great. Unlike spaniels from the sporting group the Cav is content with a romp in the backyard with the children or a moderate leashed walk once or twice daily.

CURRENT FUNCTION

The modern Cavalier King Charles has much the same color and conformation as the original and serves its families in many of the same ways. It's a nearly ideal house pet and family companion that socializes well with other family pets and is particularly good with children. It's a straightforward companion with few quirks in its personality and infrequent hang-ups.

ATTITUDE

The active and high-spirited Cav has a penchant for pleasing its family in every way. It's a long-lived, loving, and lovable little dog that adapts well to its environment, and its grace and beauty can't be faulted. Intelligence and obedience are among its assets. It's always ready for a walk or a play period and it likes games but will content itself to doze on a soft lap when asked. This charming and usually undemanding little dog is companion to senior citizens, young families, and singles alike.

APTITUDE

The Cav enjoys consistent training and bonds well with its entire family. It's a people-pleasing little dog blessed with an even and predictable temperament that adjusts well to

Spaniels were and are sporting dogs, designed to flush and retrieve game birds. Although the Cav of the 1600s may have served a similar function, the principal purpose for which this spaniel was developed was to provide pleasure for its English royalty owners. The little dog brought warmth to its master's feet, served as a hot water bottle in the beds of kings and noblemen, and provided companionship for dukes and earls. It was accepted by the English Kennel Club in 1945 as a separate breed and was distinguished from the King Charles Spaniel by the addition of Cavalier to its name. After a long period of discord among American Cav fanciers, the breed was recognized by AKC in 1996.

most situations. Spaniels are historically fine athletes, a heritage that should prove useful when training for agility and obedience. The gentle nature and sociability with both humans and other animals make it a viable competitor in off-lead activities.

Origin

Although the Cavalier King Charles Spaniel claims origin in seventeenth-century England, the roots of most if not all true spaniels are found in Spain. This breed probably has some of the ancient Oriental toy breeds among its progenitors as well. At one time the Cavalier type favored by King Charles II evolved into a dog with a shorter muzzle and lighter body, but in the early 1900s concentrated selective breeding created a swing back to the original head and body type.

APPEARANCE

The Cavalier King Charles stands 12 to 13 inches tall (30 to 31 cm) and weighs 10 to 18 pounds (5 to 8 kg). Its appearance is that of a miniature hunting spaniel with a moderately long, full muzzle, long, high-set ears, and a long or docked tail.

Its coat consists of soft, gently-waving longish hair that's almost silky. Feathering is abundant but not excessive. Its red and white color type is called Blenheim after the Duke of Marlborough's estate. Other acceptable colors include ruby, which is a solid red; black and white; and tricolor, which is a combination of black and white with russet brown accents.

Cesky Terrier

The Cesky Terrier is a relatively rare small dog from the Czech Republic and Slovakia that's also known as the Bohemian Terrier or Czesky Terrier.

Its silky coat requires a fair amount of care. Frequent combing, brushing, and regular trimming is required to keep this terrier in shape.

The Cesky is a working terrier and its need for exercise exceeds that required by many small breeds. It will settle for leashed walks, romping with children, and training, but lack of exercise will predispose it to obesity and melancholy.

CURRENT FUNCTION

The Cesky retains its aggressive hunting instincts but is much less assertive toward its humans and is normally a gentle and trustworthy pet. It's employed in rural Bohemia as a ratter, but in America it's a prize possession of rare breed fanciers and their families and is primarily found in backyards and on sofas.

ATTITUDE

The Cesky is a fearlessly tough but happy pet. Its adaptability is well established and it makes an athletic and robust companion to those who prefer a sporting terrier. This loyal and obedient little dog gets along beautifully with people, other dogs, and cats when introduced to them as a puppy and allowed frequent contact with them. The Cesky has a good rapport with kids and is most appreciated by the family's active older children. This dog is somewhat cautious around strangers and is a vigilant watchdog. Owners should remember that the Cesky was specifically developed to hunt and kill rodents and shouldn't be trusted around pet guinea pigs, gerbils, hamsters, or other small pets of that type even when they are housed securely and separately in the same household.

APTITUDE

This breed is adept at hunting small varmints but has found its way into American backyards

Origin

Dr. Frantiesk Horak, a Czechoslovakian dog breeder and geneticist, created this breed in the former Czechoslovakia, which is now divided into the countries of Slovakia and the Czech Republic. Development began in 1949, and by 1963 Dr. Horak's terrier was recognized by the FCI (the principal European dog registry). The Cesky Terrier's forefathers are difficult to discover, but Dr. Horak was a Scottish Terrier and Sealyham breeder, if that offers a clue.

where varmints have given way to grass and gardens. This intelligent little dog socializes easily with other dogs and should prove an excellent competitor in timed activities such as flyball and agility. It is not eligible for AKC registration, but obedience training should be possible, and this dog's trainability and aptitude should serve it well.

APPEARANCE

The Cesky stands about 11 inches tall (27.5 cm) and weighs about 15 pounds (7 kg).

Puppies are born black, and the final color and shading of the Cesky isn't fully developed until two years of age or older. This is a short-legged, sturdy terrier with

long hanging ears, long muzzle, and a 7- or 8-inch natural tail.

Its coat is copious and grows to the ground if allowed. The thick shiny hair is softer than many other terriers' coats and is trimmed over the back, sides, and neck. Its colors are various shades of blue-gray. Some are seen in café au lait or pale coffee tan or brown, and a few also have small white chest markings but they aren't necessarily preferred over solid or shaded colors. The coat is trimmed with clippers to produce a profuse moustache and beard, thick eyebrows, and leg and lower body feathering.

Original Design

The Cesky was designed to hunt, catch, and destroy rats, foxes, rabbits, ducks, pheasants, wild boar, and moles. It's an aggressive hunter with a fine talent for doing its job superbly. Its secondary function was that of a watchdog and companion, and those duties also are performed exceptionally well. The Czechoslovakian Kennel Club officially recognized the breed in 1963. The Cesky was introduced to the Western world late in the 1980s when the USSR's influence on Eastern Europe was unwound and the Czech Republic was separated from Slovakia. Its population has reached more than 200 in the United States, and it's slowly making inroads with Western small-dog fanciers.

The Cesky is shown in the National Cesky Terrier Club shows in America, and other breed registries are considering its registry as well.

C h i h u a h u a

The state of Chihuahua, Mexico, lends its name to the world's smallest breed of dog. The Chihuahua has been popular north and south of the Rio Grande for many years and is undoubtedly the oldest purebred canine native to the North American continent. This tiny dog knows no other name.

The Chihuahua appears in a short- or smooth-coated variety and another that has a long coat. The shorthaired variety is kept tidy with brushing several times a week with a rubber slicker or grooming glove. The longhaired type requires frequent combing and brushing to remove dead hair and keep the coat free from tangles.

Exercise requirements for the Chihuahua are minimal although it is quite agile and ambitious. Use of a litter tray is common for fecal and urinary eliminations, and paper training often sometimes takes the place of housebreaking. Many of these tiny dogs are never allowed outside but that's a practice that suits the owner more than it pleases the Chihuahua. These diminutive pets are able to

obtain needed exercise inside by following their owners about the house or apartment.

CURRENT FUNCTION

The Chihuahua has no claims of ties to royalty and no hunting heritage but is known primarily as a wonderfully sociable human companion. This little dog is quite content to have literally no work assigned to it. It fits nicely into even the smallest spaces and is content to pass the day lying in the sun or being fawned over by its humans. It can travel anywhere in your coat pocket, doesn't set off the security alarm in airports, and is almost invisible to strangers who would interfere with its passage. It can be fed for a few cents a day, is very little trouble to its owners, and needs no special care beyond a warm place to sleep and its treasured human companionship.

This breed doesn't fit well in families with preschoolers, toddlers, or young adolescents. Preschoolers try to grab it, toddlers step on it or fall over it, and young adolescents injure it

The purpose behind developing the world's tiniest dog presents a paradox. Certainly the Chihuahua is a loving and lovable little companion, but its microsize precludes romping and playing in the backyard with children or adults. It's an unlikely companion for a long walk in the country or hike in the mountains, and it's an improbable candidate for a game of Frisbee in the park. However, the bravado exhibited by some Chihuahuas is alarming and attests that this tiny dog has the spirit of a Mastiff.

Immigration across the border came quickly after the Chihuahua's discovery in the state of Chihuahua in 1850 and the breed was well established in America by the early 1900s. It rose in popularity subsequent to 1930, and the breed was entered into the AKC studbook in 1942. Today there are few if any serious Chihuahua breeders in Mexico. Americans have adopted this breed for better or worse and are quite proud of their tiny adopted friend.

when attempting to play tug-of-war. A Chihuahua usually is quite comfortable with seniors and other adult families.

ATTITUDE

This little dog often claims ownership of one family member with whom it bonds tightly.

It's a living, breathing canine, not a stuffed toy, and deserves no less attention than is given to its larger cousins. It's a brave, loyal, affectionate, and intelligent companion that can be highly sensitive and a little stubborn. Often the highly trainable Chihuahua's training is neglected because of its small size. It's easier to pick up and carry the little dog than teach it to walk on a leash. It should be emphasized that pampering is done without regard for the dog's opinion on that matter.

A few are taught some party tricks and love to perform for guests, but most are simply household adornments. What a shame!

APTITUDE

If given an opportunity the Chihuahua will respond beautifully to commands and make a fine obedience competitor. It does well in conformation shows and appreciates the training associated with these events. When consistently taught the Chihuahua loves to play hide-and-seek and some have a reliable nose for searching for hidden items or playing fetch. Its terrierlike temperament should be emphasized and developed to get the most from the world's tiniest dog.

APPEARANCE

This tiny breed has no height standard but it usually stands about 5 inches tall (13 cm) and weighs no more than 6 pounds (2.7 kg). It's slightly longer from stem to stern than its height, although shorter bodies are preferred in males. Its skull is described as an apple dome shape, with or without a molera (soft spot). Its muzzle is short and pointed, and its bite is level or scissor without any hint of over- or underbite. Its body is muscular but balanced and its uncropped ears are held erect.

It's shown in smooth- and longhaired varieties. The smooth variety's coat should be soft, glossy, and close. The longhaired variety coat has a soft texture with or without waves or curls, its ears are edged with fringes, and its tail, feet, legs, and neck are well feathered.

Colors permitted are any color or combination of colors, solid, marked, or splashed.

Origin

This breed's origin is filled with fantastic tales and extends back to the Toltec civilization of Mexico in the ninth century. Those ancient people possessed the Techichi (meaning prairie dog or gopher), which was actually a mute, longhaired dog of somewhat larger stature than the present-day Chihuahua. Toltec fanciers may have developed the modern-day Chihuahua from the Techichi. A paradox is met when we realize that Toltec communities were located in the region of present-day Mexico City and that discovery of the earliest specimens of the Chihuahua was in the state of Chihuahua. Mexico City's weather is notably cool because of its high elevation and should be relatively unsuitable for the diminutive little dog.

Progenitors of this breed might include a small hairless Chinese dog. That could account for the size reduction of the original and perhaps supports more recent development of the Chihuahua.

Tales abound of the uses of this tiny dog in Toltec and later Aztec religious rites, but nearly all fanciers accept one fact: the modern Chihuahua that was discovered in Chihuahua, Mexico, in the mid-1800s stands apart from all other canines. This tiniest breed prefers its own kind to all other dogs and although sociable with other dogs, it's most content when surrounded by other Chihuahuas.

Chinese Crested

This breed is also known as the Chinese Edible Dog, Chinese Ship Dog, Chinese Hairless, Chinese Royal Hairless, Pyramid or Giza Hairless, South African Hairless, and Turkish Hairless. As the secondary names imply, it was carried by sailors from Africa to China and nearly every other port of call.

Fanciers are found everywhere but the breed has never reached great popularity. It has often been exhibited in circuses and carnivals as a freak, but this little dog has many merits that go unrecognized.

The Crested is seen in two types, one hairless and the other with a full coat. The Powderpuff type is nearly identical to the hairless (except for coat) and the two are interbred and shown together. Breeding a hairless to a hairless or breeding a Powderpuff to a hairless may result in either type or both types of puppies, but breeding a Powderpuff to a Powderpuff will always produce the haired-type pups.

The Powderpuff's coat care is probably less demanding than the skin care of the hairless type. Brushing and combing occasionally and bathing when dirty is about all that's needed to keep the Powderpuff looking spiffy.

The hairless type is a different story and requires well-planned attention. Moisturizing creams are applied daily, sunblock is especially important in light-skinned dogs, a coat is needed in cool weather, and routine bathing with special shampoos is important to control blackheads.

Neither type is comfortable in cool climates but luckily this small breed can obtain sufficient exercise indoors. This active and nimble dog is a unique and energetic house pet that's content to follow its owners around the house, play games with the children, and join in family activities.

CURRENT FUNCTION

The Chinese Crested has earned the credentials of a superior family companion, a better-than-average alarm dog, and a good choice as an older child's playmate.

ATTITUDE

This breed is a nimble and cunning playmate, a vigilant and sensitive house dog, and a loving and obedient pet. It socializes well with other pets and is only a little cautious with visitors.

APTITUDE

This lively and active breed is rarely seen in agility contests but is still a viable candidate for timed events. The Chinese Crested is very trainable and should shine in obedience work. It's imminently qualified to be a spirited family companion who likes to share its master's bed whenever possible.

APPEARANCE

This fine-boned and graceful little dog stands 11 to 13 inches tall (28 cm) and weighs

Original Design

The Crested has enjoyed a pampered life with few duties except those associated with being a good companion and occasionally as a sideshow exhibit. It was probably employed as a ratter on trading ships and sometimes was found as an edible delicacy.

5 to 12 pounds (2 to 5.5 kg). It's an athletically built little dog and is well muscled for its size. Its legs are straight and strong. The crest referred to in its name refers to a rather copious shock of silky hair that graces the dog's head. Hair is absent over

much of the remainder of its body, except for tufts of hair on the tail and feet.

The Powderpuff has a flowing double coat of silky hair that covers its entire body. It is seen in any coat color or combination of colors. A dark skin is preferred by many because of its natural resistance to sunburn but any colors and patterns are admissible.

Origin

Origin of this dog depends on the history being read. Some authors claim it was first seen in Africa, whereas others find its origin in Mexico or any of several other warm countries. Its actual origin remains shrouded by sea tales because it's known to have been carried by trading ships from and to many different ports where it was bought and sold.

Its date of origin and development usually is considered to be during the thirteenth century, but one author puts its origin at 100 B.C. and the American Chinese Crested Club lists its origin (as recorded by explorers) in the sixteenth century.

Its progenitors also are unknown but hairless mutations are found worldwide in practically all canines and these mutations sometimes are fertile breeders. Oriental countries often concentrated on breeding miniaturized dogs, so Chinese husbandry of small, hairless mutations is a probability.

Coton de Tuléar

This little white companion dog is perhaps closely related to the Bichon group and has no other names. Its long cottony coat requires brushing and combing every few days to prevent tangles and remove dead hair.

Exercise needs are easily met by active owners. The Coton is an energetic little dog that thrives on outdoor activities. It has the endurance and interest to accompany its family everywhere. The dog loves to swim and, when given the opportunity, will display those talents in sea, lake, or pool water.

CURRENT FUNCTION

This small dog is a wonderful companion and playmate and has amazing stamina and courage. It's willing and ready to accompany its family on all-day outings, trotting alongside its master's horse for miles. The Coton's attachment to its handler is significant and its devotion to family is treasured by one and all.

ATTITUDE

This breed is friendly but alert and vigilant around strangers. It is intelligent and quite trainable but has a stubborn streak that must be understood. The Coton definitely has a mind of its own but it's a sociable little dog that's an excellent playmate for children. Fun-loving and active, the Coton is always ready for a game. This loving little dog is loyal and obedient–most of the time.

APTITUDE

The Coton de Tuléar is an alert watchdog that readily adapts to family activities. It learns rapidly and should be well equipped for flyball, agility, and possibly freestyle training. Its happy-go-lucky attitude sometimes leads to obstinacy but this shouldn't interfere with consistent and careful obedience training. The breed isn't recognized by the AKC but can enter in formal activities sponsored by other clubs.

APPEARANCE

The Coton stands about 10 to 12 inches tall (25 to 31 cm) and weighs about 9 pounds (4 kg). It appears quite similar to the smaller Maltese and to an untrimmed Bichon.

Its body is covered with a curly, white, cottony, single coat that's unsculptured and shown in its natural state. Shades of apricot or fawn sometimes are seen on its head, ears, and loin.

Original Design

The Coton de Tuléar was bred for a specific purpose as were others of the Bichon type. It was developed as a superior family companion. It's somewhat rare outside its native land but was introduced into the United States in the early 1970s.

Origin

The city of Tuléar in southern Madagascar is the place where the Coton was developed sometime in the 1600s. Its progenitors are in common with those of the Bichon Frisé and were introduced to Madagascar by French military.

Dandie Dinmont Terrier

Former names sometimes used during the development of this breed include Charlie's Hope Terrier and Mustard and Pepper Terrier. Those names were taken from Sir Walter Scott's fictional town of Charlieshope and the principal character's six dogs, named Auld Pepper, Young Pepper, Little Pepper, Auld Mustard, Young Mustard, and Little Mustard. The novel, *Guy Mannering*, was published in 1814 and the hero was named, of all things, Dandie Dinmont.

Although the Dandie appears strange to some, and clumsy to others, a good look into its facial expression tells you that this dog is neither awkward nor peculiar. Its intelligence emanates from its wise, serious eyes, and its dignified composure.

Coat care with comb and brush is accomplished regularly to prevent mats, and hand plucking should be done several times annually.

A Dandie loves long walks but will settle for a big backyard filled with playful children. This is a sophisticated little dog with a calm demeanor that may become melancholy and gloomy when its exercise is neglected.

CURRENT FUNCTION

Because canine varmint control is almost a thing of the past, the Dandie now functions as a devoted and loyal companion both indoors and outside. This ambitious terrier is quite sociable but generally ignores other dogs. It has the vigilance, voice, and inclination to sound the alarm when strangers are identified. It usually has good manners around cats and other pets, providing it's raised in contact with them. Terrier trials are available for a return to its original design, but they aren't terribly popular among Dandie fanciers.

ATTITUDE

This breed generally is a self-sufficient companion that's loyal but not an adoring pet. It is high spirited, yet it's calm in strange situations.

Its intelligence and staunch loyalty to its master are undoubtedly among its greatest qualities. Its loving nature is especially seen toward its children, with whom it will play endlessly. Generally the Dandie is a bold, independent hunting terrier that's reserved and dignified in most situations.

APTITUDE

The Dandie is biddable and sensitive with a built-in independent or slightly obdurate streak that shows up occasionally during training. It should be considered for energetic timed activities such as agility and flyball, but because of its short legs its speed may be less than desirable. Formal obedience training is mastered without difficulty, although its stubborn streak may occasionally get in the way of perfection.

Origin

The Dandie breed type dates to the beginning of the eighteenth century and was well established before Scott's book was published. One author says the Dandie type possibly resulted from crosses of the Otterhound with a now extinct Scottish terrier. It probably was selectively bred from the Border, Skye, and Scottish Terriers that resided in and around the Cheviot Hills country. Its looks are similar to the Bedlington Terrier, which may be a descendant of the Dandie. One fact that can't be disputed is that this breed was found in the Teviotdale hills for many years before Sir Walter Scott made it famous.

APPEARANCE

The Dandie stands about 8 to 11 inches tall (20 to 28 cm) and weighs a solid 18 to 24 pounds (8 to 11 kg). At that point the typical terrier description stops because the Dandie Dinmont Terrier is composed of curves with virtually no straight lines in its conformation.

This breed is nearly twice as long as it is tall, measured from shoulders to rump. It has a muscular build that begins with a large, sturdy head and leads to a well-developed and moderately long neck, thence to a well-sprung chest and muscular body. Its hindquarters are taller than the forequarters because its hind legs are longer than the forelegs. The total effect is that of a series of gentle curves from muzzle to tail tip. If the length of the Dandie's curved, pointed tail, which is 8 to 10 inches, and the length of the neck and head are added to the previously stated body length, the overall length of the Dandie is significantly greater than its height.

The Dinmont's double coat is about 2 inches long and consists of both hard and soft hair. Colors include pepper that is a bluish black to light silver gray with leg hair of tan, reddish brown or pale fawn. The other color combination is mustard that is reddish brown to pale fawn. Topknot and ear color is a creamy white.

Original Design

The Dandie Dinmont's earliest duties were involved with going to ground in pursuit of otters, foxes, badgers, rats, and other agricultural pests. In spite of its humorous, somewhat unorthodox looks, the Dandie was developed to be an efficient, aggressive hunter that's both tough and tenacious.

French Bulldog

Bouledogue Français is the name that the French would prefer us to use, but the French Bulldog Club of America overruled the proposal.

This bat-eared little dog's coat is easily cared for. Its slick and shiny appearance can be maintained by frequent brushing with a rubber slicker or grooming glove. Sometimes the facial creases need cleaning and drying to prevent topical infection.

Exercise requirements are minimal and can usually be met with short leashed walks, playtime, and an occasional romp in the yard. Because of its short muzzle, the dog often snores, occasionally snorts, and drools, and its exercise should be limited during hot weather to prevent heat prostration. Don't expect this short-nosed breed to handle vigorous activity like a terrier.

CURRENT FUNCTION

As is the case with many small dogs, the Frenchie is an excellent companion and house pet. It holds great appeal for children because of its humorous, stuffed-dog appearance. Its bright and alert demeanor and its quick response make for an excellent alarm dog. The smaller French Bulldogs are often uncomfortable around preschoolers and toddlers because of the kids' clumsiness, but this dog isn't apt to become shy or aggressive.

ATTITUDE

The Frenchie is nimble and always ready for a game yet is quiet and reserved. It's quite sociable and family oriented. A few have the reputation of being domineering toward other dogs, but that's not a general attitude. This intelligent little dog's clownish antics win the heart of everyone, and tales of the Frenchie sense of humor are manifold. It's a lovable and loving lapdog that dotes on affection.

APTITUDE

The French Bulldog is well adapted to quiet lives of retired folks as well as fanciers who

The breed was begun as a companion dog, but because of its intelligence and vigilance it is also a fine watchdog. It came to America late in the nineteenth century and was shown in New York in a specialty show in 1898. Although its progenitors were probably bred for pit fighting and bull baiting, the Frenchie seems to have few instinctive pugilistic inclinations.

want to exhibit their companions. The Frenchie is unsuited to speed activities and will do best as a pet with a wonderful personality. It's a well-behaved dog and an avocation as a therapy dog, or perhaps an obedience competitor, are well within reach.

APPEARANCE

The French Bull Dog stands about 12 inches tall (30.5 cm) and weighs up to 28 pounds (12 kg), although most weigh less. The dog has heavy bones, is compact, and is of medium or small composition. It is muscular and well balanced and has a large head with a flat skull between its characteristic rounded bat ears. Its legs are short, sturdy, and straight and are set wide apart.

Its coat is dense and flat, and acceptable colors include brindle, white, fawn, brindle and white, and any other color except solid black, mouse, liver, black and tan, or black and white.

Origin

As one might suppose, the Frenchie originated in France and has existed since the mid-1800s. It was probably bred from smaller-than-normal English Bulldogs that were unpopular in England but appealed to French fanciers at that time. These small, sometimes erect-eared English Bulldogs were probably crossed with French breeds to produce this interesting little dog. It's unknown how the Frenchie's flat skull and large, rounded, erect, batlike ears were introduced, but these features are now among the identifying characteristics of the breed. These features have been promoted and relentlessly guarded in France and America, but the English breeders disagreed and supported the rose ears of the English Bulldog.

Klein German Spitz

The Klein German Spitz also is called the Deutsche Spitz and is a miniaturized version of a northern sled-pulling dog. This breed is next-to-smallest of four German Spitz breeds that differ from one another only in height. This little dog is unknown in most of the Western world but is gaining in popularity in Europe.

Its coat requires considerable grooming much like the other northern breeds, and even more attention to combing should accompany seasonal shedding.

The Klein requires a moderate amount of exercise, though not nearly as much as its bigger brothers. Daily walks, romps in the yard, and playing take the place of pulling sleds and skijoring.

CURRENT FUNCTION

The Klein German Spitz is a responsive, alert, playful, and happy small dog that's an all-weather pet and one that can live outside in a doghouse or in the family parlor. It's an interesting, active, and mischievous little lapdog.

ATTITUDE

The Klein Spitz is a fine older-children pet that will accompany them everywhere when allowed. Not a bit delicate, this happy little dog takes snowy trails in stride. This small Spitz is a tiny dog with a big attitude and is always ready to go for a walk or a run, especially in cold weather.

APTITUDE

This athletic little German breed is independent and a bit stubborn when it comes to training. It might do well in agility trials if trained properly. However, the Klein does best when it's playing in the yard, taking long walks, and spending a good deal of lap-time in the evening.

APPEARANCE

The Klein German Spitz stands about 10 inches tall (25.5 cm) and weighs about 20 pounds (9 kg). All German Spitz are cut from the same cloth relative to conformation. Of course the Giant is more muscular and generally stronger than the smaller varieties. The Klein is a typical huskylike miniature that has small, pointed, erect ears, a full brush tail that is carried over its back, and short, sturdy legs. It's a muscular little dog with well-balanced anatomical features that lend to its quickness and agility.

The Klein's double coat is heavy for the size of the dog. It's seen in virtually every color pattern.

Origin

The forefathers of this breed are no doubt the same progenitors of the other northern European sled dogs that were probably bred in Holland, then traveled to Germany with the Vikings. The Samoyed may have figured in this dog's background. Little specific knowledge is recorded in American dog literature, but the huskylike appearance is noteworthy.

Original Design

The little Klein variety appears to be a miniature sled dog probably having origin in the German Spitz Mittel and Giant sizes. This little dog couldn't have been bred to pull sleds, but like its smaller cousin, the Pomeranian, it was probably selectively bred or crossed with other small breeds to produce this little variety. Its larger brothers sometimes serve as herding dogs in Germany and this trait is sometimes seen in the Klein.

Mittel German Spitz

The next-larger variety of the German Spitz is the Mittel, sometimes called the Standard Spitz or Deutscher Mittel Spitz.

It has all the characteristics of the other sizes and is very similar in color to the Giant, Klein, and Pomeranian. It's rarely seen outside of Western Europe but is more common in England.

Its coat is typical of northern dogs and requires a fair amount of combing and brushing to prevent mats. A bath helps remove dead hair and is indicated at the end of seasonal shedding.

Its exercise needs are nominal and can be met with a few walks each day or a serious romp with children in a fenced yard.

CURRENT FUNCTION

The Mittel is a fine, attentive small companion that's often found on German farms. This breed is exhibited in its native region of the world but has limited following elsewhere.

ATTITUDE

Like the larger and smaller Spitz breeds it's a loyal and brave companion that will keep up with its human handlers. The Mittel is a bit reserved and is cautious toward strangers, making it an excellent alarm dog.

APTITUDE

This little German breed is a notably vigilant and alert dog that serves both as a watchdog and companion. Its trustworthiness and loyalty are seen and may relate to its herding ancestors. If those characteristics dominate the personality of your Mittel, it might excel in various canine endeavors. Although this intelligent and athletic little dog isn't recognized by the AKC, with proper training it should perform well in agility and flyball contests.

APPEARANCE

The Mittel stands 12 inches tall (30 cm) and weighs about 20 pounds (9 kg). This is not a

Original Design

Like its smaller cousins, the Mittel Spitz is too small to pull a loaded sled or participate in skijoring. This little dog was produced as a companion dog for those who admire the form and appearance of northern dogs but have no functional use for them. There is some question about the Mittel's value as a sheepdog, but like the Klein its progenitors were herding dogs and this genetic trait is occasionally seen.

delicate little dog but one that can hold its own in most companion dog endeavors and in adverse weather. Its well-muscled body, strength, and excellent balance is typical of a working sled dog. Its small, pricked ears, narrow muzzle, and wolflike appearance are characteristic of the Spitz type.

Its thick wooly undercoat is covered with straight, harsh guard hair that is weather resistant. It's bred in a variety of wolflike solid colors, some with darker or lighter overtones or masks.

Origin

The Mittel German Spitz originated in Germany and the Netherlands, where it was undoubtedly bred from the northern sled dogs sometime during the Middle Ages. Smaller breeds may have been crossed with the Giant Spitz to produce its height, but breeders were careful to propagate the body type, coat, and disposition of this breed.

Havanese

The Havana Silk dog, Bichon Havanais, White Cuban, or Habenero, is another shaggy little dog of ancient European lineage.

Its coat is long and silky and tangles easily if grooming isn't carried out frequently and diligently.

Its exercise needs are easily met in its role as companion dog. All it takes is a few romps a day with the kids, a walk or two, and ideally a backyard to play in.

CURRENT FUNCTION

A Havanese's cheerful demeanor and clever intelligence combine to form a top-notch companion dog. It's a good children's dog when parents teach the children to respect the Havanese's need for its own space. It's a sociable little dog but resents constant handling, teasing, or harassment.

ATTITUDE

The Havanese attitude is nearly flawless except for a slight propensity to vocalize when it's startled. It's sensitive, playful, friendly and accommodating, affectionate, and has a great sense of humor. Its outgoing and rarely timid nature finds acceptance with practically every adult. Its sociability with other animals is pronounced, and rarely does it have a problem with other dogs or family pets.

APTITUDE

The Havanese is highly trainable but responds poorly to yelling and shouting. It wants to please, and its intelligence and gentle nature carries well into obedience and dog-show training. Its fine memory and quick learning capacity should make it adept at timed event participation. Freestyle competition should be easily taught because the breed usually is quite sensitive to voice modulation and intonation.

APPEARANCE

The Havanese stands about 10 inches tall (25.4 cm) and weighs about 10 pounds (5 kg). It is a sturdy little dog, not delicate

Origin

The ancient Havanese breed has common ancestors with the Barbichon, Bichon, and Maltese. It probably traveled with Mediterranean trading ships from Europe and the Canaries to the Caribbean islands. The Havanese developed during the 1700s in Cuba, where it was bred and owned by rich landowners and the plantation aristocracy. When the Havanese lost its popularity in these circles, many of these clever little dogs earned their living performing in circuses.

or frail, and is quite athletic. Its short legs are straight and strong. Its nose rubber, lip, and eye margins are always black or solid dark brown on chocolate brown individuals. Its drop ears, straight topline, high tail set, and animated gait gives the Havanese a happy appearance.

Original Design

Like related breeds, this little dog always has been most admired for its intelligence and adaptability. The Havanese's heritage as an excellent companion dog is unquestioned. It migrated in the 1950s from Cuba to the United States, where it received a warm welcome and was admitted to AKC recognition in 1999.

Its 6-inch-long, double, wavy, and profuse coat isn't trimmed except for nominal scissoring of foot hair. It's seen in virtually all colors from black to white.

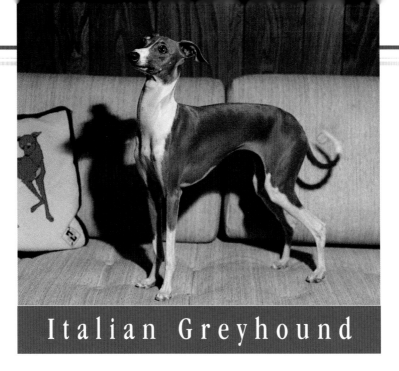

Italian Greyhound

This smallest sight hound is known in its native land as Piccoli Levrieri Italiani. It's an ancient breed that appears to be a miniature version of the Greyhound with all the talents of its big brother. It's as streamlined and speedy as the Greyhound and even more cold sensitive because of its tiny size, the virtual absence of fat insulation on its body, and its scant and slick coat.

The Italian Greyhound's coat presents no grooming problems and can be kept in prime condition by wiping it down every day or two with a chamois cloth.

This dog loves to run, whether in pursuit of small game or just for the fun of it. Its exercise needs can be met by long walks, backyard games, and play.

CURRENT FUNCTION

The Italian Greyhound has sporting qualities but is best known as a diminutive and classic companion pet. It appreciates the comfort of apartment living and a soft bed but can be seen speeding across a yard in pursuit of imaginary or real quarry.

ATTITUDE

This breed is universally affectionate, cheerful, and intelligent and with consistent handling is a superior pet. Its size restricts the kind of playmates it enjoys because rowdy dogs and children can overwhelm this tiny breed. Older children should be taught not to treat the Italian Greyhound as a carry-around toy or a roughhousing companion. Not known as a watchdog, the bark of this breed sounds like that of a much larger dog. The Italian Greyhound is often timid toward strangers, but makes up with properly introduced visitors quickly.

APTITUDE

The Italian Greyhound's elegant beauty pleases the eyes of everyone who meets this charming little dog. The lovable good nature of the Italian Greyhound suits it best for just what it is,

Originally the progenitors of the Italian Greyhound probably came from Egypt, Turkey, and Greece, where they later found favor with medieval European royalty. Similar dogs were depicted in Roman art as regular companions of the imperial court. Mummies, paintings, and carvings of dogs with similar form and function indicate that this tiny dog probably arrived on the scene thousands of years before the Christian era. Remains found in Pompeii tend to lend credibility to that assumption. It probably descended from Greyhound blood and shares progenitors with that breed.

The Italian Greyhound became popular in southern Europe, especially in Italy, during the sixteenth century and eventually was the darling of queens and princesses throughout Europe.

the streamlined Greyhound, only in smaller proportions. Its muzzle is long and tapered, and its ears are small and folded back at right angles to its head.

Its single coat is fine and lies flat. It's seen in practically every color pattern and hue, much the same as the Greyhound.

Original Design

This tiny, personable miniaturization probably was bred on purpose as a lady's companion but later gained a reputation for having sufficient speed, endurance, and determination for coursing small game.

and being a superior companion is no crime, although owners may claim this little dog is the essence of a sight hound. Seeing this tiny hound being walked on lead is like taking a trip back in time to a place where it accompanied Mary, Queen of Scots, on her rounds.

An Italian Greyhound is easy to train, providing the handler is consistent and gentle. This little dog often wins obedience trial points. It loves to chase anything that runs and may exhibit this propensity if exercised off lead.

APPEARANCE

The Italian Greyhound stands about 13 inches tall (33 cm) and weighs about 8 pounds (3.5 kg). Its conformation is quite similar to that of

Jack Russell Terrier

This breed is sometimes known as the Jack or JRT. A variation of the Jack Russell Terrier is the Parson Jack Russell Terrier, or simply the Parson Jack.

The differences between the Parson JRT and the JRT are mainly the dog's length of leg and the attitude of the fanciers.

Many owners and breeders aren't terribly happy with AKC recognition and prefer to breed their Parson JRT dogs for function rather than conformation.

The Jack Russell Terrier is seen in a smooth or broken coat, either of which is easily cared for. Minimal combing or brushing is required, in addition to periodic bathing.

Exercise requirements for this active and energetic little terrier are difficult to meet in the average family.

This is a working dog, and its energy must be spent regularly to prevent boredom and related mischief. A couple of walks a day won't begin to satisfy a Jack's demands.

CURRENT FUNCTION

This wonderful little dog is perhaps the most misunderstood breed in America today. Because of its fantastic intelligence, agility, and trainability, JRTs have captured television and movie audiences' hearts time and again. This public exposure of a few highly trained and talented dogs have subjected the breed to all the vices inherent to notoriety. This tough little terrier is still a working dog with a hunting dog's attitude and characteristics. It's true that the active and lovable little scamp is a fine pet in its own right, but that fact doesn't address the problems that come with the territory.

JRTs are phenomenal companions because they have the strength of a larger dog, the fun-loving nature that children enjoy, and the propensity to play by the hour. They've gained all the vices that accompany boredom and neglect when the new wears off and the children tire out. Some JRTs are experts in terrier trials, but because foxhunting isn't a major sport in America, even trials aren't necessarily the answer to this dog's great energy.

ATTITUDE

The JRT's attitude is about what you would expect in a working dog. It's intelligent, ambitious, a bit stubborn, and an independent hunter. It will rout any cats except the family feline and will destroy all rodents that aren't securely caged, regardless of their cost or pet status. A JRT will test the household rules and often will tip the family's standards of decorum to suit itself. It's an enterprising and self-confident companion at best and a resourceful escape artist at worst. This dog is brave and vigilant and a bit temperamental, but lovable even when turning the household upside down.

APTITUDE

This aggressive little hunter is beautifully suited for the purposes for which it was developed, and in the bargain it has a well-developed sense of humor that thrives on activity. It often excels in agility and flyball contests and won't back off from hikes that might test the endurance of larger dogs. It is well suited to an athletic and active family who wants an equally athletic canine companion. Terrier trials are another way to test a JRT's skill and endurance, and these trials also whet the little dog's problem-solving ability. This relentless little dog has been known to stay in pursuit of its quarry through the night, and reports abound of JRTs that have stayed underground for several days.

The JRT learns quickly, performs with expression and enthusiasm, and is quite trainable when receiving consistent and persistent instruction. The freethinking little dog often anticipates handler's direction and thus creates raucous humor where somber decorum was intended.

Original Design

In Parson Jack's design, this breed's sole purpose was to follow the horses and foxhounds until the quarry went to ground. The small terrier's job was to follow the fox into its lair and either bolt or kill it. The JRT's ancillary duties included hunting small rodents, raccoons, and other farm pests that inhabited the Devonshire hills and dales. The JRT's popularity grew until Reverend Russell died in 1883; then the type waned for many years. Although Parson Jack wasn't keen on seeing his creation competing in Kennel Club shows, it was admitted into English registry in 1991, and gained AKC recognition about seven years later.

Origin

The JRT was originally bred in Devonshire, England, by one Parson John Russell, nicknamed "The Hunting Parson." He was a foxhunting aficionado, an early member of the English Kennel Club, a judge, and a breeder. He developed his new breed from predominantly white terriers, including the Wirehaired Fox, Smooth Fox, and other working terriers, and through careful selective breeding created the JRT in about 1870.

APPEARANCE

The JRT stands 12 to 14 inches tall (30 to 32 cm) and weighs about 15 pounds (7 kg). Its legs are straight and strong under a slender body that's well muscled and hard. Its slightly-taller-than-long conformation assures the endurance necessary to keep up with fox hunters.

The broken coat of the JRT is made of wiry guard hair that lies over a tight undercoat. The shorthaired variety's coat lies flat and is coarse, straight hair that also lies over the weather-resistant undercoat. Most Jacks are white with only a few black and tan markings, especially around their heads and tails and occasionally on their backs.

Japanese Chin

This tiny Oriental dog was formerly known as the Japanese Spaniel and has been associated with China, Japan, and Korea.

Its long coat doesn't tangle and can be kept beautiful by careful combing and brushing several times a week.

The Chin requires a nominal amount of exercise and usually finds outlet for its energy in a yard or on a couple of walks per day. It is well suited to apartment living because of its lapdog heritage and low-maintenance exercise requirements.

CURRENT FUNCTION

This regal-appearing little dog has but one function, that of a lively and lovely companion. The Chin is happiest when it graces the lap of its owner and will seek its pleasure while pleasing the person to which it is most attached.

ATTITUDE

A Chin's cheerful, calm, and quiet demeanor bonds it quickly and securely to its handler and the little dog goes to great lengths to please this person. Though dogs of this breed prefer to be the center of attention, they are undemanding and devoted. A Chin is a fine companion for older children who have been instructed in this tiny dog's care and handling.

APTITUDE

Training is taken in stride and a Chin is easily housebroken and trained. It has an obstinate streak that occasionally rears its head, but generally it is quite accommodating. Its will to please governs its response to its owner. This tiny toy breed is rarely seen in canine sports but should do well in obedience work if the handler is dedicated and consistent.

APPEARANCE

The Japanese Chin stands about 8 to 10 inches tall (20 to 25 cm) and weighs about 5 pounds (2 kg). The breed standard lists no actual standard height and weight but generally, if all other points are equal, the smaller the better.

Original Design

The purpose for creating the Chin was to provide lapdogs for Japanese fanciers within the imperial aristocracy's ranks. This breed had no other purpose but to act as a loving and affectionate companion and in that role they were wonderfully disposed.

They were carried to Europe and America in the mid-1800s, and in the late 1800s the breed gained AKC recognition as the Japanese Spaniel. The name was changed to Japanese Chin in 1977.

It's a dainty little dog with an Oriental pug face and a lively, high-stepping gait.

Its coat is long, straight, soft, silken, and flowing. Most are seen in black and white patterns, but lemon and white, red and white, or brindle and white is allowed.

Origin

According to two writers the Japanese Chin originated in Korea. Another gives Japan as its native land, and the remainder of references agree that the Chin came from China, where it was bred and maintained for the aristocracy. Its date of origin is sometime before 700 A.D., at which time accounts reveal that several dogs of this type were presented to the emperor of Japan. From that time hence, the Japanese Chin was adopted and developed by the Japanese into a lapdog par excellence.

This little dog resembles the English Toy Spaniel and may have common origins with that breed or may have been crossed with the English dog during development.

King Charles Spaniel, aka English Toy Spaniel

A good deal of confusing information exists concerning the King Charles Spaniel, the English Toy Spaniel, and the Cavalier King Charles Spaniel. Other names associated with this breed were the Spaniell Gentle and the Comforter. Books from other parts of the world describe the King Charles and the English Toy Spaniels as name variations of the same breed. The Cavalier was covered previously and has similar features to those of this dog. The Cav is a heavier dog with a longer muzzle. For the sake of simplicity the following discussion is based on composite information available for the King Charles or English Toy Spaniel.

The coat of the King Charles is easily kept free from tangles with a comb and brush a couple of times weekly. This little companion is a low-maintenance pet and is ideally suited to apartment living.

This breed's exercise needs are minimal beyond the normal family activities in which the devoted little dog is included. It's always ready for a short romp in the yard or parlor, but doesn't require physical exertion purely for the sake of exercise.

CURRENT FUNCTION

Perhaps its hunting instincts are becoming rusty, but there is little doubt that the English Toy Spaniel is a fantastic family companion. It's small enough to be welcome in apartment and condo complexes throughout the world and is seen in the backyards and homes of suburbia. It's not known for its hardiness in extreme cold, and its long coat makes it equally unsuited to hot climates. This dog shouldn't be banished to the backyard or kept outside the family circle.

ATTITUDE

This little dog is a dyed-in-the-wool lapdog. It delights in bringing joy and companionship to properly instructed children and adults alike. It's easily socialized with other dogs and small pets and even lends an alarm dog quality to its residence. It frequently announces visitors although it rarely barks at other times. Its usual calm and quite demeanor makes it an excellent family pet.

APTITUDE

The intelligence of this little spaniel is unquestioned and it could be trained for obedience work, CGC work, and possibly timed events. Properly trained English Toy Spaniels are often a hit among residents of nursing homes, hospitals, and therapy facilities. Their alert and affectionate temperament is stable and their loving nature is ideal.

APPEARANCE

This little dog stands about 10 or 11 inches tall (25 to 27 cm) and weighs 8 to 14 pounds (4 to 6 kg). The English Toy Spaniel's body is solidly compact and basically square. Its domed head, short muzzle, long ears, dark eyes, and black lip margins add to this dog's soft and expressive countenance.

Origin

Most historians agree that this little dog's progenitors lived in the Orient or, more specifically, in Japan or China. A Japanese spaniel that originally came from ancient Korea may have been among the ancestors of the English Toy Spaniel. Oriental aristocracy could have presented this toy to European heads of state or the tiny dog may have been carried on cargo ships and traded at many ports of call. How the breed came to England is a matter of conjecture, but that's where the breed gained its lasting popularity. It was known in England at least 100 years before the reign of King Charles I, which ended in 1649. Mary, Queen of Scots, during her reign in the sixteenth century was a strong supporter of the tiny comforter spaniels that included the English Toy. The breed was afterward a particular favorite of King Charles II during the seventeenth century. The black and tan variety was known as the King Charles Spaniel.

Original Design

The oriental Cocker Spaniel progenitors of the breed probably provided the hunting instinct genes that exist today. Speculation exists that these tiny spaniels were used in the field even after they had risen to great popularity among the English gentry, but size alone very likely limited their general use.

The English Toy Spaniel was primarily a small, decorative companion dog that brought love and affection first to the courts of kings and noblemen and later was adopted by the public at large. Its ancestors were called comforter spaniels, and that synonym tells us a great deal about their nature and use.

The Toy Spaniel Club of England recognized four separate varieties, but since 1923 all four varieties have been known in Great Britain as King Charles Spaniels. The breed was known and admired in the United States throughout the nineteenth century and was among the earliest breeds shown in shows after the AKC's inception in 1885.

Its coat is long, silken, and wavy but should never be curly, and its body is heavily fringed with feathers on ears, legs, and chest. The Blenheim and ruby varieties are usually shorter coated than the Prince Charles variety.

The Prince Charles variety is tricolor that includes black, tan, and white. The ruby variety is red chestnut, and the Blenheim variety is red and white. The Blenheim variety probably includes the blood of Oriental Cocker Spaniels that lend excellent hunting instincts to the English Toy.

Lhasa Apso

The Lhasa is also known in Tibet as Abso Seng Kye, which translates to Bark Lion Sentinel Dog. The breed was called the Talisman Dog or Sheng Trou when it first appeared in Great Britain and later it was known as the Lhassa Terrier or simply as the Apso.

Because of the length of this little dog's coat it must be groomed thoroughly at least once a week. Care should be taken to comb the undercoat with equal vigor. Pet Lhasa Apsos are often clipped short instead of spending so much time at the grooming table.

Some yard exposure is preferable to total inside living. This breed is generally happy to find its own exercise while it's following its family, but it also enjoys leashed walks and romps in the park.

CURRENT FUNCTION

The Lhasa Apso's intelligence, loyalty, and cheerfulness makes it a very desirable family companion. It does quite well in almost any family circumstance and is equally at home in small apartments and more spacious abodes.

ATTITUDE

It's a calm and independent little dog that maintains a reserved attitude toward strangers and, when allowed, will bark its warning when intruders approach. It socializes well with older children that show mutual respect and are careful in their handling. The Lhasa socializes well with other family pets and lives with them quite amicably.

APTITUDE

Lhasas are quite trainable with consistent and competent handlers. It's quite sensitive to voice intonations and won't respond to yelling, shouting, or nagging. It's stubborn at times and perhaps a bit obstinate. This intelligent little dog is easily led to obedience work, providing it isn't bored by it. The Lhasa understands commands and other rules and responds well to treats when a course of training is begun. It's rarely entered in timed events but often is seen doing quite well in obedience trials.

APPEARANCE

The Lhasa Apso stands 10 or 11 inches tall (25 to 28 cm) and weighs 13 to 15 pounds (6 to 7 kg). Its bite is either level or slightly undershot and its muzzle is medium length. Its body, face, legs, and tail are well feathered and its tail is carried over its back in a screw.

Its extremely long and dense topcoat is heavy, straight, and hard and neither wooly nor silky. It lies over a medium-length softer undercoat. Its coat acted as insulation to the exceedingly harsh climate of Tibet. It's seen in virtually any color or color combination.

Original Design

This dog's place in history stems from its fantastic auditory capacity and its alertness and propensity to sound an alarm when intruders are heard. Its secondary design was to bring joy and peace to its family. One legend tells of the Lhasa's ability to receive people's souls at the moment of their deaths. The Lhasa Apso is the oldest and most popular of the four Tibetan breeds commonly recognized in the Western world and was first shown in London in 1929. Recognized by the British Kennel Club in 1933, it was admitted to the AKC's rolls in the Terrier Group in 1935 but was changed in 1959 to the Non-Sporting Group.

Origin

Tibet lies north of India. It's a country filled with tall mountains, severe slopes, and deep valleys. This terrain variation causes its climatic conditions to reach extremes in severe summer heat and terribly cold winters. *Lhasa* probably refers to the Tibetan capital, and *Apso* is thought to refer to this breed's goat-like appearance. The progenitors aren't known but the breed is documented as early as 1580. It's an indoor alarm dog that's credited with having super-acute hearing. That faculty found its niche in Lamaseries and in the homes of the common Tibetan people. The Tibetan Dalai Lama sometimes presented Lhasas to members of the Chinese imperial families and other countries' royal families.

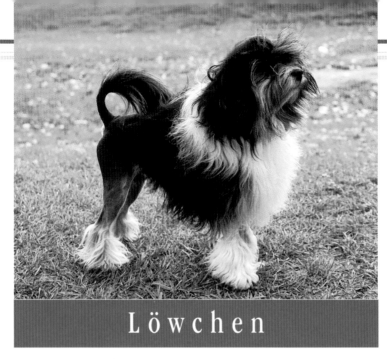

Löwchen

Other names for the Löwchen (pronounced Lirvchun) are Little Lion Dog or Le Petit Chien Lion. This member of the Bichon group is usually seen in its trimmed exhibition or fancy dress costume by which it's recognized.

Its coat requires regular, daily brushing and combing to prevent tangles.

This little dog needs an average amount of exercise for good health but can accommodate to its family's activities. It truly enjoys a long walk or romp in the park and can keep up with most people's gaits.

CURRENT FUNCTION

Löwchen's duties today include the same as were intended several hundred years ago. The little dog is a fine and playful children's companion and lovable family pet.

ATTITUDE

This breed is cheerful, intelligent, and eager to learn. It is gentle and sensitive and even tempered. Its propensity as an alarm dog endears it to its family, and its obedience and loyalty are recognized as well.

APTITUDE

The Löwchen's trainability is well known, and little trouble is encountered when teaching it manners and commands. It's anxious to please its handler and usually responds well to low-key and consistent training. It resents shouting and arm waving but will quickly learn if a calculated and systematic approach is used.

This reliable little dog should do well at obedience and in timed events. CGC training should be easily accomplished and the dog's interesting appearance and soft coat should recommend it as a visitation or therapy dog.

APPEARANCE

The Löwchen stands 12 to 14 inches tall (30 to 36 cm) and weighs 8 to 18 pounds (4 to 8 kg). It has a sturdy frame and carries its head and tail alertly. It has a broad and rather short

This little breed's original function was no doubt as a companion and family pet. It had some watchdog characteristics and was often kept as an alarm dog but its petite size would prevent it from being a guard dog of any consequence.

Its numbers reached a dangerously low level in the 1960s, and at that time it was considered the rarest breed in existence. It was revived by the efforts of British breeders and in 1996 it joined the AKC miscellaneous ranks and was admitted into the Non-Sporting Group in 1999.

muzzle, dark, intelligent eyes, and an attentive expression.

The Löwchen's coat is long, straight, or wavy, and without undercoat. Clipping is no big chore but it should be accomplished about every three months. The pattern is relatively simple. Foot hair is rounded and the forelegs are clipped short from elbow to pastern, using electric clippers. The hind legs are also clipped short from the hocks upward, including entire hindquarters, half the tail, and the abdomen forward to the last rib.

Löwchen colors vary and include solid black, white, and lemon, and markings of every hue are permissible.

Origin

The Löwchen's origin is reported to have occurred sometime in the sixteenth century in France although Germany or Russia may have equal claim. A Goya painting of a duchess of Arabia depicted a dog that resembled the Löwchen, but that's based upon its general size, clipping pattern, and length of coat more than any specific breed identification. Its progenitors are probably from the Bichon group but no data exists to confirm this.

Lundehund

The Lundehund, which in Norwegian means Puffin Hound, is one of the most interesting small dogs around. It's a Spitz-type dog that's extremely uncommon in America and is almost unheard of except in its native Norway.

The Lundehund's coat requires minimal brushing and combing except during seasonal shedding.

This active little dog requires a nominal amount of exercise to stay in good shape. A couple of leashed walks per day, a game or two, and a backyard to play in is sufficient.

CURRENT FUNCTION

Puffin hunting (see page 154) has reached a low ebb in America but this dog is gaining popularity because of its other attributes. The lively Lundehund has a great sense of humor and is an intelligent and independent little family pet.

Some researchers are convinced that this dog isn't a card-carrying member of *Canis familiaris* but instead belongs to a wild-dog species. It's a curious breed because of several features that aren't seen in other domestic dogs. These features include five-toed feet plus dewclaws on the inside of each foot, eight foot pads, the ability to completely close its ear canals, possession of a collarbone that allows its forelegs to extend 90 degrees from its body, and extra cervical vertebrae to allow it to bend its head back over its neck. (Please note that domestic dogs have only a vestige of a collarbone.)

ATTITUDE

The sharp-witted and clever Lundehund becomes bored easily. It is playfully alert, reluctantly obedient, and loves the outdoors. It tolerates other pets and children if introduced when the pup is still young. You should move slowly and have patience when bringing other pets into the household. Generally it is a loyal dog with a protective attitude, and barking is often a vice that needs attention.

The Lundehund originated on the Loefoten Islands of Norway sometime during the sixteenth century. Its specific progenitors are unknown, but because of this dog's conformational similarity to the northern Spitz breeds it's assumed to be related to that dog group.

Its coat is dense and rough, relatively short, and lies back. Its colors are white splashes on fawn to red or gray and sprinkled with black-tipped hairs.

Original Design

This little dog was bred and developed to serve a specific need. It was trained to climb the islands' steep cliff faces and return each time with a puffin in its mouth. Puffins' soft feathers were used in pillows and comforters, and the meat of the puffin was a great delicacy on Norwegian tables. The Lundehund began its decline and the breed neared extinction when puffin hunting became illegal, and this decline was hurried by a Norwegian distemper outbreak. By careful breeding the Lundehund eventually returned and today it's estimated that there are about 2,000 in the world. About 300 of these dogs are presently living in the United States but they haven't been recognized by the AKC. The Lundehund is recognized as a primitive breed by the American Rare Breed Association.

APTITUDE

Training a Lundehund requires skill, consistence, and patience. This breed is somewhat stubborn, and housebreaking will benefit from installation of a doggy door. The dog is a natural athlete and should do well in timed sports such as flyball, agility, and Frisbee. Obedience training should be taken in short sessions with a good deal of diversion interspersed.

APPEARANCE

The Lundehund stands 12 to 15 inches tall (31 to 38 cm) and weighs about 13 pounds (6 kg). Its Spitz-like body is small, rectangular, and muscular with triangular, erect, very mobile ears that are controlled to fold and be held in a tight position that effectively closes the ear canal. Its tail is coiled over its back except when alert, at which point it hangs behind in a hook shape.

Maltese

In about 1800 this popular European dog was known as Chien de Malte, or Bichon Maltaise. It was sometimes called the Shock Dog, which apparently referred to the dog's shock of white hair. European literature sometimes called this little white companion dog the Maltezer, early American dog lore listed it as the Maltese Lion Dog, and in England it was known as the Maltese Skye Terrier or simply the Maltese Terrier.

Its copious white coat requires substantial grooming to prevent tangles and sometimes once-a-week bathing to maintain the snow-white color.

Exercise is easily supplied by normal family activities, but this diminutive little dog truly enjoys getting out of the yard for a leashed walk.

CURRENT FUNCTION

An indisputable fact about this pint-sized dog is its present form and function. The Maltese is a delightful pet. It has a stuffed-toy appearance that wins the hearts of fanciers and onlookers alike, and its natural animation makes it appear as a beautiful little mechanical dog. The Maltese is typically a friendly, lovable pet that's accepted as a companion by anyone, anywhere.

ATTITUDE

It's filled with positive features including charm, affection, and trainability. A Maltese's attitude is described in the most flowery terms imaginable, such as friendly, playful, sociable, eager learner, sensitive, trainable, and loyal. It's excellent with older children and those who are carefully taught the proper manner in which to handle tiny breeds. It's an energetic little dog that often shows its propensity to not only announce but to challenge strangers who happen by.

APTITUDE

This tiny dog is well suited for training and is blessed with an excellent memory. It usually does well in obedience training, and if taught

Origin

Phoenician sailors may have introduced this breed's ancestors to Malta and that would make it one of the oldest European toy breeds. The Maltese has been in existence in a model similar to its present form for hundreds of years and possibly much longer. Its origin is muddled in literature by language variations and interpretations. Some writers claim the Maltese's origin to be around 1500 B.C. and use Ye Ancient Dogge of Malta in reference to the modern breed. Others claim that the breed described by ancient historians appeared far differently from the petite little canine that we know as the Maltese. One writer studied every work on Malta contained in the British Museum and found no references to a Maltese dog. Greek artists' works can be used to place the Maltese's origin at about 500 B.C.

Its progenitors are equally unknown but because of European references to its early form the Maltese is generally believed to be of spaniel heritage like the Bichon. In America it's sometimes believed to be more closely related to European terriers.

Original Design

This tiny breed was once called the Maltese Terrier in England and was a renowned rat catcher. More recently it has the reputation of a lady's favorite lapdog and a wonderful little pet. The Maltese was in great demand as a family dog from the beginning whether or not it has terrier or spaniel genes flowing in its veins.

Its more recent history is well documented regardless of how and when the Maltese breed was born. Positive facts place the Maltese in Europe during the eighteenth century and the first class for Maltese was in London at the Agricultural Hall in 1862. Maltese were exhibited in Westminster's first show in 1877 and the AKC accepted its registration in 1888.

gently and consistently it might compete in timed sports. The Maltese is one of the best therapy and visitation dogs and earns its reputation by its loving nature.

APPEARANCE

The Maltese stands about 9 inches tall (22 cm) and weighs between 4 and 6 pounds (2 to 3 kg). Its square body conformation is solidly constructed and set upon straight legs. Its dark eyes, black lid margins, lip margins, and nose rubber are characteristics of the breed. Its long plumed tail is carried over its straight back.

Its snowy white coat parts along the spine and covers its body from stem to stern with long, flat, and silky hair.

Toy Mexican Hairless

Sometimes this breed is referred to as the Xolo, Tepeizeuintli, or Xoloitzcuintli to designate its Mexican heritage. The last two terms very likely once referred to guinea pigs and other rodents that were reported by observers to be doglike.

The hairless dogs obviously have no coats to worry about, but they require substantial skin care to prevent flaking, sunburn, and dryness.

The Xolo is a small, barkless dog that requires no significant amount of structured exercise. A backyard and plenty of shade will suit it fine. It's a strong and vital dog that appreciates games and leashed walks, but it suffers greatly from cold weather and must be provided a coat.

CURRENT FUNCTION

If you can find a Mexican Hairless it is probably still the dog it once was. Specific breed rescue groups are always on the lookout for it, and when found it's a good watchdog, a fine companion (especially for people who are allergic to animal dander), and a quiet pet.

ATTITUDE

This intelligent, clever, and affectionate little dog is peaceful and adaptable. It has no bark but often sounds off with a rather lame howl. It's sociable with other dogs and household pets and its attitude toward children is consistently peaceful, although common sense dictates that it should be introduced to older children rather than toddlers and preschoolers.

APTITUDE

The Mexican Hairless is anxious to please its handler and responds to training quickly. It's a rare breed that adores its family and participates in all activities. It's not presently recognized by the AKC but should do well in obedience training and timed events.

The Mexican Hairless was a food animal when it reached the zenith of popularity in its native country and it was in demand as an entrée at Mexican tables. It's said to have served as a sacrifice in ancient Mexico. Another interesting use was that of a bed warmer or living heater. Its larger or standard variety was recognized as a fine watchdog in spite of its lack of barking ability. It received recognition by the AKC in 1959, but has since faded into relative obscurity in America.

APPEARANCE

This breed stands about 11 inches (28 cm) tall and weighs about 10 pounds (5 kg). Its erect ears add to the dog's alert appearance. Its legs are straight and its body is smooth and refined. It is totally hairless except for a few hairs or a little tuft on the top of the head and tip of the tail.

The Mexican Hairless dog's skin may be any shade of black, bronze, or gray, but darker colors are preferable.

The Mexican Hairless was once more popular in America than the similar Chinese Crested dog but has recently declined in favor. Some writers claim that the propagation of all hairless breeds began in Africa and migrated by means of trading ships to Guinea, Manila, China, and thence to North America. The Mexican Hairless is said to have been delivered to Mexico from the Orient toward the last of the sixteenth century. Others make a case for the Mexican Hairless being a mutant in origin and a product of Mexico before the Spanish invasion. The Hairless's progenitors and history is clouded by the fact that very little has been recorded about them.

Miniature Dachshund

Teckel is the name by which the Dachshund is usually known in Germany and this breed's founding club is known as Deutscher Teckel-klub. The Zwergteckel is the miniature of the two Dachshund varieties. The German word *dachs* means badger and *hund* means dog, so the combination means badger dogs. The three coat varieties (wirehaired, longhaired, and smooth) and two sizes of Dachshunds (standard and miniature) are all registered as one breed.

The amount of grooming needed by your Dachshund depends on whether you own a smooth, wirehaired, or longhaired variety. The smooth variety takes only a quick brush with a rubber slicker and a wipe with a chamois cloth to finish. The wirehaired Dachshund must have its coat combed or brushed on a weekly basis and plucked periodically. The longhaired Dachshund needs weekly combing, and occasionally tangles must be clipped from its long flowing coat.

Exercise needs for the miniature Dachshund is nominal. If a backyard is available to run in, it will accomplish its own exercise requirements, but the energetic Dachshund is always ready for a romp in the park, a game of fetch, or a leashed walk.

CURRENT FUNCTION

Originally this little dog's ancestors were sporting dogs, but in America it became a household companion pet as soon as it arrived. Some Dachshunds enter field trials and a few even go rabbit hunting, but these activities are forsaken by most owners, who would rather have a wonderful pet instead of a few bunny hides. One must remember this little dog's instinctive hunting traits and forgive their companion when it disappears on the trail of a chipmunk or squirrel.

ATTITUDE

The Dachshund is so devoted to its family that it has no time for strangers and treats them with suspicious reservation. The Miniature Dachshund is above all a clean, odorless, and easy-keeping family dog. It dotes on the family's children, providing those kids are taught reasonable manners and proper handling of a small dog. A miniature Dachshund has a mind of its own and is brave, cunning, and vigilant. This courageous little dog is strong and strong willed and is a wonderful and loyal companion.

APTITUDE

The modern American Dachshund is best suited for family companion duties. Its inherited hunting prowess lends tenacity and single-mindedness to its personality and this sometimes gets in the way of obedience training. It's an intelligent, curious little dog with an active mind and body that you shouldn't sell short. Introduce every conceivable type of situation to your Dachshund at a very young age and it will remember these events as it ages. Train it with consistency and persistence and try to overlook its stubbornness. Obedience is eventually taught, but not without patience.

Original Design

Its quarry often outweighed the intrepid little Dachshund, but it persevered in its duty to follow, dig out, fight, and dispatch the awesome badger. This furnishes us the key to the true identity of the original Dachshund. It was one tough little hound! Early in the breed's development smaller Dachshunds were born with equal fight, and these were used to hunt rabbits and other smaller farm pests.

Dachshunds were established in America by 1885, and in 1895 the Dachshund Club of America was established. The breed thrived in the United States until the early 1900s, when its name and long association with Germany caused popularity reversals throughout the Western world during World War I and less so during World War II.

It's occasionally found in field trials, obedience trials, CGC tests, and other events but its principal role is that of a tough little friend to the family.

APPEARANCE

The Miniature Dachshund stands about 5 to 9 inches tall (13 to 23 cm) and weighs less than 11 pounds (5 kg). The Dachshund standard fills more than four pages because of the coat varieties and sizes and the specificity of its body parts. Suffice it to say here that its body is much longer than tall, and its short legs are somewhat crooked but strong and muscular.

Its coat is either smooth, wirehaired, or longhaired, and the color of each is immaterial, but it's usually found in red interspersed

The original Dachshund type was found in various European locals intermingled with that of French basset types. From the fifteenth century onward, short-legged, long-bodied hounds were used to hunt the pesky badger and kill it or drive it to the guns of European maize farmers. One theory connects the original Dachshund with the turnspit dogs that worked in the outdoor kitchens of Europe. In the early 1600s the name Dachshund was associated with the German breed type used for going to ground to bolt or kill burrowing crop pests.

The Dachshund breed as we know it today was developed in Germany sometime late in the nineteenth century. This is the national dog of Germany but England had a specialty club for Dachshunds before a similar German club was formed.

The Dachshund's forebears probably include small pointers and German terriers such as the Pinscher. These and other small fearless European hunting dogs have been mentioned by various writers as contributors to the gene pool of today's Dachshund.

with darker or sable hairs. Dachshund colors also include black, chocolate, wild boar, gray, and fawn.

Miniature Pinscher

In its native Germany this breed is called the Zwergpinscher (dwarf pinscher) or the Reh Pinscher after the small roe deer of the same name, but in the United States it's usually called the Minpin.

The Minpin's satin coat needs no special care except for a few swipes with a slicker brush and finishing off with a damp chamois cloth to add a shine.

A Miniature Pinscher is the ultimate apartment dog. It's small enough to carry to the park or exercise ground and between times it gets plenty of exercise in its duties around the apartment. When a backyard is available this energetic little companion will make good use of the space.

CURRENT FUNCTION

Ratters aren't in high demand in America, but the Minpin is. This breed has gone beyond its original role and has gone on to excel in its primary job of taking care of its families.

It's one of the most popular breeds found in apartments and condos of the big cities because of its size, personality, and cleanliness.

ATTITUDE

A Minpin is an energetic and lively little dog that takes its job seriously. It's more courageous than befits its size and is loyal to a fault. It wishes only to please its handler and best friend and will perform practically any feat to prove it.

This small dog gets along fairly well with other small house pets, and like other little breeds it loves the family's children, providing they respect its size and don't try to lift and carry it. Its original breeding as an alarm dog lends barking to its life, which if not controlled will become a vice. The Minpin is independent and normally suspicious of strangers, but this trait can be reduced or expanded by early exposure and training.

APTITUDE

A Miniature Pinscher is a natural student that displays intelligence and trainability that will boggle the mind of a novice trainer. The Minpin has the capacity to learn a great deal that isn't taught to the average toy breed. Despite the tiny stature of this toy breed it acts like its terrier ancestors and is usually quite at home supervising the family and watching out for them. It's generally a reluctant lapdog.

APPEARANCE

The Miniature Pinscher stands 10 to 12 inches tall (25 to 30 cm) and weighs about 8 to 10 pounds (4 to 5 kg). It's a well-balanced, muscular, smooth, and clean-lined little dog that moves with a characteristic hackney gait (pronounced flexion of the stifle). Its naturally erect ears may be cropped, and its dark

almond eyes and intelligent expression are noteworthy. Its coat is slick and glossy, and its colors are black and tan, solid red, and stag red (intermingled black hairs).

Origin

Although it looks like a miniature Doberman Pinscher, those looks are deceiving. In fact the Minpin's ancestors were bred in Scandinavia at least a century before the Doberman and the two breeds aren't related. Progenitors of the Minpin were no doubt small German pinschers (terriers) and possibly Scandinavian Klein pinschers, and some writers claim the Minpin gene pool included the Italian Greyhound. Although some paintings and canine literature puts the origin of this breed type in the 1600s, the contemporary breed was developed in Germany during the nineteenth century, and by 1895 selective breeding had produced what we recognize today as the Miniature Pinscher.

Miniature Schnauzer

This breed got its name from its beard or muzzle (schnauze) and is separate from the other two sizes that bear the same name. It's called the Zwegschnauzer in Germany and in America is classed as a terrier by the AKC.

Coat care for the Miniature Schnauzer differs from show dog to pet because the show dog coat must be plucked by hand and is never shorn with electric clippers. Pet Schnauzers usually are clipped about every six to eight weeks and a brief twice-a-week combing will suffice between clippings.

The Miniature Schnauzer has a great capacity for exercise and is rarely satisfied with confinement to a backyard. It prefers long walks in the country or park but will burn energy playing games with the family as well. Exercising must be provided or your Schnauzer will become bored, melancholy, and may even become despondent.

CURRENT FUNCTION

The Miniature Schnauzer's ratting ability emerges occasionally but its family orientation is always present. Its affinity for children is stronger than that of most small breeds, probably because it doesn't consider itself a small dog.

Our two sons were quite small when we were given Delilah the Miniature Schnauzer. This little five-year-old dog followed them around constantly, possibly to lick cookie frosting from their faces. They immediately learned to respect her teeth, not because she ever snapped or bit them, but because whenever they became too rowdy she pulled up her lips, showed her shiny teeth, and growled for a second. This ample warning got their attention and taught them more about a Schnauzer's likes and dislikes than we could have hoped. She was alert to strangers who happened by, played with the kids all day, and slept in their room every night. She was a great little companion.

On the one hand the Schnauzer's quite sociable, but on the other it's an excellent alarm dog that is bold and vigilant and not easily backed down. It's rarely aggressive and even when guarding is easily called to heel.

ATTITUDE

This small breed is one of the best all-round companion dogs available. Its attitude is bright and alert, and its character is lively, curious, and loyal. It's fun-loving and always ready for a game, small enough to accept apartment or condo living, and yet sturdy enough to romp with the children in the backyard. This clever and intelligent little dog can solve mind games and come out a winner most of the time. It's an adventurous companion with a great sense of humor that keeps its handler always alert.

APTITUDE

The Miniature Schnauzer is an athletic little terrier with extraordinary ambition that's easy to train in the bargain. It's a bit stubborn, but inherited working dog characteristics temper that independence if it's trained with gentle consistency. This wise little dog has been known to switch roles with its trainer, and owners should watch for this tendency. It accepts commands quite easily and is a good competitor in obedience trials. Its athletic ability should serve this breed well in agility and flyball events. An adult Miniature Schnauzer also is an excellent therapy dog because it's clean, well mannered, and sheds minimally.

APPEARANCE

The Miniature Schnauzer stands 12 to 14 inches tall (30.5 to 35.5 cm) and weighs about 13 or 14 pounds (6 or 6.5 kg). Its head is strong and rectangular with either cropped or folding, small, V-shaped ears. Eyes are dark, and it has black eyelid margins, lip margins, and nose rubber. Its muscular and

Original Design

The ancient German farm Schnauzer was an accomplished ratter, watchdog, and destroyer of vermin. Its small size endorsed it as a clean house dog and family companion. It carries the genes of a superior working dog because the Standard Schnauzer was used to hunt vermin, pull farm carts, and guard farm flocks. These working traits were mixed with those of the Affenpinscher, a terrier in toy clothing.

The Miniature Schnauzer's immigration to England probably came about the end of the nineteenth century, and it has been known in America since about 1925. In 1933 the AKC separated the Miniature from the Standard Schnauzer at its shows.

Origin

Most experts agree that the Miniature Schnauzer was produced by crossing the Standard Schnauzer with the Affenpinscher. The breed was developed on German farms, which may account for its human sociability. In one form or another, it may have been around since the fifteenth century, but it has been exhibited as a distinct breed since 1899 in its native country.

athletic body is short and deep, and it doesn't have a tucked-up abdomen. Its legs are straight and well muscled.

The Schnauzer coat is double with a hard and wiry outer coat. Its colors are salt and pepper, black and silver, and solid black. No pink skin pigmentation is allowed. The salt-and-pepper color results from black and white bands on hairs mixed with solid black and solid white hairs.

Norfolk Terrier

The discussion of the Norfolk and the Norwich terriers is identical with the exception of the Appearance section. Both breeds are occasionally referred to as Jones' Terriers after an early breeder and Trumpington Terriers after a Cambridge professor in England who supplied students with these little terriers for pets.

Both the Norwich and Norfolk breeds have hard wirehaired coats that are easily groomed with comb and brush. Plucking is required about twice a year to keep the coats in prime condition.

These breeds are terriers to the core and require more than average exposure to outside exercise. They'll be happy with a few turns around the block but will greatly prefer to be taken to the woods or park occasionally.

CURRENT FUNCTION

These sturdy little dogs with the lovable countenance are sporting terriers and not stuffed toys in spite of their adorable appearance. They have earned a new role because Americans rarely have need for a ratter or rabbit hunter. They are wonderfully loyal and active pets for energetic families who will spend time training, exercising, and playing with them. The Norwich and Norfolk Terrier puppies are quite tiny and for that reason shouldn't be given to toddlers or preschool children for playmates.

ATTITUDE

They love to follow trails and are right at home digging for moles in your garden or going to ground for chipmunks in a sandbox. Don't allow a headstrong Norwich or Norfolk to follow a trail off lead or you'll spend hours finding where it has gone. Both of these breeds are friendly, cheerful, lively, and cunning little companions that often prove to be quite enterprising and inventive pets. Boldness and independence may get them in trouble because they will tackle almost any quarry they meet, including larger vermin such as skunks and porcupines.

APTITUDE

Their inherited aptitude is realized when you enter one of these breeds in terrier trials; but if you aren't so inclined, by all means keep them busy. A Norwich or Norfolk with nothing to do is a little dog in trouble. They become bored and melancholy when left alone in an empty backyard. Providing the space for activity just isn't the same as taking part in their play.

These intelligent little dogs are well qualified for timed sports such as agility contests. Their independence and interest in fetching balls make them fine flyball competitors. Some have made their marks in obedience competition because they learn quickly when trained consistently and firmly. They respond to treats well and training should progress in spite of their willful streak.

Original Design

Both the Norwich and Norfolk dogs were bred to be rugged, feisty, and game little terriers that welcomed every opportunity to dig out rats or rabbits anytime and anyplace. They were designed as fierce and persistent little combatants that would anxiously go to ground after any adversary.

APPEARANCE

The Norfolk stands 9 to 10 inches tall (23 to 25 cm) and weighs 11 to 12 pounds (5 to 5.5 kg). It is a sturdy little dog with good bone substance and short legs. Its dropped ears

O r i g i n

The Norfolk and the Norwich Terrier began as one breed and were registered and shown as the same breed until 1964, when the British Kennel Club separated them and called the dropped-ear variety Norfolk Terriers and the erect-ear variety Norwich Terriers. In 1979 the AKC followed suit and separated the varieties into Norwich and Norfolk Terriers. The apparent reason for separating the two varieties was logical enough. The ear carriage of the offspring was unstable when one variety was bred to the other. In other respects the breeds are nearly identical but a few differences are noted.

The two dogs were developed in Cambridge, Market Harborough, and Norwich, England, sometime during the nineteenth century. They were first and foremost tough and tenacious little farm terriers that may have the much larger Irish Terrier as their principal ancestor.

that fold in a break at the skull line enhance its expression. Its ears are carried close over the cheek and are V-shaped with slightly rounded tips.

It's hard, wiry, and straight coat is about 2 inches long and lies close to the body. The Norfolk is shown in all shades of red, wheaten, black and tan, or grizzle.

Norwich Terrier

This breed is discussed with the Norfolk because virtually all facts are identical except the Breed Standard, which is somewhat different and partially interpreted below.

APPEARANCE

The stocky little Norwich is among the smallest terriers and stands 10 inches tall (25.5 cm) and weighs 12 pounds (5.5 kg). This little dog has substantial bone structure that's in balance with its overall build.

Its coat is hard, wiry, and straight and lies close to the body. It's shown with a natural coat and little plucking is required. Its medium-sized, prick ears give it a foxlike expression that quickly identifies this breed. Its ears are set well apart and have pointed tips that are always upright when the dog's alert. Acceptable colors are all shades of red, wheaten, black and tan, or grizzle.

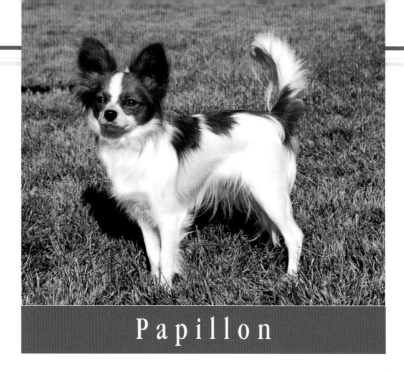

Papillon

The Papillon (French for butterfly) was named for its erect butterflylike ears that frame its face. Another French moniker is Le Chien Ecureuil (squirrel dog) because of its bushy tail. The drop-eared Papillon variety is called the Épagneul Nain or Continental Toy Spaniel in Europe and the Phalene (French for moth) in America.

The dainty Papillon's long coat requires regular and thorough combing and brushing to prevent matting and tangles. Its exercise requirements are met without much effort because it is an active and energetic companion that follows its people everywhere they go.

CURRENT FUNCTION

Papillons are excellent companions and are much hardier than they appear. They are relatively comfortable in all climates and love the out-of-doors. The Papillon is said to be an excellent mouser although not usually put to the test. The Papillon's delicate appearance stimulates the desire to pick up and hold it to protect it from the environment, but it prefers to romp in the yard or take a leashed walk in the park.

This tiny dog is quite sociable with small pets and children who have been properly instructed in small dog care.

ATTITUDE

A Papillon is lively and intelligent and has an inherent desire to learn. It's a loving and lovable little dog that's sometimes suspicious of strangers and prefers the society of its family. It generally likes to play ball and is an obedient pet.

APTITUDE

Train your smart little Papillon with gentleness and consistency and it will respond beautifully. It wants to please you and looks to you for its rewards, both verbal and edible. This breed usually is well represented in obedience classes and often surpasses larger dogs in learning ability. It might be a good candidate for flyball contests and if it works well off lead in the presence of larger dogs, it should be competitive in agility trials. The Papillon makes an excellent therapy or visitation dog after minimal obedience training.

APPEARANCE

The Papillon stands 8 to 11 inches tall (20 to 18 cm) and weighs about 9 to 10 pounds (4 to 4.5 kg). Its elegant appearance is both dainty and refined, and its fine bone structure serves to provide plenty of action in this toy breed. Papillon's legs are straight and feet are elongated. Its eyes are dark and not bulgy and its lip margins, nose rubber, and eyelid rims are black. Its tail is long, high set, and arched over the body.

Origin

Apparently the Papillon evolved in France during the sixteenth century from a small, long-eared dog known as the Belgian Spaniel or simply the Dwarf Spaniel. At that time such spaniels were popular in Spain, Italy, and France. Through what has been termed a mutation by one writer, Dwarf Spaniel puppies sometimes were born with erect ears. The genetics of this transformation apparently haven't been proven but the fact remains that both the down-ear and erect-ear types exist today and are judged by the same breed standards in AKC shows.

Original Design

This diminutive breed was quite popular with European landed gentry and royal courts' ladies for many years before the mutation created the Papillon known today. The petite Papillon was designed to be a decorative lapdog that cherished attention from its owners. It has been reported that Madame Pompadour and Marie Antoinette both owned Papillons, but ownership isn't limited to the upper class today.

Papillons migrated to Great Britain and from there to the United States, and the Papillon Club of America was organized in 1935.

Its coat is long, silky, flowing, and straight with feathering on the chest, legs, and tail. It's seen in all color combinations and is parti-colored with white appearing anywhere in any amount except that color must cover both ears and extend over both eyes.

Patterdale Terrier

This game little terrier is also known as the Black Fell Terrier, and in the *AKC Complete Dog Book* Patterdale is said to be another name for the Lakeland Terrier. Whether the two currently exist as separate breeds is problematic because, in America, Patterdale is referred to as a type of terrier rather than a distinct breed. In one British reference the Patterdale is discussed as a specific breed and a number of American breeders were found on the Internet.

The coat of a Patterdale is easily cared for by weekly brushing and combing.

Exercise is very important for this active little dog, and it will become melancholy and bored if left to its own devices.

CURRENT FUNCTION

Today in America this solid and stocky little terrier is recognized as a specific breed by the UKC and the Continental Kennel Club, and according to their standards it hardly resembles the contemporary Lakeland. The Ameri-

can references extol the persistence and hunting ability of this hardy little terrier and the Patterdale Terrier Club of America has been formed to disseminate information about this breed. The American Working Terrier Association also recognizes the Patterdale. Its primary function is to hunt and dispatch vermin such as the fox, raccoon, possum, groundhog, rat, and other animals that are considered agricultural pests.

Although it is kept as a companion pet by some, little is said about its sociability except that the Patterdale is bred to be nonaggressive toward people and other dogs.

ATTITUDE

If the Patterdale is kept busy doing what it was bred to do, it will undoubtedly prove to be a loyal and steadfast companion. It is a clean little dog with a friendly attitude toward its family and it lives inside and outside the house with equal comfort. It isn't aggressive toward strangers and is only an average watchdog but it is quite intelligent and trustworthy.

APTITUDE

Working, hunting, digging after its quarry is the driving force behind this dog's life. The breed needs very little training for those duties and has the inherited propensity to tackle any vermin that it's set upon. Its training ease is virtually unknown at the present time because this dog is among the rarest breeds in America. It's probable that its working terrier abilities would qualify it for the timed canine contests with a minimum of training.

APPEARANCE

The Patterdale stands less than 12 inches tall (30 cm) and weighs about 12 pounds (5.5 kg).

Origin

The Patterdale originated in the lake districts of northern England in the sixteenth century where it was named for the village of Patterdale. The steep bare hills of the border country between Scotland and England are sometimes called the fells, and the cold, windy, and rocky ground of the fells is quite inhospitable to man and beast. Foxhunting was a popular sport and was done on foot because the terrain was too dangerous for horses. The Patterdale Terrier has been bred there continuously for centuries, although its popularity has been associated with working and not with shows. It shares progenitors with the Border, Bedlington, Fox, and Elterwater terriers.

Original Design

The Patterdale was and continues to be used to bolt and kill vermin of every variety. It routinely goes to ground in pursuit of its quarry and is one of the gamest of the working terriers. In its native country this tough little dog was used in horseless foxhunts to bolt or tackle the pesky fox.

It is a sturdy little terrier with a strong body, a high-set tail, and straight legs. Its ears fold to the sides of the cheek and its muzzle is powerful.

It has a short coat that's coarse and very tough and is either broken or smooth. Its colors are black, chocolate, red, grizzle, bronze, or black and tan. The UKC standard says that 95 percent of the breed is black, but other colors and markings are allowed.

Pekingese

The Pekingese is also known as Peking Palasthund and Little Lion Dog of Peking. This little dog is also referred to as a sleeve dog because it's said that the Chinese royalty carried the diminutive little Peke in the sleeves of their robes.

Its coat requires a great deal of grooming that should begin as a puppy. The fine coat tangles easily, and care must be taken to straighten or clip out mats as they form.

Pekingese are active puppies, but as they mature they usually don't demand much exercise and will be contented with a short walk a few times daily if housed in an apartment. If allowed backyard privileges, this little dog will obtain needed exercise from a few trips to the yard every day.

CURRENT FUNCTION

The Pekingese is among the favorite American pets of the twenty-first century. It is quite a sociable little dog that loves to romp with its family but usually is seen in a less than frivolous demeanor. Like other miniature breeds this little dog is better suited to adult families or those with older children who understand the necessity of careful handling of such a small dog.

ATTITUDE

This somewhat stubborn little dog never loses its courage or dignity for a moment, even during training sessions. It's an even-tempered pet that's both intelligent and affectionate as long as its whims are understood and agreed upon by everyone. It's a loyal companion and doesn't ask more from its family than necessary for its comfort and will sometimes even condescend to sit on a lap.

APTITUDE

The Pekingese is best trained with gentleness, consistency, and great patience. The best technique is to reward every appropriate action with a kind word and a special treat. Never scold or shame a Peke and it will be your friend, but it will choose its best buddy for itself. The Peke usually isn't known as an effective alarm dog but it resents strangers, is bold and brave, and may develop a watchdog tendency if encouraged.

APPEARANCE

The Pekingese is a toy breed that stands about 7 or 8 inches tall (17 to 19 cm) and weighs about 10 to 12 pounds (4.5 to 5.5 kg) with an upper limit of 14 pounds (6.3 kg).

Its head is wide and thick by comparison to its hindquarters. Its muzzle is short and flat, and its eyes are large but not bulgy. Its short forelegs are slightly bowed and sturdy. Its drop ears are well feathered as well as its legs and tail. Its mane is profuse and forms a long ruff around the neck.

Original Design

Pekingese haven't changed all that much since they were residents of the royal palace of China. They're still small and compatible little dogs that maintain their blue-blooded dignity in carriage and attitude. They were bred to please their royal owners and grooming wasn't a problem because slaves abounded for those chores.

Following the looting of the Chinese palace in 1860 they were seen in Great Britain and were exhibited there in 1893. The AKC registered the Peke in 1906 and the breed has grown in popularity since that time.

Its coat is abundant, long, straight, and flat and flowing. All colors are allowed and most Pekes have a black mask that extends to the ears.

Origin

There were no lions in China but the Lion of Buddha was a sacred symbol from about the first century A.D. Artists' portrayals of these Buddhist's symbols were remarkably like the emperor's palace dogs, probably because those dogs were the artists' models. Until 1860 the Pekingese was kept only by the imperial family, who designated the three types as Lion Dogs for their manes and large forequarters, Sun Dogs because of their golden red coats, and Sleeve Dogs because they were often carried inside the rather large sleeves of the royal families.

History tells us that when the British raided the Chinese Imperial Palace in 1860, they carried off five of these little dogs, one of which was presented to Queen Victoria and subsequently named Looty. The remaining four were given to Admiral John Hay and in his Goodwood Castle became the foundation stock for today's Western Pekingese. Toward the end of the nineteenth century other Pekingese were given to Americans Alice Roosevelt and J. P. Morgan, but few of these dogs were bred.

Little is known or available about the progenitors of the Pekingese, but Oriental breeding was common to produce miniature pug-faced dogs with flowing coats.

Pembroke Welsh Corgi

Si Sawdl and the Welsh Heeler are other names used for this little dog from Wales. Some confusion arises about the two breeds of herding dogs known as Welsh Corgis. The Pembroke name differentiates this little dog from the Cardigan Welsh Corgi, which was developed in another part of Wales at an earlier period in history.

Corgi coat care is relatively easily accomplished with a weekly stiff brushing or combing to remove shedding hair.

The Pembroke Corgi needs time and space in which to exercise unless its home is a ranch where it has opportunity to work cattle. This little herding dog quickly becomes bored and melancholy if allowed to loaf around in a big empty yard. A ball the size of a basketball is a wonderful adjunct to Corgi exercise, but the game isn't a spectator sport and involves human participation. Don't choose a Pembroke Corgi if you think you can manage only a couple of turns around the block each day.

CURRENT FUNCTION

This little dog has become a wonderful companion for active and energetic American families, although the average Pembroke would probably rather spend its time on a farm with a herd of cattle. It's a great child's dog when grown, but don't forget that this tough herding dog puppy is quite tiny and should be handled with care by toddlers and preschoolers.

Our Pembroke Corgi had an aversion to infants and small children, and Mike disappeared from sight when visitors came with their toddlers. After our company had gone, little Mike could be found hiding well out of reach, burrowed between bales in the hay shed. However, his herding instincts surfaced when school-age children came. He kept himself busy herding the kids together wherever they wandered.

ATTITUDE

This hardy little dog is a playful, affectionate, and energetic playmate for adults and kids

Original Design

The Pembroke Corgi's original purpose was singular and very important. It was developed in Pembrokeshire on Welsh farms to herd their cattle and in this role it performed superbly! Its tiny stature allowed it to dash in, have a bite of a reluctant steer's ankle, and flatten out or retreat without being kicked.

alike, but it hates being teased. It's intelligent, confident, and bonds tightly with its family. The Pembroke isn't overly suspicious of strangers and for that reason is probably not a good choice for a watchdog. It has great loyalty and truly enjoys about any type of play.

APTITUDE

Training this little dog is easily accomplished if patience and consistency are practiced. The Pembroke is anxious to learn and tries hard to please. This breed should do well in timed canine endeavors such as agility and flyball because it's speedy, clever, and persistent.

APPEARANCE

The Pembroke Corgi stands 10 to 12 inches tall (25 to 31 cm) and weighs less than 28 or 30 pounds (13 to 13.5 kg). The measurement

Origin

Historical accounts give the Pembroke's origin as sometime between 900 and 1100 A.D. when many Flemish weavers immigrated into southwest Wales. These people kept the dog on their farms to tend their herds, and the Pembroke Corgi has existed in Wales since that time with little change in attitude or conformation. The Pembroke's progenitors were possibly the same as those of the Keeshond, Samoyed, Chow Chow, Norwegian Elkhound, and the Finnish Spitz. The breed bears remarkable resemblance to the Swedish Vallhund and might be a progeny of this breed. Because the Pembroke Corgi and Cardigan Corgi were developed in neighboring Welsh shires there can be little doubt that they were occasionally crossed either purposefully or accidentally.

from the tail base to the withers is 40 percent greater than the height from withers to ground. Its short stature, deep chest, and foxy-appearing head give it an interesting overall appearance. Its eyelids, lip margins, and nose rubber are all pigmented black, and its eyes are various shades of brown. Its ears are erect and of medium size with rounded tips. Pembroke Corgis occasionally are born without tails but others' tails are docked quite short.

The Pembroke's coat is short and thick with a dense undercoat. It lies flat and is full on the back of the forelegs and the underparts. Colors include red, sable, fawn, black and tan, with or without white markings on legs, chest, neck, muzzle, or underparts, and a narrow white blaze on the head.

Podengo Portugueso Pequeño

This tiny dog is also known as the Small Portuguese Hound and is nearly as small as a Chihuahua.

Coat care is simple, requiring only occasional combing or brushing. For the smooth-coated variety a rubber slicker brush is the only tool needed.

This active little dog is an accomplished hunter and as such requires regular exercise to stay healthy and trim.

CURRENT FUNCTION

Rabbit hunting using sight hounds is relatively uncommon in America today, although the sport does exist in many rural regions of the nation. The Pequeño is rare in America, but where it's found it proves to be an excellent companion for active families with limited space available for a dog. Like other tiny breeds the Pequeño puppy isn't a proper pet for small children because of accidental falls and injuries.

ATTITUDE

It's a very active, intelligent, courageous, and affectionate little dog that bonds well with its handler and family. This little dog loves children and makes a wonderful pet for older kids that have been properly instructed in handling small dogs. The Pequeño is an amazingly healthy dog that hasn't developed inherited deformities that stem from overbreeding and extreme popularity.

This little sight hound is easily socialized with other small pets but should be introduced carefully to domesticated rodents because of its instinctive chasing propensity.

APTITUDE

Podengo Portugueso Pequeño is best at chasing rabbits and other fast-moving small game, but it is also a remarkable all-round family pet. This tiny dog is also well known for its courage and value as an alarm or watchdog. The dog is well suited to hot climates and somewhat sensitive to cool regions of the country where inadequate shelter is provided.

Although not recognized by the AKC, this little dog should be a remarkable competitor in agility trials and other timed activities. It is quite trainable and easily handled.

APPEARANCE

The Podengo Portugueso Pequeño stands 8 to 12 inches tall (20 to 31 cm) and weighs 11 to 13 pounds (5 to 6 kg). Its general conformation is similar to larger sight hounds, and it is slim and athletic with straight legs. Its pyramidal head supports large pointed ears, its muzzle is straight, and its expression is alert.

Its coat is either smooth or wirehaired and ranges in color from yellow and fawn with or without white markings, to dark gray and white. The smooth coat is a bit harder and longer than on other sight hounds and the wirehaired coat is medium long, coarse, and shaggy.

Original Design

This dog somewhat resembles a tiny Greyhound and is a working sight hound. The Pequeño is used in Portugal for hunting small game such as rabbits and hares. They work alone or in a pack and are extremely efficient in their efforts.

Some Pequeños have immigrated to America and are registered with the CKC (Continental Kennel Club) and the NKC (National Kennel Club).

Origin

Portugal is the country of origin of this dog, and three sizes of this dog are found there. The Pequeño or miniaturized breed was developed sometime in the nineteenth century by selective breeding from smaller versions of the Podengo Portugueso Grande and Podengo Portugueso Medio. All the Podengo Portugueso breeds' ancestors are thought to have descended from the Pharaoh Hound of Africa and the Iberian Peninsula, but it's also speculated that this hound may have evolved directly from the small Iberian wolves.

Pomeranian

This little dog is occasionally referred to as the Miniature Spitz dog or European Spitz. In its native land it's the smallest member of the German Spitz group and sometimes called the miniature German Spitz.

Care of its somewhat coarse coat is vital if the Pom is to be kept in show condition. Excessive combing with a fine comb will damage the soft, thick undercoat.

Exercise is usually provided with a few short walks per day and plenty of backyard time, but this energetic little dog is not easily tired and can keep up with longer walks.

CURRENT FUNCTION

The Pomeranian is sometimes too courageous for its own good. It's a vigilant alarm dog but its barking sometimes becomes habitual if not well discouraged as a puppy. Its primary purpose in life is to please its owners, and it accomplishes this task very well. It sometimes shies from children because of their boister-ous play. It socializes easily with cats and other small family pets.

ATTITUDE

This big dog in a tiny package usually won't back down from a much larger dog, and this aggressiveness is sometimes self-destructive. A Pom is eager to learn and devoted to its family; its affection and loving nature is well documented. It has a delightful temperament and is always ready for a quick game before lap-time.

APTITUDE

Training an intelligent and interested Pom is easily accomplished if you remember that this tiny pet is still a dog. It responds to commands if they are consistently given and it is rewarded with tidbits or kind words. When its bad habits or lack of responses are ignored, it becomes a spoiled brat. Rarely seen in agility trials, the Pom often does well in obedience trials.

Original Design

Other Spitz types were used as herding dogs and sled pullers but this little dog has always been able to find a lap to sit on instead and is an energetic companion in the bargain. It immigrated to America late in the nineteenth century and was shown in the AKC miscellaneous class in 1892. It was officially recognized by the AKC in 1900 and has since that time become quite popular as a pampered little pet.

APPEARANCE

A Pom stands about 7 to 8 inches tall (18 to 20 cm) and weighs from 3 to 7 pounds (1.3 to 2 kg). The tiny Pomeranian has a short-coupled body, straight legs, and well-balanced overall appearance. Its erect ears and foxlike expression give the dog an alert, almost anxious expression. Nose rubber, lip margins, and eyelids are always dark, usually black.

The Pomeranian coat is double and profuse. Feathering of this diminutive ball of fur is also abundant, especially on the tail and ruff. Acceptable colors are red, orange, cream and sable, black, brown, and blue.

Origin

The Pomeranian developed in Germany and was bred to its present size in Pomerania during the nineteenth century. Its progenitors were of the Spitz type and were much larger dogs such as the Samoyed, Norwegian Elkhound, Chow Chow, and other northern European breeds. It possibly was miniaturized from the large white sled dog that originated in Iceland and Lapland. Its exact time of origin is unknown, but its English popularity was enhanced when Queen Victoria brought a Pom to her palace in 1888.

Pug

This toy breed is known as the Carlin in France, Mopshond in the Netherlands, Mops in Germany, and Chinese Pug or sometimes the Dutch Pug in Great Britain. The interesting and fitting name Pug may have come from the shape of the dog's head, because the Latin meaning of pug is clenched fist. Another theory is that the name refers to the dog's resemblance to a marmoset or monkey.

The Pug's coat is short, lies flat, and requires regular brushing and combing to control shedding, which may be profuse. A rubber slicker brush is quite effective in removing loose hair and a grooming glove is often used as well.

Pugs love to run and play in a backyard and usually will provide for their own exercise needs if space allows. They enjoy a leashed walk and are tough little hikers in cool weather or shady environments.

CURRENT FUNCTION

A Pug is forever a wonderful companion. This little dog fits in nicely with young families if the small kids are well indoctrinated in handling small dog puppies. It's often a companion to the geriatric set as well and is sufficiently active to be a buddy to a young adult.

Muggs was probably more than six or seven years old when she came to us from an animal shelter. She quickly adapted to our rural life, loved to boat with us, was curious about livestock but always gave the horses a wide berth. When we moved to Arizona she took the long trip in stride and accepted her apartment confinement until we found a house. When neighborhood dogs barked, she tipped her head and quietly listened but didn't offer to join in the bedlam. She understood our moods and knew just how to cheer us up or calm us down. Muggs's history was never discovered but whoever gave her up lost a treasure. Her trainability was phenomenal. She knew dozens of tricks when she arrived and learned more quite easily. She made a poor trainer look like a champion.

ATTITUDE

This breed is affectionate, anxious to please, and sensitive. A Pug will anticipate the owner's happy moods and will sympathize with you, sometimes making you laugh out loud with its crazy antics. When you're sad it will lie at your feet with a woebegone look on its face. The amazingly solid little Pug is always ready for a quick romp or a leashed walk, and usually will play ball or race you around the backyard. It's gentle, trustworthy, and loyal, easily socialized with other pets, and always well mannered around visitors. The Pug may pout when ignored and is jealous when not given enough attention but doesn't carry a grudge.

APTITUDE

The Pug is always looking for a way to please its handler and is extremely trainable. It usually has a good appetite and will perform

Origin

The little Pug is an ancient Oriental breed and was probably developed in Tibetan monasteries prior to the first century A.D. It slightly resembles the Pekingese and other Oriental breeds and was seen in Japan in early years. It is claimed by some to have originated from Mastiff stock progenitors, but this isn't proven and is doubted by many because several other toy breeds with large heads and curled tails came from the Orient. The Pug probably was carried from China by Holland's trading ships and immigrated early to the Netherlands where this mischievous little dog became the Clown Prince of many European courts in the sixteenth and seventeenth centuries.

wonderful feats for treats, but take care not to overfeed because it has a propensity to become obese. The even-tempered and intelligent Pug understands and responds quickly and should be an excellent obedience dog, and is often used as a therapy dog.

APPEARANCE

The Pug stands 10 to 11 inches tall (25 to 28 cm) and weighs 14 to 18 pounds (6 to 8 kg). Its body is compact and well muscled and its head is massively dignified and roundish. Its eyes are dark and eyelids, lip margins, and nose rubber are black. Its button or rose ears are small, soft, and velvety. Its tail is curled tightly over its hip and its legs are straight.

Its coat is fine, smooth, soft, and short, and its colors are silver, fawn, or black. In the colors other than black, its black mask is well defined.

S c o t t i s h   T e r r i e r

The Scottish Terrier is sometimes known as the Aberdeen Terrier after the city and region in which it presumably originated. The most familiar American nickname for this little dog is Scottie.

The hard nature of its coat makes it easy to care for with brush and comb, and usually pet Scotties have their coat clipped.

Scotties are energetic terriers who thrive on exercise but apartment pets should be able to satisfy their exercise needs running about the house and taking several daily leashed walks outside.

CURRENT FUNCTION

Scotties retain plenty of their old ratting instincts but few are given the opportunity to pursue them in earth-dog trials. Today's Scottish Terrier is generally found in a backyard, apartment, condo, and sometimes in a presidential mansion. It's a superb companion dog that requires a little extra compassion to deal with its independent and aristocratic attitude.

Children should be introduced carefully and with ample training in handling a small dog with an independent nature. The Scottie requires respect in order to communicate with youngsters.

ATTITUDE

This sometimes sensitive little breed definitely has a mind of its own. The Scottie is a sober and vigilant companion that's brave and loyal to its handler. Attachment to its family comes early and is a strong bond but this dog is quite independent. It resents teasing by children and adults and may isolate itself from those whom it learns to distrust. It's a tough and steadfast pet that often may overestimate its own capabilities.

APTITUDE

The Scottie is quite trainable if consistency and fairness is applied. This self-reliant little dog can be a big handful if the wrong attitude is used in its training. Start young and treat the

Original Design

Terriers were first and foremost vermin destroyers, and the Scottie is no exception. It was developed specifically for hunting and digging out foxes and weasels from their burrows. This tough little dog is an excellent ratter as well and has always held a special place in the family.

Scottish Terrier Clubs in England and in Scotland were formed in 1882 and Scotties immigrated to America in 1883. In 1925 an American standard was adopted and the popularity of this sturdy little terrier has thrived since that time.

Origin

The exact time and place of our present-day Scottie's origin is lost in antiquity, but probably the type was developed in Scotland's Blackmount region of Perthshire, Moor of Rannoch. Early Scottish terrier breeds include the one known today as the Scottie, as well as the Skye, Cairn, Dandie Dinmont, West Highland White, and sometimes even the tiny Yorkshire Terrier. All these breeds originally were shown together under the generic name of Scottish Terriers. They resembled each other only slightly, but all may have been descendants of the now extinct Highland Terrier sometime prior to the middle of the nineteenth century.

The splitting of show classes into specific breeds came about after Scottish Terrier breeders became involved in a verbal battle that resulted in a Scottish Terrier standard written by J. B. Morrison in 1880.

Scottie to evenhanded and objective lessons and you will gain its respect. From there, the sky is the limit. This seemingly stubborn dog is occasionally seen performing well in obedience trials and other such canine endeavors.

APPEARANCE

The Scottie stands about 10 inches tall (25 cm) and weighs about 20 pounds (9 kg). Its body is short, strong, muscular, and deep chested. Its head is long and equipped with exceptionally strong jaws. Its pricked ears are small and pointed but never surgically clipped.

Eyes are dark and lip margins, eyelids, and nose rubber are black. Its legs are heavy-boned, straight, and quite strong.

Its coat is composed of wiry and hard guard hair over a dense softer undercoat. It grows rather profusely over the body and is hand plucked periodically for shows. Scotty colors are various steel or iron gray, brindled or grizzled, sandy or wheaten, or black. White markings are always objectionable.

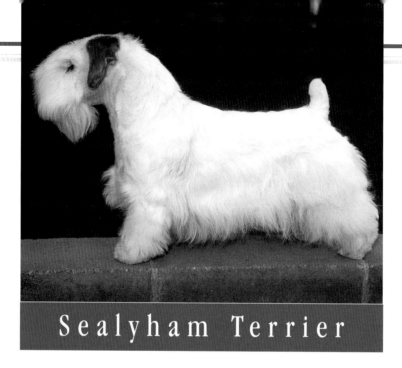

Sealyham Terrier

The Sealyham Terrier was named for the district in which it was developed, Sealyham, Haverfordwest, Wales, and has never been known by any other name.

Its coat responds well to regular combing and brushing. Clipping and trimming are required a couple of times a year to keep the coat in good repair.

Exercise requirements for this terrier are average, but it will appreciate several leashed walks every day and loves to journey on unbeaten paths in the woods or parks. A Sealy often digs after varmints that invade flower gardens for exercise and chases errant rodents that happen into its backyard.

CURRENT FUNCTION

American farm pests are hardly a nuisance or threat to our lifestyles, but Captain Edwardes terrier still has hunting blood flowing in its veins. Terrier trials are becoming more popular as urbanites obtain terriers, realize their potential, and wish to see them compete in a natural terrier endeavor.

Aside from its hunting ability, the Sealyham is and always was a wonderful and playful companion pet. It enjoys children who are properly introduced and those who aren't likely to tease, torment, or handle it roughly.

ATTITUDE

A Sealyham is active, brave, and tough as nails. It's an intelligent little dog with a bit of a stubborn streak that crops up occasionally. It socializes well with other dogs and bonds with its handler easily and quickly. It's quite sociable if introduced carefully to other family pets, but domesticated rodents are always at risk around this breed and should be housed well away from the Sealy's reach. The Sealy has a big bark that it uses when it perceives danger, but generally it is a calm and dignified companion.

Original Design

The Edwardes estate flourished with vermin of various types, including foxes, badgers, otters, rats, rabbits, and polecats. All these agricultural pests gave Captain John plenty of quarry on which to test his Sealyham Terrier. It's said that he used a polecat as a final test, and a dog of merit would go to ground to challenge and bolt or destroy this odoriferous creature.

Badger-digging trials and weasel-hunting contests were instrumental in obtaining the Sealy's recognition prior to conformation shows. The British Kennel Club allowed Sealyham's entry in 1910, and in 1911 Sealyhams were introduced to America, where they were immediately recognized by the AKC. The American Sealyham club formed in 1913 and a standard was accepted in 1935.

Origin

Captain John Edwardes lived and hunted on an estate in Sealyham where he and possibly other breeders created this breed between 1850 and 1891. Possible progenitors of the Sealyham include the Corgi, Dandie Dinmont, West Highland White, and Bull Terrier. This unlikely combination was carefully chosen, and offspring were strictly tested for hunting ability before they joined the gene pool.

APTITUDE

The Sealyham learns quickly and easily but its hereditary instincts may be in conflict with

human commands. The Sealy's independence often rears its head and takes over its actions. It's a strong and sometimes willful breed that must be trained with consistency and rewards. The Sealy never forgets the time the trainer allowed it to take the dominant role.

It's best fitted to compete in earth-dog trials but with careful training should excel in obedience work and possibly in timed canine contests.

APPEARANCE

This little breed stands about 10 inches tall (25 cm) and weighs about 20 pounds (8 kg). Its head is long and powerful, and its well-rounded ears are folded level with the top of the head. Its legs have good bone and are straight and muscular.

Its weather-resistant coat has a soft undercoat and hard, wiry guard hair. The Sealyham can be totally white or with lemon, tan, or badger markings on its head and ears. Body marking is undesirable.

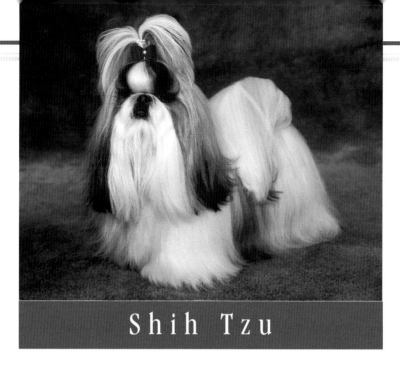

Shih Tzu

This ancient Chinese court dog has been known as the Chrysanthemum Dog because the hair around its face grows in every direction. *Shih Tzu* means Lion Dog and it's so called because of its similarity to pictures and carvings of the Lion of Buddha.

The Shih Tzu coat requires lots of combing to prevent matting. A hairband is used to keep the profusely growing hair from its eyes. Coat care may be a reason for choosing another breed, but the reward of owning this wonderful companion might well compensate for this.

A Shih Tzu is not an overly ambitious or active little dog, and it is usually content to take short leashed walks, play in the backyard if one is available, and follow its owner around the home.

CURRENT FUNCTION

The sweet disposition of the Shih Tzu is the principal reason it has evolved as a favorite American companion. It bonds well with its handler's family, is sociable with dogs and other small pets, and gets along fine with well-trained children. It's known to be a little standoffish with strangers but rarely ever barks.

ATTITUDE

A little Shih Tzu puppy is extremely playful but an adult is a little more reserved. The Shih Tzu is an intelligent and lovable pet that has a tiny obstinate streak. As an adult, it's always sophisticated and conducts itself with great dignity and poise most of the time. It's outgoing, friendly, alert, cheerful, has a good sense of humor, and always treats its family and friends affectionately.

APTITUDE

The stubbornness that's occasionally seen in this breed doesn't mean it can't be trained. If consistency and gentleness are used, you're probably in for a surprise. The diminutive size and regal stature of the dog sometimes defeat

Original Design

The Shih Tzu was undoubtedly meant to be just what it is today—a lovable, affectionate, and pleasantly agreeable companion.

It immigrated to England in 1930 shortly before its standard was adopted by the Peking Kennel Club in 1938. At that time it was confused with the Lhasa Apso but this problem was solved by the British Kennel Club, and the Shih Tzu Club of England was organized in 1935. It was registered by the AKC in 1969, and this little dog has spread its personality across America ever since.

the trainer, but persistence will win out. Yummy treats will help as well.

If you watch obedience trials closely you'll see an occasional Shih Tzu being exhibited, and that should reinforce your faith. This little dog is a perfect visitation or therapy dog for nursing homes and hospitals. The Shih Tzu's exceptional beauty and pleasant personality is bound to be appreciated by shut-ins wherever they are found.

APPEARANCE

This little dog stands about 9 to 10 inches tall (23 to 24 cm) and weighs about 10 pounds (4.5 kg). Its body length slightly exceeds its height and its broad body has a level topline. Its head is round, broad, and

The Shih Tzu was originally a product of Tibet, where it's known to have existed since about the first century A.D. It was brought to China in the seventeenth century and was bred in Peking imperial courts to be a pet and companion for royalty. Its history and progenitors were probably similar to other short-faced, longhaired, Chinese breeds such as the Pekingese. The Shih Tzu was extremely popular during the Ming dynasty and suffered a great loss when the British sacked the royal palace in 1860.

wide between the eyes. Its eyes are large and round and dark. Its short muzzle is square and unwrinkled. Its nose rubber, eyelids, and lip margins are black or dark except on liver-colored or blue-colored dogs. Its legs are short and straight, and its tail is heavily plumed and carried in a curve over the back.

The Shih Tzu's coat is long, fine, copious, double, and flowing but never curly. All colors are permissible, and markings may be seen in any patterns.

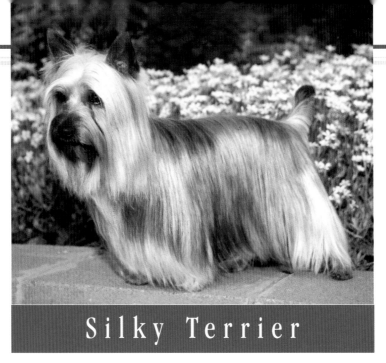

Silky Terrier

This tiny breed sometimes is called the Australian Silky Terrier or the Sydney Silky Terrier.

Its long coat requires daily grooming if the Silky is not clipped. Many pets are clipped every couple of months to minimize daily grooming.

Exercise requirements are minimal, and most Silky Terrier pets find ample activity in following their family about the house and playing in the yard. This lively little dog burns excess energy readily with its normal household chores, but a turn around the block is appreciated.

CURRENT FUNCTION

The Silky's main job is to keep its family happy and entertained. This tiny breed excels at these duties because it's an energetic and active companion. It loves children, especially those who are introduced while it is still a puppy, but the usual precautions apply. Preschoolers and toddlers who tend to see the Silky as a stuffed toy rather than a living animal will cause the dog to be shy and distrustful of kids in general.

ATTITUDE

A Silky has a territorial sense that governs much of its daily activity. It must bark to guard its home against all interlopers, both canine and human. In spite of its diminutive size, this dog has been accused of being physically aggressive toward strange people and dogs and more protective of its family than many large breeds. Within its family circle the Silky is a clever, affectionate, docile, and fun-loving little dog that likes to keep its favorite people within reach at all times.

APTITUDE

This energetic and active little dog is an accomplished ratter by instinct. It is easily trained for other jobs because of its intelligence and eagerness to please its handler. No encouragement needs to be given to the hereditary alarm and guard dog traits. The clever

Silky should perform well in obedience work and is sufficiently athletic to compete in timed activities such as flyball and agility. It should be a shoo-in for visitation and therapy work because of its pleasant character and love of petting.

APPEARANCE

The Silky stands 9 to 10 inches tall (23 to 24.5 cm) and weighs 8 to 11 pounds (4 to 5 kg). Its body is longer than tall, and it has refined but not delicate bone structure. Its head is strong and wedge shaped, its ears are small, erect, and set high on the head, and its eyes are dark and almond shaped.

O r i g i n

The popular little Silky was developed toward the end of the nineteenth century in Sydney, Australia, from crosses between the Australian Terrier and Yorkshire Terrier.

Its eyelids, lip margins, and nose rubber are black.

The Silky's single coat doesn't touch the floor and is parted down the spine. The coat is straight and quite silky in nature, and is all types of blue and tan.

201

Original Design

The reason for the development of this breed was to improve upon the colors of the Australian Terrier. The new type produced suited breeders, and the offspring were bred together until the Silky type was genetically fixed. The Silky Terrier is mid-sized between the Australian and Yorkshire, and its coat is not nearly as long as the Yorkie's, but its bone structure is sturdier.

Both terrier ancestors are adept at ratting, but the primary role of the Silky from the time of its inception has been that of an outstanding family companion.

A revised standard for the breed was established in 1926 and after that time no further crosses were allowed. The Silky came to the United States in the 1950s and was officially recognized by the AKC in 1959.

Skye Terrier

Known by no name other than Skye Terrier, this ancient breed is a working dog of great repute.

The Skye's coat requires minimal care in spite of its appearance. Weekly brushing usually is sufficient.

Exercise is important to all working dogs and the Skye is no exception. It thrives on long walks and particularly when it can be taken off leash in the country to pursue its instinctive quarry. Its playful nature will help fulfill its exercise requirements, but all active and energetic terriers will pout and become melancholy if exercise needs aren't met.

CURRENT FUNCTION

The Skye is generally assumed to have changed little since Dr. Caius presented its first reviews to the world. It's a tough little vermin-destroying dog that also serves well as a companion pet. It gets along with other dogs but may show a bit of aggression. It should be introduced to other family pets with caution, and rodents should never be housed within reach of this terrier.

Children and the Skye make a good combination, but the kids should be cautioned never to tease this dog if they wish to continue the pleasant relationship. Typical small-dog precautions should be taken with preschoolers and toddlers to prevent injury to both kids and dogs.

ATTITUDE

The Skye is affectionate and calm, noble and vigilant, loyal and reserved with strangers and their pets. This game little dog has a tendency to choose one person with whom to bond, but it is an excellent family dog as well. Its propensity to announce visitors is legendary, and its bark is quite distinctive.

APTITUDE

If trained with respect and consistency, this

Original Design

The Skye was developed to go to ground with the express purpose of bolting or destroying vermin of all types, principally foxes, otters, and weasels, all of which are vicious brawlers. This breed was common in England during Queen Victoria's reign and was a popular companion to British royalty for many years.

The Skye immigrated to America and was registered with the AKC in 1887. It has continued to be relatively popular in the United States although is only occasionally found at shows.

intelligent dog is capable of performing well in many endeavors. The Skye shouldn't be pressed or hurried and should be allowed time to fully understand what is being asked of it. Losing one's temper will always be counterproductive and may set training back significantly.

This little dog is a tough competitor that should do well in timed activities, and it will excel in earth-dog trials if put to those tests.

APPEARANCE

The Skye Terrier stands 10 inches tall (24.5 cm) and weighs about 20 pounds (9 kg). It is twice as long as it is tall and its body is sturdy and muscular. The Skye's head is

Origin

The Sky Terrier had its origin during the seventeenth century in the Scottish Inner Hebrides and more especially on the Isle of Skye, west of Scotland. It's been mentioned as a progenitor of many other Scottish terrier breeds, but the ancestors of the Skye are virtually unknown. This intrepid little hunting terrier was already news in the mid-1700s when Dr. John Caius wrote *Of Englishe Dogges,* the first book devoted totally to domestic canines.

long with powerful jaws. Its ears are either pricked or dropped and are covered with long hair. The tail is long and well feathered and is carried behind the rump without twist or curl.

The coat is double and the outer coat is hard, straight, and flat. It's parted along the spine and hangs straight down but not to the floor. Colors may be black, blue, dark or light gray, silver, fawn, or cream, but no markings are allowed except for black points on the ears, muzzle, and tail.

Swedish Vallhund

This small herding dog is called the Svensk Vallhund (meaning herding dog in Swedish) or Väsgötaspets elsewhere in Scandanavia after Väsgötasland, which is on the Vara Plains in southern Sweden. It is quite similar in appearance to the Welsh Corgi.

Its coat is easily maintained by occasional brushing and combing that's increased in frequency during shedding season.

All small working dogs require significantly more exercise than other small breeds, and the Vallhund is no exception. If kept in an apartment or without a big backyard it deserves several lengthy leashed walks daily and regular weekend romps in the country or in a park. Remember that mental exercise is equally important for energetic little herding dogs. Training challenges or some type of work is a fundamental requirement. The lack of sufficient exercise will result in depression and loss of interest.

CURRENT FUNCTION

This little dog wears many hats. It's a hardy, working herd dog and if you live in the city is an excellent vermin destroyer. It has been in a supervisory role on Swedish farms for centuries and has great versatility, stamina, and intelligence. It's been used by the Swedish army for search and rescue and by common folk as a truffle sniffer. Last but not least the Vallhund is a superior family pet and children's companion.

ATTITUDE

Its long association with humans has provided the Vallhund with an even temperament and the ability to socialize well with children and other pets. It's a brave and vigilant natural watchdog and is well suited to pal around with its family in everyday activities. It's loving and obedient and always wants to please its handler and family. The Vallhund's pack mentality makes it an ideal all-round pet.

APTITUDE

Any experienced trainer who uses consistency, rewards, and an even tone of voice can easily train this smart, clever, and instinctive herd dog. The Vallhund is capable of obedience work and should fare well in timed activities such as flyball and agility contests. It will also do well in tracking and rescue work.

APPEARANCE

The Swedish Vallhund stands about 12 inches tall (30.5 cm) and weighs about 25 pounds (11 kg), although some dogs are an inch taller and a bit heavier. It has a typical Spitz-type head with erect ears and a long muzzle.

Original Design

This little herd dog was developed with watchdog characteristics and it relentlessly guards its herds from humans and four-legged predators on Swedish farms. It herds livestock, chickens, or other poultry instinctively and holds a part-time job as a super ratter. Like many dogs that developed in rural environments this dog is also a fine family pet.

The Swedish Vallhund isn't terribly popular in America but it is seen occasionally, and several American breeders are found on the Internet. It isn't recognized by the AKC but was recognized as a purebred by the Swedish Kennel Club in 1948.

Eyes are dark, and eyelids, lip margins, and nose rubber are black. Its body is long and straight, and its legs are straight and powerful. Its chest is quite deep as befits a herding dog.

Its wiry, coarse, guard coat lies smoothly over a soft and wooly undercoat. Its color is a steely wolf gray with lighter patches on the belly and underside of the neck and feet, and in the mask.

Origin

The Vallhund was developed from the Spitz-type genetic pool in Sweden and might be the ancestor to Welsh Corgis, or the Corgis might be progenitors of the Vallhund, depending on which side of the fence you sit. Norsemen were known to make frequent raids on the coast of Wales during the eighth and ninth centuries, and those northern seamen might have taken a few dogs with them, but nothing of this sort is documented. One reference gives the origin of this breed as sometime during the 600's A.D., which would seem to lend credibility to that theory because the Pembroke Corgi was known well before that time.

Tibetan Spaniel

This Tibetan toy breed's name is a misnomer, but the dog is nevertheless a sweet, loving companion. No other names are known to apply to the breed, but it falls into the same lion category as the Pekingese and Lhasa.

Its coat requires minimal combing and brushing to maintain.

Exercise is necessary in minimal amounts. The active little dog likes to take frequent walks or play in a backyard.

CURRENT FUNCTION

Most little dogs of today can be classed primarily as companions, friends, and family pets and the Tibetan Spaniel fits well into this arbitrary class. It's quite sociable with other pets and children, if introduced to them as a puppy.

ATTITUDE

This Lilliputian spaniel is a vigilant little character that's retained its alarm quality and will let you know when a stranger approaches. It isn't always yappy but is cautious and reserved around visitors until properly introduced. It's a loving and lovable little dog that exhibits poise and self-confidence and one that has great intelligence combined with a strong nature.

APTITUDE

Training a Tibetan Spaniel shouldn't create problems because it wants to please its handler and grasps its lessons readily. Like all toys, this little dog will attempt to appear smaller than its stature when it's to the dog's advantage. It can be obstinate and is known to reverse the trainer-student roles when given the opportunity. Consistent treatment, kindness, and ample treats will win the day. This tiny dog can be considered for obedience training, competition in timed canine activities, and as a visitation or therapy dog.

APPEARANCE

The Tibetan Spaniel stands 10 inches tall (25.4 cm) and weighs 9 to 15 pounds (4 to 7 kg). Its head is small in proportion to its

Original Design

Historically this breed was developed by Tibetan holy men and served as symbols of Buddha's lion. Apparently it was an alarm dog whose duty it was to sit on the top of a monastery wall and warn inhabitants of interlopers with its shrill barking. It also walked on treadmills or prayer wheels that were used to select bits of parchment on which one's fate had been written. Probably the little Tibetan Spaniel's most lasting duty was being a loyal and obedient companion to its handler.

The Tibetan was introduced to England in about 1800 and was there modified by selective breeding to produce a longer muzzle. It immigrated to America in the 1960s and received AKC recognition in 1984. Since that time this little breed has slowly gained popularity with its American fanciers.

Origin

The Tibetan Spaniel probably is closely related to the Japanese Chin and Chinese Pekingese and was developed in Tibetan monasteries where it was revered and protected. Carved representatives of the Tibetan Spaniel have been found fashioned from jade and bronze dating to the Shang Dynasty in 1100 B.C. The Tibetan Spaniel has little in its history to indicate that its progenitors were from Spain, from whence came the word *Spaniel,* or that it's related to gun dogs or water retrievers, as are most true spaniels. Its actual history and exact origin are lost in antiquity because it was introduced to the Western world relatively recently in the early nineteenth century.

sturdy body and it has slightly bowed forelegs and hare feet. It has dark eyes, pendant, feathered ears, a medium-length muzzle, and a slightly undershot jaw. Its richly plumed tail is set high and carried over the back in a curl.

Its coat is double, silky in nature, of moderate length, straight, and flat. All colors and mixtures of colors are allowed, although the typically seen color is golden with black points.

Toy American Eskimo

This toy variety of the American Spitz, or Eskie as the American Eskimo is affectionately known, is indeed a tiny dog.

Its coat is somewhat difficult to maintain. Grooming should be performed at least several times weekly and more often during shedding season.

Exercise is essential, and regular short walks and brief runs in the park or country are needed to keep this little dog fit and happy.

CURRENT FUNCTION

It's safe to say that the little Eskie is primarily a family companion and is better known for its personality than for its dog show skills. It's a fine kids' pet but should always be introduced gradually to small children and other pets.

ATTITUDE

The Toy American Eskimo is bright, clever, and quite active. It bonds tightly with its owners and is a loyal companion that isn't as independent as other northern breeds. The Eskie welcomes mental challenges more than physical ones and has a more placid temperament than its sled-dog ancestors.

APTITUDE

This little dog is eager to please and will accept training easily if consistency and patience are used. It's primarily interested in activities such as lap sitting and leashed walks, but its intelligence and trainability can be harnessed to provide good basic obedience work. Like other tiny breeds it will work for yummies but not for scolding or nagging.

APPEARANCE

The Toy American Eskimo Dog stands 9 to 12 inches tall (23 to 30 cm) and weighs 6 to 10 pounds (3 to 5 kg). Its head is typically Spitz-like with a medium muzzle, small, erect ears, and a bright and alert foxy expression.

Origin

The American Eskimo Dog breed is divided into three sizes: the Standard, Miniature, and Toy. Most all Spitz breeds originated in northern Europe, especially in Germany, and the Toy Eskimo is probably no exception. The Toy variety is the result of Eskie fanciers' selective breeding efforts, but all three sizes apparently originated from a single type, and all three are judged by the same standards except for height.

Keeshond genes may be lurking behind the Eskie, which might account for the little dog's gentleness and companion dog value. The Toy American Eskimo was developed in Europe during the early 1900s and came to the United States soon afterward. It was first known as the American Spitz and was often found among circus groups, where these dogs demonstrated their trainability and unique agility.

The eyes are dark and lid margins, lip margins, and nose rubber are jet black. Its body is proportional and well muscled.

Its double, thick coat is plush to the touch. Its usual color is pure white but cream-colored dogs are occasionally found.

Original Design

The northern Spitz breeds are among the best sled dogs in the world, but the Toy American Eskimo probably never saw a dogsled over its shoulder. Its value as an energetic and independent companion pet is well established by all who own these little dogs.

First seen in America in about 1910, this little dog was first registered by the UKC and later by the CKC. The breed was recognized by the AKC in 1994, but the Toy Eskimo hasn't gained much attention in shows since that time.

Toy Manchester Terrier

The Standard-size Manchester Terrier is often referred to as the Black and Tan Terrier. That larger dog and the Toy Manchester are registered and shown as varieties of a single breed although their sizes differ significantly. The Toy Manchester is also known as the English Toy Terrier. The height, weight, and ear carriage are the only features that differentiate one variety from the other, and both are registered and shown as varieties of a single breed.

The Toy Manchester's coat is short, sleek, and glossy and requires minimal care. Brushing every few days with a rubber slicker or a grooming glove is quite sufficient, and finishing these chores with a chamois will keep its coat shiny.

Exercise and mental challenges for this tiny dog are important. Its heritage demands long walks, runs in the park, and plenty of games and activities. Although the toy variety was nearly inbred into extinction at one time, the present-day Toy Manchester is an active, hardy little companion.

CURRENT FUNCTION

The Toy Manchester retains many if not all the attributes of its ancestors and, regardless of its size, this little dog is a quick, energetic vermin catcher. Its usual occupation is that of companion to adult families. Although the Manchester personality and sociability are well established and it does love to play, a Toy Manchester's fine bones render it somewhat problematic as a child's companion, especially where preschoolers and toddlers are involved.

ATTITUDE

The Toy Manchester is a clever, alert, and vigilant house dog that wants to please its master. It sounds an alarm whenever visitors approach, but when they are introduced the dog accepts them readily. In spite of its size, it relates to children very well, and in some families Toy Manchesters and kids live together in harmony. This breed has a propensity to be

From its Black and Tan progenitors and its big brother, the Toy Manchester's attitude is all terrier. It's an athletic, determined, and swift rabbit hunter and a rat and mole killer. At the same time it's an intelligent, high-spirited, and cunning playmate and family companion.

Cats are probably safe around a Manchester if they are properly introduced to the little dog, but rodent pets are at risk unless kept well out of reach.

APTITUDE

The Toy Manchester is a very trainable pet if its handler retains the dog's focus and proceeds consistently. Although the Standard Manchester is more often seen in agility and flyball contests, the aptitude is there for the Toy as well. Obedience shouldn't be overlooked, and Toy Manchester Terriers are often trained for therapy work.

dominant toward other small dogs and it isn't easily discouraged once its mind is made up.

Origin

The foundation for both Manchester Terrier sizes was undoubtedly the English Black and Tan Terrier, a fantastic ratter that was apparently a coarser and less streamlined dog than the present-day Manchester. During Manchester development, the Black and Tan was interbred with the Whippet, Greyhound, and Italian Greyhound to produce the sleek, aerodynamic body style, but the terrier attitude and aptitude was retained. Many fanciers lived in and around Manchester, England, as the modification of the Black and Tan progressed. In the 1860s the new Manchester breed spread from that center across Great Britain and to America. Toy Manchesters were popular among Manchester fanciers and were probably the result of the crossings with the Italian Greyhound.

APPEARANCE

The Toy Manchester stands about 11 inches tall (28 cm) and weighs about 6 to 8 pounds (2.5 to 3.5 kg). The Toy's muzzle and skull are equal in length, and its neck is slender and slightly arched. Its abdomen is tucked up and its chest is deep. Its legs are straight and its loin is muscular. The Toy has small, thin, naturally erect ears that are never cropped.

The Toy Manchester coat is smooth, short, dense, tight, and glossy. Its color is black with mahogany markings. The mahogany to tan-colored markings appear in a symmetrical pattern on its lower muzzle, over each eye, on each cheek, on its chest, and on its lower legs.

Toy Poodle

The Toy Poodle is another of the toys that is actually one of three varieties or sizes of a breed and is judged in shows by the same standard as the miniature and standard sizes. It is sometimes called the Caniche, Chien Canard, or Barbone. The name *Poodle* probably is derived from the German word *pfudel* that means puddle, or *pudelin,* after the sound of the splash when an oar hits the water.

Your Toy Poodle's coat should be trimmed and shaped every five or six weeks by an experienced groomer if you want it to look like a traditional Poodle. At home the Poodle should be brushed and combed every few days to prevent matting and knotting of the coat. Another option is to keep your Toy Poodle in a puppy or sporting pattern, which is done by clipping the dog's coat to the same length all over its body, then shaving the face a little shorter and trimming the topknot, tail, and ear hair with the scissors. This is by far the most practical and attractive pattern for the active and playful Toy Poodle if you have no interest in dog shows.

The Toy Poodle is capable of providing for its own exercise if it has active owners and a backyard to play in. Providing the space for exercise isn't the same as encouraging or participating in your dog's activities. A tiny dog that's alone and ignored in a big backyard or home is about the same as one that spends all its time in a kennel. The Toy needs people contact to balance and enjoy life. Play scent games with your intelligent little Poodle, toss the ball, play tug, begin obedience training, and include yourself in your little dog's daily activities.

CURRENT FUNCTION

The Toy Poodle has emerged as one of the finest companions available, and yet it has nearly been ruined by those breeders who have inbred their stock to produce teacup Toy individuals. Generally these microtypes are delicate, quite fragile, and often unhealthy and inactive. Some of those seen are nearly as small as a Chihuahua, but this isn't contrary to the breed standard that gives no minimum height for the variety.

Normal-sized Toy Poodles are robust little dogs that make excellent pets for older children and adults of all ages.

ATTITUDE

The Toy Poodle is a superintelligent little dog that's playful and active. It's sensitive and bonds quickly with its family, although it may be reserved toward strangers until they're properly introduced. It responds ideally to its handler and is quite sociable with other dogs and small household pets. Toys often have the propensity to bark but this habit can be curtailed with gentle training while it is still a puppy.

APTITUDE

This loyal and affectionate little dog thrives on pleasing its owner and is therefore a cinch to train. With the inheritance of a working retriever the Toy Poodle understands commands quickly and complies almost automatically. It requires consistency and gentleness and will respond to treats but not to scolding or nagging. It has inherent scenting abilities and will succeed in hide-and-seek games and retrieving. This Toy should be an excellent obedience competitor and can hold its own in agility or flyball activities. Because the Toy is quite sociable, one of the best avocations for it is visitation or therapy.

APPEARANCE

The Toy Poodle stands less than 10 inches tall (25.4 cm) and weighs about 8 to 10 pounds (3.5 to 4.5 kg). The breed has a long, straight muzzle that's accentuated by bright, dark eyes and pendulant, heavily haired ears. Its eyelids, lip margins, and nose rubber are either black or dark in color, depending on the coat

Origin

The origin of the Poodle is generally assumed to be France, but actually it was first seen in Russia and Germany where the Standard size was used as a water retriever. It immigrated to France where it captured the hearts of the public and it's the National Dog of France. The Standard's origin is placed in the fifteenth century, but the Toy variety came 300 years later.

The progenitors of the Poodle were probably the Barbets and other ancient curly-coated breeds. The Toy evolved at about the same time as the tiny Maltese and may be related to it.

Original Design

A Toy Poodle's original purpose was that of a companion and friend and in France it was sometimes used as a truffle-scenting dog. Its tightly curled coat was developed to capture shedding hair, making the dog a very clean house companion. It's doubtful that the Toy was ever used as a water retriever but the inherited scenting ability remains.

The British Poodle club was established in 1886 and soon thereafter Poodles were seen in America. The Poodle Club of America adopted standards that were approved by the AKC in 1940. In the standard, three varieties are listed, and the Toy's height is stated to be under 10 inches tall at the shoulder.

pigment. Its back is short, its body is muscular and athletic, and its legs are straight and stylish.

The coat is clipped into a particular pattern and is expertly shaped by scissors to provide a show-dog appearance that's one of the most beautiful of any small dog. The various styles are termed Puppy, English Saddle, Continental, and Sporting. Hair clipping has progressed from utilitarian to elegance and grace that's appreciated by fanciers everywhere.

Colors are all solid and are seen in shades of blue, gray, silver, brown, café au lait, apricot, and cream. Sometimes darker points or shading is seen on ears and the ruff.

West Highland White Terrier

The West Highland White Terrier's lengthy name is often shortened to Westie, and in many references the breed is called the Highlander. It occasionally is known as the Poltalloch Terrier after the region in which it was developed, or the Roseneath Terrier after the Roseneath Estate of the Duke of Argyll, who was an early fancier of the breed. This dog also has been called the White Scottish Terrier, Little Skye, or Little Cairn Terrier.

The Westie coat is relatively easy to care for. Ideally, long hair should be plucked two or three times annually, but in pets this is often forsaken in favor of clipping. Show dogs need more attention to keep them in tiptop shape.

A typical Highlander demands ceaseless commitment to lessons, exercise, and games. Exercise for a hardy little Westie often takes the form of playing ball and romping in the yard, but it also has the endurance for long walks in the country where it can pursue animal scents at length. Always walk your Highlander on a leash unless you have time to search for it as it trails or digs out some quarry deep in the woods.

CURRENT FUNCTION

The hardy West Highlander enjoys great popularity as a rugged outdoor hunting dog that holds its own in earth-dog trials. Its amusing, lighthearted, and mischievous ways have made it one of the finest companion dogs in America.

ATTITUDE

A Westie is bold and energetic, self-assured, yet exceptionally loyal. The Highlander is a clean, personable house dog. It's quite sociable and the merriest and most cheerful of the Scottish breeds. This little dog has the endurance of a much larger dog, and owners need not pamper or carry it home from a long walk. It's loyal and extroverted, an independent thinker with a stubborn streak. The Westie is a cunning and self-confident little dog that's wild about balls and other small toys.

O r i g i n

Scotland was the birthplace of the Westie, more specifically the town of Poltalloch, which is slightly south of Kilmartin, about sixty miles northwest of Glasgow. That region generally is called the Highlands. The breed was developed in the nineteenth century and claims the same progenitors as other Scottish terrier breeds, namely the Skye and Cairn.

Boredom and lack of human attention stimulate barking and digging vices. The Highlander is generally sociable with friendly dogs and cats, but big dogs won't intimidate the Westie.

APTITUDE

The Westie is a game earth dog and has the traits to serve it well in trials. It's trainable but a bit headstrong and willful. Its amusing antics will make correction extremely difficult if you let it get the upper hand. The Westie should be a relatively good obedience dog, and its love of play should provide it with a basis for flyball. It might do well as a therapy dog after basic obedience training has been absorbed and it has mellowed and matured.

APPEARANCE

The Westie stands about 11 inches tall (28 cm) and weighs about 20 pounds (9 kg). Its general appearance is that of a curious and personable, cheerful little terrier. It's strongly built with a deep chest and strong legs. Its head is compact and roundish, and its sharply

The Westie was developed to follow, bolt, or destroy the many agricultural pests residing in the rocky terrain of its homeland. As is often the case, it found its secondary niche as a wonderful companion pet because of its personality and hardiness.

In London's Crufts dog show in 1907 the Highlander made its first appearance as a show dog. From the very first Westie to arrive on United States soil, these lovable little dogs established their reputation as excellent companions with a built-in propensity to rid their surroundings of vermin.

The West Highland White Terrier Club of America was admitted to AKC membership under the name of Roseneath Terrier Club in 1908, and the following year its name was changed.

pointed ears are small and carried erect. Its muzzle is blunt and its eyes are dark with black eyelid rims, as well as black lip margins and nose rubber.

The Westie coat is double, hard, and never fluffy or soft, and is plucked for showing. Color is pure white with no trace of markings or shadings.

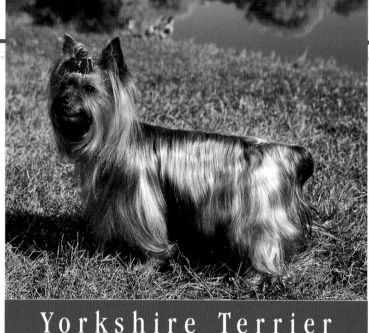

Yorkshire Terrier

The Yorkshire Terrier is affectionately known by all as the Yorkie. The beauty of its long, flowing coat adds to its ostentatiously grand appearance that's a striking contradiction to its terrier temperament.

The fully developed coat of a Yorkie requires daily, intensive grooming with brush and comb, and its topknot must be retained by some device to keep it from obscuring the little dog's vision. The pet Yorkie's coat can be clipped to a manageable length and kept short, but this will never do for a show dog.

This breed takes its exercise where it finds it and usually is satisfied with scurrying from here to there while keeping track of its human family. A little Yorkie will always appreciate a walk around the block and backyard play times.

CURRENT FUNCTION

Its capability as a ratter is rarely employed in America today, but owners shouldn't be surprised when this little character finds an opportunity to dispatch a wayward mouse or gerbil. The inherited terrier trait remains.

A Yorkie is a valued companion and show dog. It's often indifferent to lying on laps and prefers a more independent lifestyle. The Yorkie has a terrier mentality instead of the typical mind-set of a decorative toy. In that regard this tiny terrier is well equipped to play with older children that have been well indoctrinated in the handling and care of a 5- to 7-pound adult dog.

ATTITUDE

Yorkie bravery and boldness is acknowledged by most owners. Here I must interject a personal observation. Rowdy was our 5-pound beautiful Yorkie with a silky coat that dragged the ground. She shared the household with Flash, our son's 100-pound Malamute. Rowdy refused to concede their size difference, and when Flash walked by, Rowdy would jump up, grab, and hang onto the white hock. Flash refused to acknowledge the tiny dog's courage or tenacity and simply shook Rowdy free without looking back.

The Yorkie is an active, intelligent, and loving little dog, vigilant and alert. It's an excellent alarm dog, and although unable to inflict significant damage to interlopers this daring little guard dog will bark ferociously and never back down.

It socializes well with people and pets, and except for its sometimes-foolhardy attitude toward bigger dogs the Yorkie has a great temperament.

APTITUDE

Training a Yorkie is a challenge only because of the dog's size. It has above-average intelligence and enjoys learning, but it has a stubborn streak that might defeat a less determined trainer. It's a terrier through and through and requires consistency and fairness in training methods. Don't train for lengthy periods, change lessons to prevent boredom, and be persistent. Maintain a positive attitude and never scold or nag.

Some Yorkies are seen in the obedience ring and many are put to work as visitation or therapy dogs. All are great companions.

APPEARANCE

The Yorkshire Terrier stands about 8 inches tall (20 cm) and weighs no more than 7 pounds (3 kg). Its small head is well proportioned and its muzzle isn't overly long. Its eyes are dark and its eyelid rims, lip margins, and nose rubber are black. Its ears are V-shaped and are carried erect. Its body is compact and sturdy, and its legs are straight. Its docked tail is carried higher than its back.

The coat of this little dog is fine, silky, and glossy. It's parted in the center and usually is trimmed even with the ground. The head hair

Original Design

It's hard to believe, but this elegant and pretentious little dog was originally developed as a ratter and lived with common working folks. The classy-looking Yorkie was quite happy living with weavers, miners, and other blue collar admirers and was eschewed by the wealthy and aristocratic English classes.

The Yorkshire Terrier came to America in the late 1800s and was shown here in 1878 in a variety of different sizes. By the turn of the century fanciers had agreed on the proper size and appearance of the modern Yorkie, and it has remained one of the favorite show dogs ever since.

is long and is tied out of the eyes with a rubber band or bow. The colors are blue and tan with the steel blue coat extending over the back of the neck to the root of the tail and the tan extending from the elbow to the head and chest.

Origin

The Yorkie's origin dates to Victoria's reign and its beginning probably came about when some Scottish Weavers carried their small dogs along when they immigrated to Yorkshire, England, in the nineteenth century. The breed's progenitors included Scottish and English terriers and toy breeds that were found in Yorkshire at that time. Among the dogs contributing to the Yorkie gene pool was the Waterside Terrier, which is similarly colored. Others include the Manchester or Black and Tan, Skye, Dandie Dinmont, Clydesdale, and Paisley terriers, the Maltese, and possibly other small terriers and toy breeds. The Yorkshire underwent many changes in size and coat color and quality during the midnineteenth century, and the final product was first exhibited in England in 1861 as a Broken-Haired Scotch Terrier. In 1870 the silky-coated breed was differentiated from the other Scottish terriers and was given the name Yorkshire Terrier.

Index

Aberdeen Terrier, 191
Abso Seng Kye, 148
Acclimation, 22–23
  bonding, 11, 23–24
  crate, 25–26
  exercise, 26–27
  fatigue, 26–27
  feeding, 26
  housebreaking, 24–25
  socialization, 23–24
Affenpinscher, 87–89
  appearance, 87–89
  aptitude, 87
  attitude, 87
  function, 87
  origin, 88
  original design, 89
Age considerations, 14
Agility trials, 31
Aging, temperament, 79
Altering, 35–36
American Spitz, 212
Antigenicity, 44–45
Arthritis, 50
Artificial respiration, 41–42
Atopy, 50
Australian Silky Terrier, 200
Australian Terrier, 90–92
  appearance, 92
  aptitude, 91
  attitude, 90
  function, 90
  origin, 91
  original design, 92

Backyard hazards, 18–20
Basset Fauve de Bretagne,
    93–94
  appearance, 94
  aptitude, 93–94
  attitude, 93
  function, 93
  origin, 94

original design, 94
Begging, 32–33
Belgian Griffon, 104
Bichon Frise, 2, 95–97
  appearance, 96–97
  aptitude, 96
  attitude, 95
  function, 95
  origin, 96
  original design, 97
Bichon Havanais, 136
Bichon Maltaise, 155
Bichon Tenerife, 95
Biting, 34
Black Fell Terrier, 176
Blindness, 80
Blood tests, 37–38
Blue and Tan Terrier, 90
Bohemian Terrier, 115
Bonding, 11, 23–24
Boosters, 47
Border Terrier, 98–100
  appearance, 100
  aptitude, 98–99
  attitude, 98
  function, 98
  origin, 99
  original design, 100
Boston Terrier, 101–103
  appearance, 102–103
  aptitude, 102
  attitude, 101
  function, 101
  origin, 103
  original design, 102
Breeders, 11–13
Breeding, motives, 73–74
Brussels Griffon, 104–106
  appearance, 105–106
  aptitude, 105
  attitude, 104–105
  function, 104
  origin, 105

original design, 106
Bulldog, French, 129–131

Cairn Terrier, 107–109
  appearance, 109
  aptitude, 107, 109
  attitude, 107
  function, 107
  origin, 109
  original design, 107
Calories, 68
Canine:
  cognitive dysfunction, 80
  compulsive disorder, 34
  distemper, 47
  Good Citizen, 30
  hepatitis, 47–48
Cardigan Welsh Corgi,
    110–112
  appearance, 111
  aptitude, 110–111
  attitude, 110
  function, 110
  origin, 112
  original design, 111
Cardiopulmonary resuscita-
    tion, 42
Caregivers, 20–21
Carlin, 188
Castration, 75–76
Cataract, 57
Cavalier King Charles
    Spaniel, 113–114, 145
  appearance, 114
  aptitude, 113–114
  attitude, 113
  function, 113
  origin, 114
  original design, 114
Cesky Terrier, 115–117
  appearance, 116–117
  aptitude, 115–116
  attitude, 115

function, 115
  origin, 116
  original design, 117
Charlie's Hope Terrier, 126
Chewing, 33
Chihuahua, 2, 118–120
  appearance, 120
  aptitude, 120
  attitude, 119–120
  function, 118–119
  origin, 120
  original design, 119
Children, considerations, 8–9
Chinese Crested, 121–123
  appearance, 122–123
  aptitude, 122
  attitude, 122
  function, 121
  origin, 123
  original design, 122
Chocolate poisoning, 61–62
Circulatory diseases, 51
Cleft palate, 51
Collars, 27, 29
Commands, 29
Congenital defects, 16
Continental Toy Spaniel, 173
Coquetdale Terrier, 98
Corgi:
  Cardigan Welsh, 110–112
  Pembroke Welsh, 181–183
Corona virus, 48
Coton de Tulear, 124–125
  appearance, 125
  aptitude, 124
  attitude, 124
  function, 124
  origin, 125
  original design, 125
Craniomandibular
    osteopathy, 54
Crates, 18, 25–26
Crossbreeds, 13–14

Cushing's disease, 38
Czesky Terrier, 115

Dachshund, Miniature,
  160–162
Dandie Dinmount Terrier,
  126–128
  appearance, 128
  aptitude, 127
  attitude, 126–127
  function, 126
  origin, 127
  original design, 128
Deafness, 79
Dental disorders, 50, 79
Deutsche Spitz, 132
Diabetes mellitus, 50–51
Diagnostic aids, 37–38
Diarrhea, 60–61
Discipline, 28
Distemper, 47
Distichiasis, 56
Dystocia, 58

Ear wounds, 64
Eclampsia, 58–59
Elbow dysplasia, 51
Energy requirements, 68
English Toy Spaniel, 145
Entropion, 57
Epilepsy, 51–52
Epiphora, 57
Erythrocytes, 37
Euthanasia, 81–84
Exercise, 26–27
Eye appearance, 39–40

Facial deformities, 54
Family, introductions, 22–23
Fat, 68
Fatigue, 26–27
Feeding, 26
  free-choice, 66
  trials, 69
Fencing, 19
First Aid, 39–42
Flyball, 31
Food:
  terminology, 67–68
  types, 69
Fractures, 64
French Bulldog, 129–131
  appearance, 130
  aptitude, 129–130

attitude, 129
function, 129
origin, 131
original design, 130

Garages, 20
Gates, 19
Gender differences, 11
Genetics, 2
Geriatrics, 77–84
  aging, temperament, 79
  arthritis, 79
  blindness, 80
  canine cognitive dysfunc-
    tion, 80
  deafness, 79
  dental disease, 79
  euthanasia, 81–84
  incontinence, 80–81
  medications, 78
  nuclear sclerosis, 80
Gingivitis, 50
Giza Hairless, 121
Glaucoma, 56
Glucose, 38
Greyhound, Italian, 138–139

Habits, bad, 32–34
  begging, 32–33
  biting, 34
  chewing, 33
  jumping up, 32
  mouthing, 33
  running away, 33
  separation anxiety, 34
Hairless:
  dog, Chinese, 121
  Toy Mexican, 158–159
Havana Silk dog, 136
Havanese, 136–137
  appearance, 136–137
  aptitude, 136
  attitude, 136
  function, 136
  origin, 137
  original design, 137
Hazards, 17–20
Health considerations, 35–42
  artificial respiration, 41–42
  blood tests, 37–38
  cardiopulmonary resusci-
    tation, 42
  circulatory diseases, 51
  dental disorders, 50

diabetes mellitus, 50–51
diagnostic aids, 37–38
elbow dysplasia, 51
epilepsy, 51–52
first aid, 39–42
hereditary concerns, 50–59
history, 36–37
immunity, 44–47
insurance, 21
kneecap luxation, 54–55
medical kit, 40–42
ocular diseases, 55–56
parasites, 43–44
precocious maturation,
  35–36
preventive medicine, 43–44
reproductive disorders,
  58–59
shock, 41
therapy, 38–39
urgent care, 60–65
vaccines, 45–47
veterinarian, 36–40
vital signs, 39–40
Heatstroke, 62
Hepatitis, 47–48
Hereditary concerns, 50–59
Heterosus, 13
Housebreaking, 24–25
Hypoglycemia, 52–53
Hypothyroidism, 53

Identification, 27
Immunity, 44–47
Incontinence, 80–81
Intervertebral disc disease,
  53–54
Italian Greyhound, 138–139
  appearance, 139
  aptitude, 138–139
  attitude, 138
  function, 138
  origin, 139
  original design, 139

Jack Russell Terrier, 140–142
  appearance, 142
  aptitude, 141
  attitude, 141
  function, 140–141
  origin, 142
  original design, 141
Japanese Chin, 143–144
  appearance, 143–144

aptitude, 143
attitude, 143
function, 143
origin, 144
original design, 144
Jobs, 9–10
Jones' Terrier, 169
Jumping up, 32

Kennel cough, 48
Keratitis Sicca, 55
King Charles Spaniel,
  145–147
  appearance, 146–147
  aptitude, 146
  attitude, 145–146
  function, 145
  origin, 146
  original design, 147
Klein German Spitz, 132–133
  appearance, 132–133
  aptitude, 132
  attitude, 132
  function, 132
  origin, 133
  original design, 133
Kneecap luxation, 54–55

Lakeland Terrier, 176
Leash, 29
Legg-Calve-Perthes Disease,
  55
Leptospirosis, 48
Lhasa Apso, 148–150
  appearance, 149
  aptitude, 148–149
  attitude, 148
  function, 148
  origin, 150
  original design, 149
Life expectancy, 16
Lifting, 23
Little Lion Dog, 151
Lowchen, 151–152
  appearance, 151–152
  aptitude, 151
  attitude, 151
  function, 151
  origin, 152
  original design, 152
Lundehund, 153–154
  appearance, 154
  aptitude, 154
  attitude, 153

function, 153
origin, 154
original design, 154

Malocclusion, 50
Maltese, 155–157
appearance, 157
aptitude, 155, 157
attitude, 155
function, 155
origin, 156
original design, 157
Manners, 28
Maturation, early, 35–36
Meals, 67
Medical kit, 40–42
Medications, 78
Metabolism, 67–68
Minerals, 69
Miniature Dachshund,
160–162
appearance, 162
aptitude, 161–162
attitude, 160–161
function, 160
origin, 162
original design, 161
Miniature Pinscher, 163–165
appearance, 164
aptitude, 164
attitude, 163
function, 163
origin, 165
original design, 164
Miniature Schnauzer,
166–168
appearance, 167–168
aptitude, 167
attitude, 167
function, 166–167
origin, 168
original design, 167
Miniature Spitz, 186
Mittel German Spitz,
134–135
appearance, 134–135
aptitude, 134
attitude, 134
function, 134
origin, 135
original design, 135
Mixed breeds, 13–14
Momma towel, 17
Monkey Terrier, 87

Mopshond, 188
Mouthing, 33
Mucous membranes,
39–40
Mustard and Pepper Terrier,
126
Muzzle, 63

Name, learning, 28–29
Neighbors, 20
Neutering, 75–76
Norfolk Terrier, 169–171
appearance, 170–171
aptitude, 170
attitude, 169
function, 169
origin, 171
original design, 170
Norwich Terrier, 172
appearance, 172
Nosebleeds, 64–65
Nosodes, 49
Nuclear sclerosis, 80
Nutrition, 66–72
calories, 68
fat, 68
feeding:
free-choice, 66
trials, 69
food, 67–69
metabolism, 67–68
minerals, 69
obesity, 71–72
overfeeding, 71–72
protein, 68–69
starch, 69
supplements, 69
treats, 70
vitamins, 69
water, 66
weight loss, 72

Obedience training, 30
Obesity, 71–72
Ocular diseases, 55–56
Ownership considerations,
1–2
age considerations, 14
breeders, 11–13
children, considerations,
8–9
gender differences, 11
genetics, 2
jobs, 9–10

life expectancy, 16
purchasing considerations,
7–16
impulse purchases, 7–8
puppy, evaluating, 14–15
quantity considerations,
10–11
temperament evaluation,
15

Paper training, 25
Papillon, 173–175
appearance, 174–175
aptitude, 173–174
attitude, 173
function, 173
origin, 174
original design, 175
Parasites, 43–44
Parson Jack Russell Terrier,
140
Parvovirus, 48
Patterdale Terrier, 176–177
appearance, 177
aptitude, 177
attitude, 176–177
function, 176
origin, 177
original design, 177
Pekingese, 178–180
appearance, 179–180
aptitude, 178–179
attitude, 178
function, 178
origin, 180
original design, 179
Pembroke Welsh corgi,
181–183
appearance, 182–183
aptitude, 182
attitude, 181–182
function, 181
origin, 183
original design, 182
Pens, 25–26
Physical exam, 36–37
Pinscher, Miniature, 163–165
Podengo Portugueso
Pequeno, 184–185
appearance, 185
aptitude, 184–185
attitude, 184
function, 184
origin, 185

original design, 185
Poisons, 18–19, 60
Pomeranian, 186–187
appearance, 187
aptitude, 186
attitude, 186
function, 186
origin, 187
original design, 187
Precocious maturation,
35–36
Preventive medicine, 43–44
Progressive Retinal Atrophy,
55–56
Protein, 38, 68–69
Puffin Hound, 153
Pug, 188–190
appearance, 190
aptitude, 189–190
attitude, 189
function, 188
origin, 189
original design, 190
Pulse, 39–40
Puppy:
evaluating, 14–15
mills, 13
rations, 70

Rabies, 48–49
Reh Pinscher, 163
Reproduction, 73–76
breeding, motives, 73–74
neutering, 75–76
planning, 74
whelping, 75
disorders, 58–59
Respiration, 39–40
Rough-Coated Terrier, 90
Round Head Terrier, 101
Running away, 33

Safety concerns, 17–20
Sandbox training, 25
Schnauzer, Miniature,
166–168
Scottish Terrier, 191–193
appearance, 192–193
aptitude, 191–192
attitude, 191
function, 191
origin, 192
original design, 192
Sealyham Terrier, 194–196

appearance, 196
aptitude, 196
attitude, 194
function, 194
origin, 196
original design, 195
Separation anxiety, 34
Sheng Trou, 148
Shih Tzu, 197–199
  appearance, 198–199
  aptitude, 197–198
  attitude, 197
  function, 197
  origin, 199
  original design, 198
Shock, 41
Silky Terrier, 200–202
  appearance, 201
  aptitude, 200–201
  attitude, 200
  function, 200
  origin, 201
  original design, 202
Sit command, 29
Skye Terrier, 203–205
  appearance, 204–205
  aptitude, 203–204
  attitude, 203
  function, 203
  origin, 205
  original design, 204
Slipped Stifle, 54–55
Socialization, 23–24
South African Hairless, 121
Spaniel:
  Cavalier King Charles,
    145
  Continental Toy, 173
  English Toy, 145
  Japanese, 143
  King Charles, 145–147
  Tibetan, 209–211
Spaying, 35–36, 75–76
Special diets, 70
Spitz:
  American, 212
  Deutsche, 132
  Klein German, 132–133
  Miniature, 186
  Mittel German, 134–135
Starch, 69
Sunburn, 59
Supplements, 69
Swedish Vallhund, 206–208

appearance, 207–208
aptitude, 207
attitude, 206–207
function, 206
origin, 208
original design, 207
Sydney Silky Terrier, 200

Talisman Dog, 148
Tattoos, 27
Tawny Brittany Basset, 93
Teeth, 18
Temperament evaluation,
  15
Temperature, 39–40
Tenerife Dog, 95
Terriers, 2
  Aberdeen, 191
  Australian, 90–92
  Silky, 200
  Black Fell, 176
  Blue, 90
  Bohemian, 115
  Border, 98–100
  Boston, 101–103
  Cairn, 107–109
  Cesky, 115–117
  Charlie's Hope, 126
  Coquetdale, 98
  Czesky, 115
  Dandie Dinmount,
    126–128
  Jack Russell, 140–142
  Jones', 169
  Lakeland, 176
  Monkey, 87
  Mustard and Pepper, 126
  Norfolk, 169–171
  Norwich, 172
  Parson Jack Russell, 140
  Patterdale, 176–177
  Rough-coated, 90
  Round Head, 101
  Scottish, 191–193
  Sealyham, 194–196
  Silky, 200–202
  Skye, 203–205
  Sydney Silky, 200
  Toy, 90
  Toy Manchester, 215–217
  trials, 31
  Trumpington, 169
  West Highland White,
    221–223

Yorkshire, 224–226
Testicular retention, 58
Therapy, 38–39
  dogs, 31–32
Tibetan Spaniel, 209–211
  appearance, 209, 211
  aptitude, 209
  attitude, 209
  function, 209
  origin, 211
  original design, 210
Tourniquet, 64
Toy American Eskimo,
  212–214
  appearance, 212, 214
  aptitude, 212
  attitude, 212
  function, 212
  origin, 213
  original design, 214
Toy Manchester Terrier,
  215–217
  appearance, 217
  aptitude, 216
  attitude, 215–216
  function, 215
  origin, 217
  original design, 216
Toy Mexican Hairless,
  158–159
  appearance, 159
  aptitude, 158
  attitude, 158
  function, 158
  origin, 159
  original design, 159
Toy Poodle, 218–220
  appearance, 219–220
  aptitude, 219
  attitude, 219
  function, 218–219
  origin, 219
  original design, 220
Toy terrier, 90
Tracheal collapse, 57–58
Training, 28–34
  agility trials, 31
  begging, 32–33
  biting, 34
  canine compulsive
    disorder, 34
  canine good citizen, 30
  chewing, 33
  collar, 29

commands, 29
discipline, 28
Flyball, 31
habits, bad, 32–34
jumping up, 32
leash, 29
manners, 28
mouthing, 33
name, learning, 28–29
obedience training, 30
running away, 33
separation anxiety, 34
Terrier trials, 31
therapy dogs, 31–32
Treats, 70
Trials, 31
Trichiasis, 56
Trumpington Terrier,
  169
Turkish Hairless, 121

Umbilical hernia, 59
Urgent care, 60–65

Vaccines, 45–47
Veterinarian, 36–40
Vital signs, 39–40
Vitamins, 69
Vomiting, 60–61

Walk command, 29
Water, 66
Weight loss, 72
Welsh Heeler, 181
West Highland White
  Terrier, 221–223
  appearance, 222–223
  aptitude, 222
  attitude, 221–222
  function, 221
  origin, 222
  original design, 223
Whelping, 75
White blood cells, 37
White Cuban, 136
Wounds, 63–65

Yorkshire Terrier, 224–226
  appearance, 225
  aptitude, 225
  attitude, 224–225
  function, 224
  origin, 226
  original design, 225